D1600618

GOD AT THE CROSSROADS OF WORLDVIEWS

GOD AT THE CROSSROADS
OF WORLDVIEWS

TOWARD A DIFFERENT DEBATE

ABOUT THE EXISTENCE OF GOD

Paul Seungoh Chung

University of Notre Dame Press
Notre Dame, Indiana

University of Notre Dame Press
Notre Dame, Indiana 46556
www.undpress.nd.edu

Library of Congress Cataloging-in-Publication Data

Names: Chung, Paul Seungoh, 1978– author.
Title: God at the crossroads of worldviews : toward a different debate
about the existence of God / Paul Seungoh Chung.
Description: Notre Dame : University of Notre Dame Press, 2016. |
Includes bibliographical references and index.
Identifiers: LCCN 2016032978 (print) | LCCN 2016033474 (ebook) |
ISBN 9780268100568 (hardcover : alk. paper) |
ISBN 026810056X (hardcover : alk. paper) | ISBN 9780268100582 (pdf) |
ISBN 9780268100599 (epub)
Subjects: LCSH: God. | Religion—Philosophy.
Classification: LCC BL473 .C48 2016 (print) | LCC BL473 (ebook) |
DDC 212/.1—dc23
LC record available at https://lccn.loc.gov/2016032978

∞ *This paper meets the requirements of ANSI/NISO Z39.48-1992
(Permanence of Paper).*

CONTENTS

PREFACE

Sometimes while listening to two parties arguing intensely, one begins to realize that they are not exactly talking about the same thing. The differences may be subtle, but the points they raise, things they emphasize, the nuances in their reasoning, or the way they use certain words seem a bit off from each other. Then, the disconcerting thought eventually dawns that their argument will not end; it cannot end, because in a sense it never really began. This is what I increasingly sensed when I delved into the intellectual debate regarding religious beliefs years ago. This book slowly took its shape as I examined where this sense was coming from.

Our world is increasingly gripped with questions about God, or to be precise, about religious beliefs in God. As I write this preface, the world is abuzz with the question regarding the role of religious beliefs—and in particular the beliefs of the monotheistic religions of the West—in wars, violence, and intolerance against minorities of every kind, and pulsing underneath that cacophony is the question of the irrationality of such beliefs. Yet what I have experienced in my life was not an easy dichotomy of, on the one hand, irrationality and intolerance of the "religious"—a term which itself is notoriously difficult to define and, I think, too often used in whatever way best fits one's polemic—and, on the other, the rationality and liberation of the "secular." Nor vice versa, I would wryly add. Rather, I encountered a bewildering spectrum of both rationality and irrationality, both intolerance and liberation, from both sides. This may be the main reason why we still engage and struggle in intellectual debates regarding religious beliefs; after all, it would be difficult to do so, at least sincerely, when one simply assumes the rationality of oneself, and the irrationality of the other.

In this book, I begin with one of the axiomatic questions in these debates, "Does God exist?," and the different reasons for the answers to that question. There are other questions—those more closely wedded to the more "urgent" social issues—that I want to explore eventually in subsequent books, but the journey begins here, and the rest of the story will unfold from this point. What I will propose in this book is that our conception of how we ought to proceed in the debate about the existence of God needs to change. Or, to put it more provocatively, though perhaps imprecisely, we are asking the wrong question when we ask, "Does God exist?," or at least, we are posing it in ways that prevent fruitful discussion and obscure the ways of reaching further answers. That is, what it is we are really asking by the question, "Does God exist?," in an intellectual debate is *not* actually "Does God exist?" What then is the question?

So I return to the same disconcerting thought with which we began. In our questions rest the seeds of our answers, yet we cannot ask the right question, let alone answer it, if those involved are in significant ways talking past each other. To begin, we must find crossroads. This is the "different debate" about God I eventually envisioned in this book—a different way of thinking about, and arguing for or against, the existence of God. However, it turned out, rather surprisingly, that such crossroads will not be common "standards of reasoning," or "bodies of facts," on the basis of which different sides may argue. Rather, in the debate I envision, the argument for the existence of God is the endeavor to find and stand at the crossroad of particular worldviews involved in the debate, in order to forge a way forward. Yet God at the crossroad is not yet "God" of the theist; rather, this "God" extends beyond the horizon seen from the crossroad—a horizon toward which those who met at the crossroad in this debate must journey together, and what this horizon will turn out to be will remain unanswered until much, much further on.

This may seem a very strange suggestion. This book traverses through a wide range of topics—from contemporary debate about the existence of God, to conceptions of rationality and intellectual inquiry, to the concept of worldviews, to Thomistic theology, to the historical emergence of modern atheism—in order to arrive at that point. Some books contain one or more chapters one can skip; this is not such a book. Each chapter leads to the next, and the conclusion remains but a proposal, a hope, at a point in a story that is still being told.

I owe thanks to many. I thank the director, editors, and the staff of the University of Notre Dame Press. I thank Nancey Murphy and Richard Mouw, who first read the manuscript that would become this book and were the first to recommend its publication, as well as Bob Sweetman, who introduced the readings in Thomas Aquinas when I was a student. The advice and encouragement of Yujin Nagasawa and Douglas Loney kept my effort for publication going. Then, there are a number of friends, family—especially my brother—and members of the community in which I belong, too numerous to list here, all of whom were an integral part of my journey that led to this point, in particular those that were with me these last three years. I am grateful to my grandfather, who taught reason, imagination, fairness, and virtue to my mother, who in turn sought to instill them—hopefully with some success—in me. I owe my greatest thanks to my father and my mother, who taught me the most important things in my life, including the motivation and values that went into this work. Most of all, the one who continues to inspire and move me in all things—to you I give my thanks.

January 12, 2016

Paul Seungoh Chung

ONE

To Step Back

Rethinking the Question

There is something odd in the way we argue about the existence of God.

Let us, however, begin with a parable. Suppose two explorers came upon some natives in the New World, performing an esoteric ritual in which each adult male enters a secluded enclosure to offer a token of petition. One explorer says that a "benevolent ruler" must govern these natives and grant their wishes. Furthermore, this ruler must be benevolent by the very definition of *what* he is, not because he merely *happens* to be charitable or kind. The other explorer is skeptical and says that such a ruler does not exist. He then asks to meet this ruler in person, but no one seems able to arrange a meeting. He also finds that the petitions are not always granted, and often remain unanswered. He even learns that though—and at times even because—this ruler supposedly governs their world, they experience poverty, disasters, and wars. How, then, the skeptic finally asks his colleague, can he still say that the "benevolent ruler" of these natives exists?

How can our explorers resolve this disagreement? Perhaps they can talk to more natives to examine their claims, or set up some tests. It may be that although not all petitions are granted, a "significant" number are.

Perhaps other compelling evidences or arguments support the existence of the "benevolent ruler." What if there are no such proofs or arguments? Then, perhaps the "believer" ought to acknowledge that the "benevolent ruler" of the natives does not exist. Or, perhaps he may argue instead that this belief is somehow not a matter of "rational" discourse, but of "feeling," or "picture preference." He may even insist that this belief can be understood only within the context of a particular mode of living practiced by the natives, a mode to which his colleague is an outsider.[1] This is largely the way we have gone about arguing about the existence of God.

However, let us shift our perception of this parable. Suppose the context of this debate is actually as follows. The "skeptic" comes from a feudal society, rather like medieval Europe or the feudal Japanese shogunate, and the "believer" is from a representative democracy, similar to that of, say, early nineteenth-century United States. Moreover—and this is important—neither explorer has any notion of other forms of sociopolitical organization. What the "believer" believes he saw in the "esoteric ritual" was the natives participating in an election or a referendum. The "benevolent ruler" he speaks of is the "president," or rather, the holder of the "highest democratically elected office," whose government is, by definition, "of the people, by the people, for the people," representing and upholding the will—or the "wishes"—of those who vote for him. The "benevolence" of the "ruler," for the believer, is defined solely in these terms. What he is saying, then, is that the natives live in such a sociopolitical system.

However, the skeptic, who has lived within a radically different form of sociopolitical organization—a feudal hierarchy—has no conceptual basis with which to properly understand these claims of the believer. He has no concept of elections, referendums, or democracy, nor the related notions of individual rights, equality, liberty, or self-government. He assumes, and cannot imagine otherwise, that the natives belong to a feudal society. The description of a democratically elected office is baffling to him, since he understands this to describe a peculiar kind of feudal rulership, which somehow places upon the ruler the obligation to "grant wishes" of peasants, which is unlike the governance of any "ruler" he knows. Therefore, when he hears about the "president," the holder of the highest office, it seems to him that the believer is *positing* the existence of a very peculiar sort of ruler, above, and *in addition to*, the existing feudal hierarchy of lords and even monarchs—a ruler whose court "grants wishes" of the lowliest peasants. It is also important to note that the very wording of our parable in the beginning would differ depending on who is telling the tale—the skeptic, the believer, or even the natives.[2]

I have not stated, quite deliberately, what it is that the natives are *really* doing. Perhaps the "natives" are really some rural nineteenth-century Americans, voting on a proposition or an election. If so, the believer is correct. Or, perhaps they are participating in some elaborate ritual to send their petitions to a distant, wish-granting ruler. It may even be that this ruler does not exist, except as a fanciful tale told by their village elders. If so, the believer is wrong. Not only does the "president" not exist, but the believer *mis*understood what was happening, *because* of his sociopolitical background. Even if the natives themselves believe they live in a democracy as the believer understands it, they too might be mistaken. Consider the society of David Brin's *The Postman*, or George Orwell's *Nineteen Eighty-Four*.[3] Or consider real-life totalitarian states that pose as democracies, with dictators who commit atrocities while being adored by their people. Thus, the skeptic is not necessarily wrong in saying that the "benevolent ruler" does not exist, just because he fails to understand what the believer is saying. What I am separating here is the question of whether the "benevolent ruler exists" from the question of how we would go about answering this. Our concern is the latter.

How then can the explorers go about resolving their disagreement in our expanded parable? A simple answer may be that unlike God, the "president" would be someone they could just meet. However, the explorers are seeking an answer *now*, and even if the "president" exists, it will likely be a long while, if ever, before they are granted a personal audience with a head of state. On the other hand, numerous religions do claim that many people have met God, and we may even quip here that everyone may yet meet him after death! The more significant problem is that simply meeting the "president" would not by itself resolve their disagreement, any more than meeting someone who is supposedly divine, such as a Hindu Guru, or, say, Jesus Christ himself, would compel a skeptic to affirm that God exists. How else can the explorers resolve their disagreement?

Consider our problem. The two explorers hold radically different understandings of state, society, governance, and so forth, and thus have different reasons for their positions, and even employ different sets of vocabulary. Each explorer, for example, understands differently what it is that defines a "benevolent ruler" *as* such a ruler. For the "believer," such a ruler is the one elected by the nation to represent the will of its people, whereas for the "skeptic," such a ruler is the one who "grants wishes" of the peasantry and to whom all other feudal lords, and even monarchs, swear fealty. For the "believer," the evidence that this ruler exists would simply be an election for such office. To him, this is what it means to have *any* government, and what the natives did—which he assumes is a referendum or an election, for what else could it be?—confirms his claims. The evidence for the "skeptic," in contrast, would be a feudal lord, such as a baron, earl, or a daimyo, who swears fealty to this ruler and attests to the ruler's "benevolence" toward the peasants by granting their wishes in the ruler's stead. He assumes that what he saw is the native "peasants offering petitions," for what else could it be?

Thus, unless both explorers adequately understand the sociopolitical *system* of the other side, any evidence each raises for his position, or against the other, will not be acknowledged nor understood as an "evidence" by the other. Furthermore, each will insist that it is the belief of the other that must be justified by sufficient evidence. The "skeptic" will demand evidence because he sees no reason—one that befits his understanding of government—to posit this ruler in addition to the existing feudal hierarchy. It seems to him that since the petitions of these natives are not granted, what he sees before him is obviously a superstitious ritual born from their "wishful thinking." The "believer" will demand evidence that the "president" does not exist, because with an election going on, the "skeptic" is incomprehensibly denying what is even now happening before them.

Still, would there not be some form of evidence about the ruler that both would recognize? What about signs of law, order, and infrastructure, such as courts, police, schools, hospitals, or roads? Or perhaps, centralized currency, taxation, or a military? However, the skeptic may easily concede that these are signs of some sort of governance, but deny that these point to the existence of the "benevolent ruler." Such evidences are insufficient because the skeptic can explain these features in other terms, namely as the economic and social infrastructure within a feudal hierarchy, without the benevolent ruler.[4] Thus, the skeptic would still "have no need to posit the existence" of the benevolent ruler. On the other hand, a similar problem occurs when the skeptic raises evidences against the believer. Places ruled by military occupation, occasions when votes—or wishes—from one region fail to sway national policies, times of poverty and suffering among the general populace, and even slavery are consistent with a society governed by a democratically elected government.[5] Thus, again the explorers cannot evaluate which "shared" evidence is valid, in what ways, and to what extent, without understanding first how each fits in the sociopolitical system of the other, as a whole.

However, is not this account so far unrealistic, or even contrived? It begins by supposing that our two explorers would be unable to understand, or even notice, the differences in their sociopolitical backgrounds from which they have formed their positions about the natives' society. Does it not seem unreasonable to suppose that the explorers who are otherwise able to communicate with each other to the extent of having this disagreement, would repeatedly fail to realize the rather obvious fact that they are arguing from, and about, very different sociopolitical systems, using manifestly different sets of definitions and arguments? This is true; the point of this parable actually lies elsewhere. That is, if such differences *were* recognized, it would change the way they view their debate and proceed in it.

First, the question of whether the "benevolent ruler," or the "president," of the natives exists would become an odd question to ask. That is, it would be odd if, even when the two explorers understood their fundamental differences, their debate still proceeded primarily in terms and questions that consist of whether or not to posit the existence of the "benevolent ruler." What the skeptic from a feudal society would more likely question is whether the believer's description of the society the two of them have encountered—with that account's strange notions of individuality, liberty, equality, self-government, and so on—which this "benevolent ruler" supposedly governs, is an accurate description of the society that the natives live in.[6] He would ask, for example, if the natives really live as equals, liberated from the constraints of feudal classes.[7] To once again argue mainly over whether the "benevolent ruler" exists would be a very awkward way to proceed in their debate.

This is not to say that the question "whether the benevolent ruler exists" is itself incoherent or illegitimate. For example, one may understand such a question to be a rather simplistic way of asking which system of government exists for a particular society. It is quite legitimate to inquire in a first contact, or in the context of, say, social anthropology, whether a particular society has chieftains, oligarchs, monarchs, clerics, presidents, or some other, as its head. One may, given the relevant sociological or anthropological data, even coherently present a case that postulates the existence of a particular kind of ruler who likely governs a society. Also, an outsider may know better what sort of society exists than do those on the inside, provided that his or her understanding of such a society is comparable to the understanding its native members have of it. For example, a modern Western sociologist may be better situated to know what kind of sociopolitical system a particular Amazonian tribe has, or if a south Asian feudal monarchy is going through the process of becoming a constitutional monarchy, or if an autocracy in the Middle East is becoming a democracy, than are the members or citizens of those groups.

The problem, rather, is that the question of "whether the benevolent ruler exists" is situated within, and inseparable from, the larger question of "what sort of society exists." That is, what is being asked is a more comprehensive question that involves numerous, inseparably interconnected issues regarding what sort of social concepts, values, organizations, systems of government, jurisprudence, and so forth operate in the natives' society. Therefore, a likewise comprehensive answer is required for the question whether the "president," or some sufficiently similar office, truly exists in their society. Furthermore, precisely because of this, the final answer need not be limited to whether the office does or does not exist, since the society may have an office that is similar in some respects to the "president," yet differs greatly in others. What would be odd then would be if the existence of the "benevolent ruler" became the primary issue of contention in the debate—that is, if this were where the debate became "stuck," so to speak. We may even say that the debate would be stuck here only if the two explorers had somehow failed to grasp, in significant ways, this difference in their sociopolitical positions.

This brings us to a second point. It would be odd if both explorers, given their sociopolitical background, did not agree—at least provisionally—that a ruler of some kind that governs the natives exists. What they would disagree about is not the existence of the ruler per se, but his "benevolence," or rather, the nature of his office. The question of contention is about the society in which the ruler governs—whether the native society is closer to a feudal monarchy or a liberal democracy, which is a *comparative* question.[8] Thus, rather than the existence of the ruler being the primary point of disagreement, it would likely be the starting point of agreement, from which further questions could be asked. Moreover, it would again be odd to expect that only one position, as stated initially, must be right regarding everything about the native society, and the other, entirely wrong. It may be that in some respects, the believer is right, and in others, the skeptic, and yet in some others, both, or neither. Indeed, we would not be too surprised if we found that the final answer was developed, at least partially, from both positions.

Third, if all this were to be so, it would be odd if the skeptic continued to consider this debate largely in terms of the believer presenting evidence for his position, which was then to be defended or refuted. That is, it would be odd for the skeptic to claim that without evidence for liberal democracy, the debate is resolved in his favor by default. Both explorers are proposing that the natives belong to their particular form of sociopolitical organization. The question is not whether to posit the existence of the "benevolent ruler," or even whether the native society is a liberal democracy per se. Rather, it is a comparative question about which of the two views—liberal democracy, or feudal monarchy—as a whole, is closer to how the native society functions, and both sides must present their cases. However, the difficulty is that an adequate answer to this comparative question can be given only by someone who is "fluent," so to speak, in both sociopolitical forms, and can therefore assess the "correctness" of each position regarding a particular aspect of native society by its own standards. For example, if the believer's position regarding the native society on the subject of, say, equality of individuals is wrong, it must be shown to have failed by his own terms of what such "equality" is and what constitutes evidence for it, and not by the skeptic's terms—that is, the standard of a feudal monarchy.

Let us finally return to my first remark: what I am proposing is that the way we argue about the existence of God is odd, and for the same reasons that the way the skeptic and the believer in the parable argue is odd.[9]

Immediately, one may object that in our parable, it is only because the two explorers argued from different sociopolitical systems that they failed not only to resolve their disagreement but even to adequately understand their rival positions. Moreover, when the nature of this disagreement is understood, the debate may move on to other questions precisely because for both sociopolitical systems there are parallel concepts of a "ruler," such as the monarch and the president. However, the crucial difference between the theist and the atheist, in contrast, is simple: the theist says that God exists, and the atheist does not. But is this the case? There are reasons to believe that their difference is much more complex. For example, Alasdair MacIntyre comments in his account of the historical development of philosophy and the university in relation to the discourse on God:

> It may be retorted that the answer [to what the theist and the atheist disagree about] is obvious. The disagreement is as to whether God does or does not exist. But this retort misses the point, for the disagreement between atheists and theists is one of those fundamental disagreements that extends to how the disagreement is to be characterized. Atheists characteristically take theists to believe in one item too many. . . . This is not however how the theists characteristically understand their disagreement with atheists. From the theistic point of view this is a disagreement about everything, about what it is to find anything whatsoever intelligible rather than unintelligible.[10]

That is, at least according to MacIntyre, the nature of their differences may be more similar to that which characterized the explorers from a feudal hierarchy and the liberal democracy; it is a disagreement about "everything."

By remarking that there is something odd in how we argue, I am proposing a shift in our understanding of what we are doing when we argue about the existence of God. Recall the example of the ambiguous duck-rabbit image used by, among others, Thomas Kuhn in *The Struc-*

ture of Scientific Revolutions.[11] To shift the perception of such an image from the duck to the rabbit, or vice versa, is to shift to a radically different understanding of the entire image. That is, such a shift requires a reference not merely to this or that part of the image, but to the whole. This shift is not only made possible by presenting a plausible alternative of the whole—that it may be a "rabbit" rather than a "duck"—but triggered by a new understanding of a particular, yet defining, part of the image, such as "coming to see" the "beaks" as "ears." Here, the "whole," in the most general terms, is the intellectual debate regarding the existence of God, particularly in regard to God as the "first cause." The goal then is to propose a shift in our understanding of what we are doing when we argue about the existence of God in such a debate, along with the relevant philosophical and scientific issues. The shift is to be made possible by proposing what the alternative is, and then triggered by presenting a particular account of the context and function of the Five Ways of Aquinas—a paradigmatic argument in this debate.

The reason why I began with a parable ought now to be clear. Since I am proposing a gestalt-shift in our understanding of the entire rational debate about the existence of God, and how such a debate ought to proceed, a parable is required in order "to take a step back" and "see" the whole picture from a more simplified perspective. The debate is too great in scope and too complex for such a large-scale proposal to be intelligible without the aid of such a device. What the parable presents is a new metaphor for understanding the nature of the disagreement between the theists and the atheists in the contemporary debate, implicitly explaining why the debate remains unresolved so far, and suggesting a different way to proceed in arguing about the existence of God.

All this sets the general contours of my argument in this book. I will argue how the debate about the existence of God resembles the state between the two explorers in our parable, and that this ought to shift our understanding of how we are to argue. That is, I will present a particular perspective of the debate, from which the way we have argued about the existence of God will begin to seem "odd" to us, in the same way the debate between the explorers seemed odd. I am, however, in no way suggesting that the question about the existence of God, nor the numerous philosophical arguments concerning it, past and present, are simply to be abandoned. What I am proposing is a different way of seeing this debate, and thus of continuing and expanding it in a direction that may be more fruitful.

Therefore, in the next chapter, I will argue that the differences between the diverse theist and the atheist positions in the contemporary debate about the existence of God are not merely incompatible, but incommensurable. By "incommensurable" I mean primarily what MacIntyre describes in the following:

> Let us consider the case where the beliefs are not only incompatible but also incommensurable. We have already seen that from the fact that two communities with such rival belief-systems are able to agree in identifying one and the same subject matter as that identified, characterized, and evaluated in their two rival systems and are able to recognize that the applicability of certain of the concepts in the one scheme of belief precludes certain concepts in the other scheme from having application, it does not follow that the substantive criteria which govern the application of those concepts—the standards, that is, by which truth or falsity and the rational justification or the lack of it are judged—cannot differ radically. The incommensurability of two schemes of beliefs in no way precludes their logical incompatibility.[12]

That is, incommensurable positions (a) consist of belief *systems*, rather than a particular belief proposition, and (b) have intelligible disagreements —that is, hold incompatible views regarding what both understand as the *same* "subject-matter"—yet (c) inhabit a different conceptual scheme, and more importantly, (d) have "radically different" standards to judge the truth or falsity, or rationality or irrationality, of their beliefs. Thus, a rational debate between incommensurable positions tends to become interminable and sterile. I will argue that contemporary debate about the existence of God is characterized by such incommensurability of rival positions, which resembles the kind of comprehensive difference that framed the disagreement between the two explorers in the parable.

In chapter 3, I will describe the philosophical background, namely the Enlightenment foundationalist epistemology, in which the very possibility of such incommensurability of the rival positions was once precluded, and then describe the contemporary philosophical developments which have overturned this position. I will argue how these developments have led to a conception of rationality and intellectual inquiry as situated within comprehensive, historically contingent networks of interconnected beliefs and concepts, exemplified by the concept of "worldview." It is within these worldviews that beliefs—or lack thereof—regarding the existence of God are also situated. The worldviews, in this sense, function like the sociopolitical backgrounds of the explorers in the parable.

In chapter 4, I will explain how the problem of incommensurability in the contemporary debate, described in chapter 2, arises *because* each position in the debate is a worldview; that is, each position argues *from* a particular worldview *against* the other. Furthermore, I will argue that insofar as the contemporary debate about the existence of God resembles the disagreement between the two explorers in the parable, understanding the rival positions in the debate as different worldviews—rather like understanding the explorers' positions as arising from different sociopolitical systems—renders their incommensurable disagreements intelligible. I will then propose, primarily from MacIntyre's account of rationality, how such comprehensive and incommensurable positions may nevertheless intersect, and resolve their disagreement, and what it would be to argue about the existence of God in such a context—namely, to argue at the crossroads of worldviews.

In the next two chapters, 5 and 6, I will give an account of the Five Ways of Thomas Aquinas as just such an argument. Among contemporary participants in the debate, there is a widespread understanding of the Five Ways as simply "proofs" for the existence of God. However, I will outline how, according to contemporary Aquinas scholarship, Aquinas's intellectual opus presents a comprehensive position in which two particular rival worldviews of his time were integrated together. Furthermore, the Five Ways are situated within this very project of integration and synthesis. I will then describe the role of the Five Ways in such a project. That is, the Five Ways do not prove that God exists per se, but identify and present the existence of a starting point—much like how both explorers would agree that a "ruler" of some kind exists—from which two comprehensive, rival worldviews may be brought together, in order to begin the debate on the other issues.

In chapter 7, I will briefly describe how atheism as a worldview emerged, and did so in such a way that it eventually seemed to be the "default" position in the debate. I will suggest how through this development the understanding of God—and more specifically, God as the first cause—has changed, and how this has further contributed to the failure of the argument for the existence of God and to the emergence of the notion that the theist belief in God is about positing God in addition to the universe. Finally, in chapter 8, I will sketch what it may mean to argue for the existence of God in our contemporary debate if we are arguing at the crossroads of worldviews to accomplish what Aquinas did in his Five Ways.

The argument from each chapter, by itself, will be largely uncontroversial. That is, what I present will be a position that summarizes what is either widely accepted or even close to a general consensus regarding that subject matter. The only exception may be found in the latter section of chapter 6, where I will argue from MacIntyre's account of Augustinian and Aristotelian conceptions of rational inquiry that Aquinas's Five Ways present God as that which is indispensable for the conception of truth, reality, and intellectual formation of both rival worldviews—and in a way that is not another transcendental argument. Yet even this, I believe, is not too far from a highly influential position of MacIntyre.

However, this is precisely my point. The arguments in each chapter, largely uncontroversial in themselves, when linked together, will present a standpoint from which the way we have proceeded in the contemporary debate about the existence of God will seem—not wrong, but "odd." The actual argument of this book as a whole, therefore, is the parable in this chapter. The following chapters simply expand on its points in order to argue one thing: if we accept what seems to be largely uncontroversial regarding the character of the current debate about the existence of God, the contemporary philosophical positions on rationality, intellectual inquiry, worldviews, and the historical account of Aquinas, we will find ourselves likewise accepting what *is* controversial—that the parable of the two explorers, with its implied critique and suggested alternative, applies to how we have argued about the existence of God.

Finally, the way of arguing about the existence of God that I will propose will be such that most of the existing arguments in the debate will remain seemingly unchanged in content and argumentation, yet the context and frame in which such arguments function, and their significance in the debate, will be different. After all, a gestalt-shift changes the perception of the whole, but leaves component parts mostly unchanged. However, I will suggest that several issues previously deemed unimportant, or even irrelevant, for the debate, such as the resurrection of Christ, will become more significant, whereas other issues, previously significant, such as whether "laws of nature" may adequately explain the beginning of the universe, miracles, or the phenomenon of religion, will simply be "dissolved." All this, however, must remain as mere speculation to be considered in the final chapter.

TWO

Where We Stand

The Contemporary Question

Incommensurability is what characterizes our contemporary discourse about the existence of God.[1] By this, I mean to say more than that there are different positions in the present-day debate regarding whether God exists, although the bewildering array and the sheer number of such positions is one of the debate's key features. Nor do I mean that the debate is merely unresolved, or even irresolvable. Indeed, the existence of God persists as a significant question in philosophy, not only because it asks about the ultimate level of our reality, but because the question has seemed tantalizingly resolvable, yet remains unresolved. Long series of different arguments, counterarguments, and refutations flow through the history of Western philosophy, and more than once the debate was declared definitively to be closed, only to be later revived. What I am saying, rather, is that if we conceive the debate simply as the question of whether or not God exists, the differences between the opposing positions—between the theist and the atheist—are such that no simple comparison or adjudication between them is feasible, and it is because of this that the debate remains unresolved. This is because these rival positions pose comprehensive systems, which differ not only in the beliefs regarding the existence of God proper, but in the standard of justification for their positions, the understanding and usage of concepts involved, and even how to start or proceed in the debate. What is claimed here is that it is both this feature of the debate and the increasing awareness of this feature that characterizes the contours of our contemporary discourse.

A number of considerations suggest this characterization, and I will divide them into three key levels. First, it has become increasingly evident that each of the opposing positions about the existence of God—mainly the theist and the atheist—formulates and presents its case from a larger philosophical standpoint containing premises, assumptions, and concepts different from those of the other position in numerous significant ways. Second, even the starting point of the debate is disputed, as is exemplified by the Reformed epistemologist critique of evidentialism, which questions the claim that it is the theist who has the burden of proof. Third, that the existence of God is subject to proofs or evidences is disputed as well, notably by D. Z. Phillips, not because such belief is not "rational" per se, but because it is inseparable from a larger "world-picture," from which one begins to reason. Due to the scope of this issue, I can provide only cursory descriptions of the significant exemplars of these disputes, and will eschew further discussion about the ongoing debate between the theists and the atheists regarding them.[2] My purpose is simply to present some very general points that have emerged in this contemporary debate, only in order to sketch out the emerging feature of "incommensurability" that I claim as characterizing the debate.

THE DISTINCTIVE CHARACTERISTIC OF THE DISAGREEMENT ON WHETHER GOD EXISTS

Consider the cases of disagreement on whether something exists. What is often overlooked is that most such disagreements begin from a larger set of agreements—that is, from within a common framework. For example, if a police officer claims that a fugitive is hiding in the warehouse, and his partner disagrees, they will still agree as to what—and usually who—is meant by "the fugitive," and they will presumably search the warehouse to find out. When some scientists hypothesized the existence of the Higgs-Boson particle—or the "God-particle," as the media are fond of calling it—and others were skeptical, they all still largely agreed as to what such a particle is, and that the Large Hadron Collider was to be used to confirm its existence. Thus, those who disagree whether x exists tend to be rather clear on what x is, and what it would be like to have confirmed whether x exists—or, differently put, on the nature of their disagreement and on how they would go about resolving the disagreement. Even the popular parodies against the theist position regarding the existence of God, such as the "Great Pumpkin," the "Invisible Pink Unicorn," or the "Flying Spaghetti Monster," depend precisely on this feature.[3] That is, despite being invisible, undetectable, and so forth, these things, by the very images that their names evoke, cause us to feel that it is rather obvious as to what it is that they are—even if obviously ridiculous—and thus what it would mean to have confirmed their existence, if it could somehow be confirmed. These parodies then assume that the case is the same for the existence of "God."

However, consider the disagreement on whether God exists. First, there are differing positions even among theists and among atheists. More striking is the breadth of such differences, which is revealed even in the most general characterization of the main positions on any given issue in the debate:[4]

(a) concerning the concept of God in relation to the existence of God:
   (i)   the concept of God is such that it is logically necessary that God exists
   (ii) no concept is such that it is logically necessary that the thing referred to by the concept exists
   (iii) the concept of God is such that it is logically necessary that God does not exist
(b) concerning the arguments that purport to prove the existence of God:
   (i)   rational arguments prove that God exists
   (ii) rational arguments fail to prove that God exists
   (iii) rational arguments prove that God does not exist
(c) concerning the arguments that present evidences for the existence of God:

(i)   evidences imply that it is probable that God exists

(ii) evidences imply that it is improbable that God exists

(iii) no possible evidence can imply that God exists

(d) concerning the relation between modern science and the existence of God:

   (i)   findings of modern science are consistent with the existence of God

   (ii) findings of modern science are inconsistent with the existence of God

   (iii) findings of science are irrelevant to the belief that God exists

(e) concerning the relevance of religious experience to the question of the existence of God:

   (i)   religious experience is a valid kind of evidence that God exists

   (ii) religious experience is not a valid kind of evidence that God exists

   (iii) it is inappropriate to understand religious experience in terms of evidence

(f) concerning the role of proofs and evidences in generating belief in the existence of God:

   (i)   it is rational to believe that God exists even without proofs or evidences

   (ii) it is not rational to believe that God exists without proofs or evidences

   (iii) proofs or evidence, and rationality as such, are inappropriate terms with which to understand the belief that God exists

(g) concerning the cognitive meaningfulness of the claims regarding God:

   (i)   statements regarding God can be cognitively meaningful and intelligible

   (ii) statements regarding God cannot be cognitively meaningful or intelligible

   (iii) neither "cognitive meaningfulness" nor "intelligibility" as used above is an appropriate term with which to understand statements regarding God

The differences are both wide ranging and comprehensive in scope; there are disagreements at nearly every level and related issue of the debate. That is, it seems there is no larger, universal, common set of agreements from which the participants in the debate can meaningfully disagree on whether God exists. More significantly, the disagreement about each issue is itself not simple: there are not only two opposing positions on a given issue, but other positions that question the very categories and assumptions with which the debate proceeds. Furthermore, these rival positions on each issue cannot be divided neatly along the theist-atheist lines. For example, a theist may disagree with other theists and agree with an atheist that (1) no concept is such that it is logically necessary that the thing the concept refers to exists, and (2) rational arguments fail to "prove" that God exists, yet this same theist may nevertheless argue that there are evidences that make it probable that God exists.[5] Another atheist may disagree with the theist above, yet also with an atheist who argues the existence of God is improbable, by arguing that no possible evidence can imply that God exists.[6] Yet another theist may agree with this atheist, yet disagree that lack of proofs or evidences implies that one ought not to believe that God exists.[7]

Again, these are necessarily oversimplified characterizations. Indeed, it is striking that such a complex web of differences seems evident even at this level of simplification. Deeper in, disagreements multiply on the definition and use of terms and on the myriad variations of the above positions. However, an adequate understanding of the incommensurability in the debate requires a closer view via particular case studies. We will therefore survey the difference at three levels: first, concerning the answers to whether God exists and the justifications for such answers; second, concerning the starting point of the debate; third, concerning whether belief in God is subject to a rational debate.

DISAGREEMENT IN THE CONTEMPORARY ARGUMENTS

Contemporary Revival of Theistic Arguments

The modern debate about the existence of God has generally assumed an "evidentialist" premise: that a belief in God is rationally justified only if there is sufficient evidence. This is not to say that if there is no such evidence, there is no God, only that if there is no such evidence, there is no rational justification for believing that God exists. From this, the debate has consisted largely of the theist presenting evidences or grounds for the existence of God, and the atheist refuting them. These rational cases for the existence of God are presented either as a deductive argument, which purports to prove that God exists, or as a probabilistic argument, which offers evidences for the case that God probably exists.[8]

There are numerous types of these arguments, each with subtypes and variations, but for our purpose here, we will mainly consider the example of three classical categories of theist arguments—the ontological, the cosmological, and the teleological—or design—arguments.[9] Ontological arguments argue that the concept of God is such that God exists by definition. Cosmological arguments argue from some very general features of the universe, such as the existence of the universe or the contingency of existence as such, that there is an ultimate or first cause of all that exists, which is God. Teleological arguments argue that there is purposiveness or order in the universe, which implies the existence of an intelligent, purposive Creator, and the most historically significant version argues that nature evinces design, and this version thereby posits a divine Designer.

Not long ago most philosophers—at least Anglo-American ones—considered the debate about God closed on account of the writings of David Hume and Immanuel Kant. Hume's *Dialogues concerning Natural Religion* was a sustained argument that experience is insufficient to establish an infinite, perfect Creator, either as the first cause or as the cause of design in nature.[10] Kant, in his *Critique of Pure Reason*, argued further that theist arguments fail, and inevitably so, because "knowledge" is limited to the spatiotemporal world of phenomena, and reason can never prove that which is beyond it, such as the existence of God. His critique of the ontological argument, and his argument that the cosmological argument fails largely because of its dependence on the flawed ontological argument, became especially influential.[11] Thus, since the time of Hume and Kant, these three classical arguments that presented "sufficient evidence" for the theist position were regarded as decisively refuted, and the theory of evolution was considered as merely dislodging the last remaining urge to posit the existence of God to explain the features of nature.

However, this has changed. In his preface to *The Non-Existence of God*, Nicholas Everitt, who himself argues against the existence of God, recalls a time when as a philosophy student, he was told by a tutor, "My interest in my maker ceased when I read Hume's *Dialogues*," and comments that this general outlook has been "transformed . . . in the last few decades."[12] Everitt credits this to the revitalization of the field of philosophy of religion by new imaginative, creative thinkers and philosophers, with new, sophisticated arguments and positions. Again, my purpose is not to describe the specifics of the critiques posed by Hume and Kant or to detail the vast array of the new contemporary theist arguments that has since emerged.[13] What is of interest is that the debate, once considered decisively closed since Kant, was revived. How?

First, contemporary philosophers reformulated their arguments so as to avoid the point of their critiques, or presented entirely novel versions. Norman Malcolm, Charles Hartshorne, and Alvin Plantinga, for example, reformulated the ontological argument, defining the concept of God in terms of *necessary* existence, or existence in all possible worlds, rather than in terms of the notion that the definition of God simply includes existence, which had been critiqued by Kant.[14] William Lane Craig presented a version of the *kalam* cosmological argument that argues for the first cause from the finitude of the universe, an argument that avoided the applicability of Hume's critique of previous cosmological arguments.[15] Alternative kinds of evidence were formalized into philosophical arguments—such as arguments from morality, consciousness, religious experience, and miracles—by William Alston, Richard Swinburne, William Wainwright, and many others.[16]

These new formulations and arguments, however, often involved revisiting or reevaluating the past—supposedly refuted—arguments for the existence of God. Malcolm and Hartshorne thus argued that there is a second version of the ontological argument by Anselm that his critics such as Gaunilo and Kant largely did not address, or wrongly criticized. Bruce Reichenbach, William Rowe, and Richard Taylor reevaluated the cosmological arguments, concluding against Hume and, later, Bertrand Russell, that the universe as a whole requires an explanation even if there is an explanation for the existence of each member, because the existence of the whole series is contingent.[17] Rowe, for example, reformulated the problem as "Why does that set (the universe) have the members that it does rather than some other members or none at all?"[18] He concluded that the cosmological argument for the existence of God is still questionable, but stated nevertheless that there is no reason to reject either of the two core assumptions of the cosmological argument: the possible existence of a necessary being—contra Kant—or the principle of sufficient reason, which demands explanation for the existence of every contingent being.

These contemporary theist positions included, or implied, a critique—and subsequently the rejection—of the underlying philosophical positions, especially the epistemology, from which the past refutations of the theist arguments were developed.[19] Such implicit rejection of Kant's epistemology in relation to the contemporary debate about the existence of God is exemplified by Graham Oppy. He does conclude, like Kant, that there are no arguments that successfully show that God exists.[20] However, he adds: "I have not discussed all of the arguments that have been constructed thus far; and, as new arguments come in, they will all need to be assessed on their merits. I do not claim to have a successful transcendental argument for the conclusion that there *cannot* be successful arguments about [God]."[21] In a Kantian epistemology, it is not that particular theistic arguments fail to demonstrate that God exists; it is simply not possible for any rational argument as such to prove that God exists. However, without Kant's theory of knowledge based on a transcendental critique of reason, there is no longer any means to justify an a priori rejection of every theistic argument. On the other hand, Hume's position, characterized by a skeptical position toward knowledge, was criticized for this very skepticism by those, such as his contemporary Thomas Reid, who argued that what is considered "knowledge" in real life—or in science—simply does not conform to such rigid standards. Likewise, a number of contemporary theists, most notably Swinburne, argue that the existence of God is rational in terms of such real-life reasoning, following the model of probabilistic or scientific reasoning.

Lastly, many new arguments drew upon new developments in fields outside philosophy since the time of Hume and Kant. Contemporary cosmology, such as the big bang theory, and thus the finitude of the universe, lent previously unavailable support to cosmological arguments, including Craig's new *kalam* variant, while the seeming "fine tuned" nature of the universe, with its set of highly specific cosmological constants, gave new life to design arguments. These factors were by no means decisive in the debate, but were sufficiently significant to have required sustained scrutiny from both sides. On the other hand, a more sophisticated understanding of scientific reasoning opened a way for less restrictive conditions to justify the theist position, thus leading to arguments that the existence of God is rationally—or even "scientifically"—more probable than not, as well as to new arguments from religious experiences, miracles, and so on.

What is relatively uncontroversial in all this so far, yet underemphasized, is how each position in the debate is set in a larger philosophical context. Hume's and Kant's critiques of theistic arguments, for example, were inseparable from their larger epistemological positions. Likewise, their refutation of prior forms of ontological and cosmological arguments of those such as Descartes and Leibniz largely involved the rejection of those earlier thinkers' epistemology. Again, the subsequent theist responses included not merely new arguments, but new understandings of old arguments and extended critiques of larger philosophical positions of Hume and Kant. Furthermore, theist arguments often even involved areas beyond the discipline of philosophy proper. All this reveals that each position is situated in a larger intellectual context or a framework. This, so far, would be uncontroversial in the present day.

I, however, am suggesting something more controversial: the rationality and the justification of each position are also inseparable from such a framework. Consider, for example, how one would refute the argument for the existence of God if Descartes's epistemology in its entirety—including the assertion that the existence of God ensures certainty regarding all knowledge of the world—were not abandoned. What would happen in a debate between such a position and Kant's epistemological position that there can be no rational proof for the existence of God? With a different account of what constitutes knowledge, how would such a debate proceed to answer the question of whether God exists? This question raises the issue of incommensurability. However, one may retort, both the Cartesian and the Kantian theory of knowledge were in fact abandoned. Indeed, even if there is a "larger context or framework," is not the contemporary debate largely conducted in a common framework? After all, most participants who present or refute rational cases for the existence of God are empiricists, share a common set of scientific claims about the universe, and so forth.

Let us then examine a paradigmatic example of such a debate.

Debate between Richard Swinburne and J. L. Mackie

Swinburne's *The Existence of God* and J. L. Mackie's *The Miracle of Theism* together constitute one of the milestone exemplars of the contemporary debate about the existence of God. Swinburne's case is one of the most influential theist positions, cited in most writings on the subject since, and Mackie's response is likewise influential as a critique. There has certainly been no shortage of newer atheist positions since Mackie that purport to critique Swinburne's position.[22] However, the influence and familiarity of the debate between the two in subsequent works, bolstered by years of secondary literature and extensive discussion regarding it, make a case study of this debate more helpful in bringing into sharp focus some key features that will underlie that extended debate.

Swinburne and Mackie begin from what seems to be a large set of agreements. Both are empiricists and share a common set of scientific knowledge-claims. Both hold that religious language—especially about God—is cognitively meaningful, coherent, and intelligible.[23] For Swinburne, the existence of God is an explanatory hypothesis, that is, it claims that God is the best explanation for the existence of the universe and its various features.[24] Mackie concurs that God is rightly regarded as an explanatory hypothesis.[25] Where then do they disagree?

Swinburne's argument, in contrast to classical theistic arguments, is not a deductive argument. An expert in confirmation theory, a field of inductive logic, Swinburne uses the probability calculus of Bayes's theorem to argue that it is probable that God exists. His argument is highly technical, but to put it very simply, it is that each theistic argument, such as the cosmological argument, teleological argument, argument from consciousness, morality, providence, miracles, religious experience, and so on, increases the probability of the existence of a unique, omnipotent, omniscient, perfectly free, and personal being—namely, God—until cumulatively, the existence of such a being is significantly more probable than not.[26] His conclusion is summed up neatly in a later book: "The existence, orderliness, and fine-tunedness of the world; the existence of conscious humans within it with providential opportunities for moulding themselves, each other, and the world; some historical evidence of miracles in connection with human needs and prayers . . . , topped up finally by the apparent experience by millions of his presence, all make it significantly more probable than not that there is a God."[27] What Swinburne is doing is formulating the theistic arguments—none of which, he concedes, is compelling by itself—so that each refers to a key feature of the world, or a kind of "data." Each of these "data," such as the existence of the universe, its contingency, its orderliness and fine-tunedness, the existence of conscious beings, morality, reports of miracles, religious experience of God's presence, and so on, confirms the theistic hypothesis in that (a) it is what we would expect if the theistic hypothesis were true, and moreover, (b) it seems less likely to occur unless the theistic hypothesis is true. The hypothesis that God exists, given all the data *cumulatively*, is then the best explanatory hypothesis supported by evidence. Indeed, this form of reasoning, Swinburne argues, is that which actual scientists, historians, and detectives use to determine which theory is best supported by observed data.

Mackie, however, retorts that arguments from miracles and religious experience are extremely weak, vulnerable to the critiques of Hume found in *An Enquiry concerning Human Understanding* and *The Natural History of Religion*.[28] That is, both miracles and religious experience may be either explained in natural terms or rejected rather than being understood as a direct experience of the supernatural. Likewise, morality and consciousness may be explained in materialist terms, and although he concedes that there is some difficulty in giving an account of how conscious awareness emerges for the materialist, the difficulty for the rival position is "at least as great."[29]

He also rejects Swinburne's cosmological argument that it is more probable that a universe, with all its complexities and contingency, exists if God exists. Although a naturalist has no answer to the question "Why is there a world at all?," if the theist is deprived of the "illusory support of ontological argument," which would have God existing necessarily, the theist has no answer to the question "Why is there a god at all?"[30] While it does seem more improbable for there to be causal regularities and orderliness in the universe on a naturalist hypothesis, and it is true that this hypothesis cannot explain why the fundamental laws of nature and constants are what they are, it is far more improbable for there to be a disembodied, omnipotent, omniscient person capable of creating the universe.[31] Furthermore, the existence of God is made more improbable, and considerably so, because of the problem of evil. Thus, Mackie concludes: "In the end, therefore, we can agree with what Laplace said about God: we have no need of that hypothesis."[32]

Why such startlingly different conclusions? A simple answer is that one is wrong. However, their differences are more complex. We will consider one example.

Comprehensive Simplicity of Hypothesis vs. Occam's Razor on Unwarranted Entities

One of the keys to Swinburne's position is his view that the theist hypothesis is simple. He identifies two forms of explanations. First is the "inanimate," which explains an event in terms of powers and liabilities— or simply, the laws of nature and initial events as cause of events. Second is the "personal," which explains an event in terms not only of powers, but of purposes, beliefs, and intentions. Both forms of explanations are indispensable in real life. He then identifies three "ultimate explanations," that is, final, comprehensive explanatory accounts of all the causes in the universe in terms of its most fundamental level. First is materialism, which states that all the factors that require personal explanation ultimately have complete inanimate explanations. Second is humanism, which states that factors that involve personal explanation cannot fully be explained in inanimate terms and vice versa. Third is theism, which states that all the factors may be completely explained in terms of personal explanation, where the "person" is God, who "keeps in existence the material objects of our universe from moment to moment, with their powers and liabilities to act."[33] Swinburne points out that in scientific reasoning, if each theory explains the relevant data equally, the best theory is that which (a) best fits "background" knowledge, or what is known to be true in other areas of inquiry, and (b) is the "simplest." He then argues that in ultimate explanations, such as materialism, humanism, and theism, the consideration of the "background" drops out, because the scope of its explanation already includes everything. Thus, simplicity becomes the crucial determinant for the hypothesis of theism. He then argues against the materialist and the humanist hypotheses: "[Materialism] remains a very complicated hypothesis—in postulating that the complete causes of things now are innumerable separate objects (coincidentally, with exactly the same powers as each other). . . . Humanism is an even more complicated hypothesis—for it postulates that current explanation terminates not merely with innumerable separate material objects, but with very many persons and their powers and purposes, all of which . . . are brute facts."[34] That is, both the materialist and the humanist position are complicated theories that require references to innumerable objects and interrelations between them for a complete explanation of all causes. He then contrasts this with the theist position, which he argues is a "very simple hypothesis," because "theism claims that every other object which exists is caused to exist and kept in existence by just one substance, God."[35] He then argues that the theist hypothesis is made even simpler because this God has infinite power, infinite knowledge, and infinite freedom—insofar as it is logically possible to act and know, and consistent with God's own character and purposes. Furthermore, it is simpler to suppose that God is eternal and possesses these divine traits essentially.

Mackie, of course, would easily retort that such a hypothesis is not "simple," because after all, it postulates an entity to explain what may be explained without it. If, say, science can eventually explain everything by reference to the relevant laws of nature, or principles, that describe the workings of the universe, what is the point of positing an additional entity like God? Furthermore, why would a disembodied, omnipotent, omniscient, perfectly free, and eternal person be "simpler"? Does this not make this unique being highly improbable? After all, we have no experience of beings with the same, or even comparably similar, traits. The only "persons" we know through sense experience are human beings, who are embodied and limited.

However, Swinburne and Mackie employ the term "simplicity" in misleadingly different ways. For Mackie, the theistic hypothesis is not "simple," because God is a postulation of an unwarranted entity—and a rather puzzling one at that—in addition to the universe. This assumption is made apparent throughout his arguments in *The Miracle of Theism*, but he makes it explicit when he characterizes Swinburne's argument—

and indeed every theistic argument other than Berkeley's idealism—as that which "adds God to the universe."[36] For Swinburne, the "simplicity" of the theist hypothesis is the simplicity of its ultimate explanation. This is a fundamental, yet seemingly oft overlooked, difference. Thus, Richard Messer, in *Does God's Existence Need Proof?*, comments: "This difference is rarely observed. Swinburne's principle of simplicity looks for the simplest possible final explanation; Mackie's Occam's razor looks for no unwarranted multiplication of entities in an explanation."[37]

Swinburne's theistic hypothesis is not only "simple" but also unitive; it is a singular hypothesis that explains every aspect of all existence. It is comprehensive in scope, unifies disparate data, yet is singular. He begins his argument this way:

> Using those same criteria [that scientists use], we find that the view that there is a God explains *everything* we observe, not just some narrow range of data. It explains the fact that there is a universe at all, that scientific laws operate within it, that it contains conscious animals and humans . . . as well as the more particular data that humans report miracles and have religious experience. In so far as scientific laws explain some of these things . . . these very causes and laws need explaining, and God's action explains them.[38]

That is, the theistic hypothesis is "simple" because *everything*—note his emphasis—that can be explained, including why there are scientific laws and why they are what they are, is explained by a reference to a *single* being with particular, unique traits. For example, there are personal beings whose interactions operate through moral principles, *and* there are intelligible, causal regularities and order that operate in the material universe, because the single, ultimate explanation of everything is personal, moral, intelligible, and orderly. In contrast, the materialist requires a large number of disparate explanations for each such datum, by reference to different laws of nature, initial conditions, and so on.

Thus, an eternal, omnipotent, omniscient, and perfectly free—and essentially so—personal being is not what is to be explained, but, what explains everything else. That is, God is the hypothesis within which everything else is explained, and this "ultimate" explanation itself is an unexplainable "brute fact." The divine traits that, for Mackie, make God "improbable" are precisely those which allow the theist to reference only one being for an ultimate explanation. Swinburne therefore argues for his position against those like Mackie's in this way: "The whole progress of science and **all** other **intellectual enquiry demands that we postulate the smallest number of brute facts.** If we can explain the many bits of the universe by one simple being, which keeps them in existence, we shall do so—even if inevitably we cannot explain the existence of that simple being."[39] What the theist position of Swinburne seeks to minimize, then, is not the number of entities, per se, but the number of unexplained "brute facts." The theist hypothesis is simple because there is only one brute fact, namely God, whereas the materialist hypothesis, even if it explains everything, requires many brute facts.

It may be asked why a hypothesis that provides a simple—that is ultimate, unitive, singular, and so on—explanation of everything is required. It may also be asked why "simplicity" of an ultimate explanation should be a reason to believe it. Then again, it may be retorted, Why not? After all, physics strives to achieve a single theory unifying quantum physics and the theory of relativity, and ultimately seeks the "theory of everything," in which there is the smallest number of unexplained brute facts. Then again, in the case of Swinburne's theist hypothesis, this "simple" theory postulates an additional entity, which does not provide any further scientific explanation beyond what the naturalist position also provides. Yet again, Swinburne argues that the theist can explain why there are laws of nature in the first place—though, then again, do the laws require such explanation? And so on and so forth.

Thus, the two positions, both empiricist, and seemingly operating from a shared body of scientific knowledge, actually hold different principles of justification. They differ on the very standards with which to evaluate the rationality of belief in God. They even differ significantly in how they use the same term, "simplicity." However, it turns out that this is just one possible example of such difference.

Oppy's Assessment of the Debate

Graham Oppy's *Arguing about Gods* is one of the recent and significant works that present a comprehensive account of the numerous arguments about the existence of God. What is important for our purpose is not his account or critique of each argument, but his analysis of the concept of argument as such. He begins by giving this account of philosophical arguments:

> I take it that the proper function of arguments is to bring about reasonable belief revision. . . . A good argument is one that succeeds—or perhaps would or ought to succeed—in bringing about reasonable belief revision in reasonable targets. The most successful argument would be one that succeeds—or perhaps would or ought to succeed—in persuading any reasonable person to accept its conclusion; good, but less successful arguments would be ones that succeed—or perhaps would or ought to succeed—in persuading a non-zero percentage of reasonable people to accept their conclusions.[40]

Thus, Oppy identifies the purpose of the argument concerning the existence of God. It is to persuade "reasonable" persons who hold a different position—all, or at least some—to revise their beliefs.

However, he argues that there are many difficulties to this goal of belief revision. First, if a reasonable person need not accept all of the premises of the argument, then he or she need not accept its conclusion. Even if every premise is acceptable, an argument may nevertheless be circular, question begging, and so forth.[41] So far, the standard of "successful" arguments seems difficult, but still not too problematic. However, Oppy argued previously that there are two significant sources of disagreement among reasonable people, aside from errors. First, rational persons in the debate may have "different bodies of evidence," which is obtained in "all manner of different ways," and even if both have the same body of evidence, each may access the evidence in "differing orders."[42] This problem is compounded, of course, when we consider the possibility that they may also disagree on what body of evidence is relevant, and why. Second, if both use the same body of evidence in the same order, there may yet be different set of "priors"—either "prior beliefs" or "prior probability"—that the evidence fits.[43] What Oppy seems to suggest then is that different arguments concerning the existence of God may be "rational" yet fail to be "successful," precisely because the same set of arguments may be evaluated very differently by different positions.

Thus, for example, Oppy rejects all versions of the cosmological argument, because no argument has premises that every atheist ought to adopt. Conversely, he rejects the argument that Hartle-Hawking's version of the big bang cosmology poses a problem for the theist position, because it assumes certain premises that theists need not accept, and even if those premises are accepted, there are many "strategies" by which to make the premises consistent with classical theism.[44] He then identifies the larger conceptual issues of "infinity," "time," "causation," "necessity," "sufficient reason," and so forth, which are inseparable from the coherence, soundness, and acceptability of cosmological forms of arguments.[45] Since there are different positions regarding these complex issues, he points out that it is "highly plausible to suppose that there is not going to be a short and simple argument that succeeds in establishing either theistic or non-theistic conclusions" without "the dozens of complex premises that would be required . . . to evade the charge that one is simply begging the question on key issues."[46]

With all this, Oppy's conclusion seems predrawn. After examining a number of contemporary arguments concerning the existence of God, he writes:

> Given the view of arguments that I have developed in chapter 1, it is not surprising that I have arrived at the conclusion that there are no successful arguments that have as their conclusion that there are—or that there are not—orthodoxly conceived monotheistic gods. After all, it is a plausible hypothesis that wherever there is substantial perennial disagreement about matters of philosophy or religion, there is no prospect that there are successful arguments that settle the matter. It is plain matter of fact that there are sincere, thoughtful, intelligent, well-informed, and reflective theists, sincere, thoughtful, intelligent, well-informed, and reflective atheists, sincere, thoughtful, intelligent, well-informed, and reflective agnostics; but this would not be the case if there were successful simple arguments of the kind that have been examined in this book.[47]

That is, the disagreement between the "rational" positions in a significant philosophical debate such as that concerning the existence of God is too complex, with differences in numerous key, related issues and premises, and differences between "prior" sets of beliefs, for any simple argument to be "successful."

We may question Oppy's conclusion. For example, from the fact that an atheist need not accept every premise of a theist argument, does it follow that the argument is unsuccessful? Even when she need not accept a premise of an argument, if she cannot refute this premise either, is the argument "wrong"? However, this overlooks Oppy's definition of a "successful" argument—that which brings about a belief revision. Thus, even in the definition of what constitutes a successful argument, there may be incompatible standards. Furthermore, the critique above also raises the problem of the burden of proof. Do we need to prove every premise of our arguments, or do others need to refute them?

This in turn raises a larger issue about the debate as a whole. If neither the theist nor the atheist position has a "successful" argument, as Oppy defines it, is not belief in the existence of God irrational? After all, the burden of proof is on the theist. Oppy disagrees, arguing instead for a weak form of agnosticism. I will, however, examine a more significant response to this question of the burden of proof, one that raises the issue of the larger context in which the debate regarding the existence of God as a whole is situated: evidentialism.

DISAGREEMENT ON THE STARTING POINT: EVIDENTIALISM AND ITS DISCONTENTS

Evidentialism and the Presumption of Atheism

Evidentialism, as noted above, is the claim that a belief is rational only if there is sufficient evidence. What has so far been unquestioned, and indeed unexplained, is why it is the theist who must present "sufficient evidence." That is, although the debate includes a number of arguments against the existence of God, it generally consists of arguments for the existence of God and their refutation. The burden of proof lies with the theist, so that a proper conclusion from the lack of evidence that God exists in the debate is not "mere suspension of belief" but "disbelief."[48]

This was the case with Mackie's argument; if there is no compelling reason to posit the existence of God, in that there is an adequate naturalist explanation for that which the theist position also explains, one ought to disbelieve that God exists.

Why is this so? A concise answer comes from Antony Flew, who argues, using the legal court analogy of "presumption of innocence," that the "presumption of atheism" ought to be the starting point in any rational debate regarding the existence of God. Flew defines the "atheist" in this presumption not as "someone who positively asserts the nonexistence of God," but as "someone who is simply not a theist."[49] Furthermore, he emphasizes the difference between his position of a purely procedural presumption and a metaphysical assumption of atheism. That is, to hold a presumption of atheism in a debate about the existence of God is not to positively assert that God does not exist; rather, it is to simply not affirm the assertion that God exists unless there is sufficient evidence. Why is the onus of proof on the theist? Flew argues that, first, it is because the onus of proof lies on those who affirm, not those who deny, or more precisely, on "the proposition, not on the opposition."[50] Secondly, it is because the goal of this debate is knowledge—in this case, to know whether God exists—and this requires not only true, but warranted, belief. Thus, any positive proposition—such as the theist claim that God exists—in a setting of knowledge-seeking inquiry requires evidences or grounds for such a claim.

This position seems to be assumed by Swinburne, who argues that before one can have a personal relationship with God, God must exist, and that one ought to test one's belief that God exists.[51] Indeed, Swinburne's rational case for the existence of God is his answer to this evidentialist challenge. However, not every theist accepts that a belief in God is rational only if there is sufficient evidence. The most significant objection is rooted in the works of Reformed epistemologists.

Reformed Epistemology and Its Critique of Classical Foundationalism

Alvin Plantinga argues that the evidentialist position, such as that of Flew, depends on what he calls "classical foundationalism." According to Plantinga, this position may be construed as a view about a "rational noetic structure" with the following three theses:

1. In every rational noetic structure there is a set of beliefs taken as basic—that is, not accepted on the basis of other beliefs,
2. In a rational noetic structure nonbasic belief is proportional to support from the foundations, and
3. In a rational noetic structure [properly] basic beliefs will be self-evident or incorrigible or evident to the senses.[52]

Thus, classical foundationalism states that a rational person holds only beliefs that either are properly basic or are supported by such basic beliefs, which form the foundation of a rational belief-system. A properly basic belief, in turn, is that which is incorrigible and obvious when one simply thinks about it, thus self-evident, or that which is directly from sense experience.

Plantinga argues that if these criteria for basic beliefs are valid, "enormous quantities of what we all in fact believe are irrational," such as the belief that "there are other persons" or "enduring physical objects" or that "the world has existed for more than five minutes."[53] None of these beliefs is self-evident, incorrigible, nor evident to the senses, yet none is entailed by what this foundationalism would consider to be properly basic. That is, sense experience alone simply cannot establish the above statements—an argument similar to Hume's skeptical position. Thus, in classical foundationalism, the "properly basic" beliefs, as the foundation of a "rational noetic structure," are unable to support significant beliefs—including discoveries of modern science—and beliefs that do are not "properly basic" by its own account. Furthermore, the tenet of classical foundationalism does not itself satisfy its own conditions, even with reformulations; it is not self-evident, incorrigible, or evident to the senses, nor is it supported by beliefs that are. Thus, a foundationalist who holds this view becomes self-referentially inconsistent.[54]

Plantinga then argues that with the collapse of classical foundationalism, theists could consider their belief in God as properly basic. Does this not imply that any belief may be claimed as properly basic, including the belief in "the Great Pumpkin"? Plantinga argues that this is not so. Belief in God is properly basic only in certain circumstances, in the same way a belief that there are other persons is properly basic when one is interacting with other persons. To be more precise, statements such as "that person is pleased," or "I had breakfast an hour ago," rather than "there are other persons" or "the world has existed more than five minutes," are properly basic." Likewise, the propositions about God that are properly basic are those such as "God is speaking to me" or "God disapproves of what I have done," propositions that ground the belief that God exists.[55]

Is a rational debate concerning the existence of God then irrelevant to a belief in God? This would be odd, since Plantinga is known for his reformulation of the ontological argument in terms of modal logic of possible worlds. He argues that arguments are "defeaters." That is, rational arguments may potentially "defeat" a position, thereby persuading an atheist to become a theist or vice versa. One way an argument constitutes such a defeater is by showing that a position that one's interlocutor holds is incompatible with other background beliefs that she also holds—such as established scientific theories, or certain logical principles. Thus, a modal ontological argument such as what Plantinga presented may be a defeater for an atheist who accepts the principles of modal logic about possible worlds and also accepts Plantinga's central premise that the existence of a maximally great being is possible.[56] Likewise, an argument that purports to explain religious experience in purely natural terms may be a defeater for a theist who accepts the psychological theories on which it is based. Also, refutations of such arguments, or further arguments, may defeat such a defeater, or defeat such a defeater-defeater, and so on.[57] Thus, for Plantinga, rational arguments function as offensive or defensive tools of the opposing positions in the debate. He insists, however, that because a belief in God is properly basic, those who believe in God are rational without such arguments.

Plantinga's position has its critics. For example, Norman Kretzmann points out that evidentialism does not depend on classical foundationalism, but vice versa.[58] He argues that Plantinga misunderstands what evidence is for an evidentialist, by equating it with a particular way of reasoning and arriving at evidence, and in doing so, misrepresents some evidentialist positions, such as that of Aquinas, who is not a classical foundationalist. Thus, Plantinga's position does nothing to argue that a belief in God is rational without sufficient evidence. Everitt questions how Plantinga's example of belief in God is properly basic. For example, if one believes God is speaking through the process of one's reading the Bible, he asks, is not the basic belief that one is "reading the Bible" rather than that God is speaking?[59] Furthermore, if a statement like "God disapproves of what I have done" is properly basic, why not statements concerning the Great Pumpkin, or Zeus? Even if one grants Plantinga's argument, this merely means that a theist does not "violate epistemic duties" in holding the belief; it does not indicate whether such a belief is true; indeed, Plantinga's position becomes largely irrelevant in practice because it still allows reason to present various theistic and antitheistic arguments that, for Everitt, still give reasons to believe either that the theist or the atheist position is true.[60]

However, while these are significant criticisms, Nicholas Wolterstorff further challenges evidentialism by proceeding from Plantinga's critique of classical foundationalism to present Reformed epistemology as an alternative account of rationality. Even if classical foundationalism collapses, evidentialists may use reliabilism, which is the thesis that a belief is rationally justified if the belief is produced or sustained by a "reliable process or mechanism."[61] Wolterstorff argues, however, that it is difficult to identify the "reliable mechanism" that produces "mainly true" beliefs in every given circumstance. Instead, he proposes that we regard rationality as a moral obligation, arguing that a belief is rational only if it is arrived at "innocently," that is, if the circumstances in which the person came to hold a belief were such that there was no reason for the person to reject it, such as a child learning from an elder. He then writes: "A person is rationally justified in believing a certain proposition which he does believe unless he has adequate reason to cease from believing it. Our beliefs are rational unless we have reason for refraining; they are not nonrational unless we have reason *for* believing. They are innocent until proved guilty, not guilty until proved innocent."[62] Flew argued that one ought not to assent to the proposition that God exists without reason, just as a legal court—Anglo-American, that is—does not pronounce a person guilty without sufficient evidence. Wolterstorff subverts this analogy. He emphasizes that rationality is "always a *situated* rationality,"[63] and that one ought to presume that the beliefs one already holds are "innocent"—that is, rational—until proven "guilty" by sufficient evidence. This resonates with the position held later by Oppy—though he holds an agnostic position on whether God exists—regarding how "rational" people may regard evidence differently, depending on their "priors."

What a Reformed epistemologist argues, therefore, is not simply that it is rational to believe without evidence, but that the starting point of the debate on whether God exists is not necessarily a presumption of atheism. Depending on the person, and his or her existing belief-system, the starting point may be a presumption of theism. This again raises the issue of incommensurability. Not only are there disagreements on *whether* God exists, and also on the standard of justification or reasoning with which to support one's position, but there can be disagreements on where one ought to start the debate. This incommensurability, of course, may not be obvious because of the piecemeal approach in contemporary analytic philosophy; that is, if we understand Reformed epistemology solely in terms of its critique of evidentialism, considered in isolation from its position on other philosophical issues, it may seem that the dispute concerns simply whether it is rational to believe something without evidence. However, Reformed epistemology is inseparable from the overall philosophical and theological position within which it is situated, along with its particular position regarding God, human nature, sin, and so forth.

First, a particular position concerning the starting point of the debate is closely tied to a person's position on what it is to be rational and what it is to know. For example, classical foundationalist epistemology is necessarily evidentialist regarding the existence of God, asserting that a belief in God is rationally justified only if there is further proof or evidence. The Reformed epistemologist position that belief in God is the starting point for a theist is rooted in an entirely different account of knowledge. For example, Plantinga elsewhere introduces the notion of "warrant" as alternative to "justification." A belief is "warranted" if the cognitive faculties involved are working properly in an appropriate environment, with the result that those faculties reliably produce true beliefs.[64] Regarding religious beliefs, he presents the Calvinist position, which emphasizes the role of the Holy Spirit in repairing the cognitive faculties—among others—that enable human beings to arrive at the truth of the Christian gospel, including, presumably, the existence of God.[65]

Furthermore, the proposed starting point of the debate is inseparable from the way in which a Reformed epistemologist, or an evidentialist, understands the point of rational argumentation, or even characterizes the debate itself. The evidentialist with the presumption of atheism, for

example, characterizes the debate about the existence of God as a theist presenting proofs or evidence, and the atheist refuting them. In such
a debate, unless the theist has an argument to convince the atheist, her
belief in God is not rationally justified. However, the Reformed epistemologist characterizes the debate as both the theist and the atheist presenting rational arguments as "defeaters" that undermine, or cast doubt
on, the opposing position, using the body of beliefs that the opposing
side already holds. Each position is rational unless it fails to defend itself against the defeaters posed by its opponent. Thus, Plantinga's arguments for Christianity in the latter chapters of *Warranted Christian
Belief* consciously follow the form particular to this Reformed epistemologist's understanding of the debate. The arguments he presents are
either outright refutations of possible "defeater" arguments or arguments
that what a Christian would accept from a seeming "defeater" to his faith
does not actually pose a reason to *abandon* the Christian belief in question.[66] Or, consider the wording of his repeated thesis in a more recent
work of his, *Where the Conflict Really Lies*: "There is superficial conflict
but deep concord between science and theistic religion, but superficial
concord and deep conflict between science and naturalism."[67] These are
primarily terms of "defeaters," regarding whether science is "in conflict"
or "in concordance" with each position. Thus, the purpose and even the
forms of the arguments are inseparable from what one considers as the
starting point of the debate.

However, all this nevertheless retains the assumption that the existence of God is a proper subject of rational debate and argumentation,
at least in some form. There are challenges, however, even to this assumption.

THE EXISTENCE OF GOD, RATIONALITY, AND THE
WITTGENSTEINIAN WORLD-PICTURE

The Challenge That Discourse about God Is Noncognitive

In the first half of the twentieth century, logical positivists and logical
atomists leveled a severe critique against theology and metaphysics—
thus, any discussion of God—by arguing that statements about these

subject matters are "noncognitive." They argued that any cognitively meaningful statement ought to be verifiable by a direct correspondence to the objects of sense experience. This was the case, they argued, for scientific statements. However, statements concerning God were not likewise verifiable. Later, Flew would challenge theists from another, though closely related, direction by asking whether theistic statements were likewise falsifiable.[68] Thus, statements concerning God, including the existence of God, became increasingly regarded as "not even false." They were neither true nor false because they lacked cognitive meaning. The concept of God was also criticized, including whether "disembodied person" is even intelligible or coherent.

Numerous accounts describe the reversal of this dominant view—at least, in Anglo-American analytic philosophy—that preceded the revival of philosophy of religion. In most accounts, two key reasons are given for this reversal. First, the positivist theory of cognitive meaningfulness precluded numerous commonsense statements and important scientific theories. For example, statements about the past, such as "I had lunch yesterday," and many modern scientific theories such as the theory of relativity, quantum physics, or the big bang theory were not verifiable or falsifiable in such a simplistic way. Second, and more to the point, even the positivist principle of verification was not verifiable by its own standards.

In *Evidence and Faith*, Charles Taliaferro adds two more reasons for the reversal in his account of the "five major moves" in the contemporary development of philosophy of religion.[69] One of the moves he describes is how philosophers of religion since have successfully argued for the intellectual coherence and meaningfulness of religious statements; for example, Swinburne, using a narrative of an embodied person becoming a disembodied, omnipotent, omniscient, omnipresent person, argues that insofar as the narrative is intelligible, the concept of God is coherent.[70] The other is that Ludwig Wittgenstein's philosophy of language undermined the positivist position by arguing that there are different "language-games" and different "forms of life" within which a given statement has meaning. A key development from this view was the notion, held by those such as Malcolm and D. Z. Phillips, that religion was its own "language-game," with different modes of speaking than rational or scientific discourse.

D. Z. Phillips and Religion as a World-Picture

Wittgenstein remarked that "God's essence is supposed to guarantee God's existence," which really means that "the issue is not the existence of [God]"; rather, he likened it to affirming a color—that is, one can talk of color only by showing a color sample.[71] This suggested that the existence of God is not a matter of proof, but something different. Phillips developed this into an argument that religious belief in God is a distinct "language-game," rather than beliefs about metaphysical truths. This view is controversial even among the followers of Wittgenstein; it seems to be a misuse of Wittgenstein's concept of language-games, a point raised by Fergus Kerr, for example, who argues that a language-game tends to be a rather specific form of activity, such as "describing, forming a hypothesis, telling a story, joking, thanking, cursing, greeting and praying," whereas religious belief seems too large-scale and comprehensive to be reduced to or identified with it.[72] However, the importance of Phillips's position is his argument regarding *why* God cannot be subject to proofs, because it reveals a number of key features about a belief in God and, consequently, further reasons for the "incommensurability" in the contemporary debate.

Phillips agrees with Plantinga's position against the classical foundationalist; his critique is that it does not go far enough by abandoning foundationalism altogether. He criticizes Plantinga's argument at various points, some of which seem indecisive—that is, Plantinga may easily defend his position against them—and unimportant for this discussion. His main critique, however, is twofold.[73] First, Plantinga still "grounds" the belief in God on a foundation of properly basic beliefs, in the forms of "God is speaking to me" and so on. Secondly, Plantinga admits that theistic and atheistic rational arguments are "potential defeaters," thus making belief in God susceptible to proofs. Phillips points out that, aside from the difficulties in arguing that these are indeed "properly basic," or that a theistic noetic structure may be supported by such foundations, this is not how a belief in God actually functions in a theist's belief system.

Phillips affirms, as does Plantinga, that belief in God is basic, but what he means by "basic" is vastly different. For Plantinga, basic beliefs are foundations, whereas for Phillips, basic beliefs are "held fast in all that surrounds them."[74] To explain, he uses Wittgenstein's concept of "world-picture":

> The way the propositions [of beliefs] hang together make up [*sic*] what Wittgenstein calls our world-picture. . . . Once again, our world-picture cannot be thought of as the foundation of our thinking. It is what shows itself by being taken for granted *in* our thinking. Similarly, we cannot think of our world-picture as the presupposition of the ways in which we think, as though those ways of thinking could be derived from it. We cannot first identify our world-picture and then go on to describe the ways in which we think, because it is only in terms of how we think that we can speak of our world-picture.[75]

The basic beliefs that constitute a "world-picture" hang together as a whole, with each mutually supporting the others. Thus, these form what we may call a web of beliefs, rather than a system with independent, isolated basic beliefs serving as foundations.[76] The web is held as a gestalt; that is, basic beliefs in a world-picture stand or fall *together*. Such basic beliefs are neither presuppositions nor foundations that support one's reasoning, but are inseparable from *how* one reasons, thinks, forms beliefs, or even understands and describes one's own position. To say that belief in God is basic for a person, therefore, is to say that such a belief is inseparable from and inherent in the everyday living and thinking of such a person.

Phillips also argues that because belief in God is basic in this way, it is not susceptible to proofs. This is because such basic belief is "held fast" by all that surrounds it, that is, by the world-picture, which operates *in* the very reasoning and thinking required to present or refute proofs in the first place. To put it differently, a particular belief *within* such a comprehensive position may be susceptible to proof or reasoning—it can be true or false. However, that which is integral to the whole position itself, that is, its basic beliefs such as belief in God, is a boundary within which the language-game of justification, rational argumentation, and so on is practiced. This is why Phillips denies that the God of religious belief is "an existent among existents," and points out that God is a necessary being.[77] God is a necessary being in that it is impossible, for those who think and reason within the particular world-picture in which belief in God is basic, to deny that God exists. For Phillips, this means belief in God is neither true nor false—it simply is basic to the "language-game" within which questions of truth can even be asked.

What then of philosophical arguments for the existence of God? Messer, in describing the position of the Wittgensteinian school on religious belief, writes: "The Wittgensteinian school does not find the Proofs worthless. If a Proof of God's existence is an attempt to find a rational justification of belief in God, then such a Proof is misconceived; but if Proof is interpreted as an attempt to give glory to God by expressing his nature, then such a Proof is well conceived."[78] Thus, the ontological, cosmological, and teleological arguments do not justify belief in the existence of God, precisely because it needs no justification. However, such arguments may be understood as attempts—sometimes misdirected—at worship and praise by expressing God's unique nature. Indeed, the design argument and the cosmological argument fail precisely because they misconstrue this nature of God "as a creator in the way that an all-powerful human being might be creator," and so "[commit] gross anthropomorphism."[79] Rather than putting forward such a misconstrual of God, we ought to express awe and wonder at the order and beauty of creation through the design argument, and come to understand that the whole world is God's and that God is radically other than the world through the cosmological argument.[80]

Thus, Phillips adds yet another dimension to the debate about the existence of God, and with it yet another level of wide-ranging philosophical issues, concepts, and questions, which even theists disagree on among themselves. Messer, comparing the evidentialist position of Swinburne and the Wittgensteinian position of Phillips, argues that the two positions operate from radically different standpoints. For Swinburne, religious language is cognitive, and God is a definable, explanatory hypothesis, whereas for Phillips, religious language is neither cognitive nor noncognitive, and God is inexpressible mystery, neither existent nor nonexistent. Even the ways they interpret and understand the classical forms of theistic arguments are different. Thus, with such wide-ranging differences even at the most fundamental levels, adjudication between them seems impossible.[81] That is, the feature of incommensurability in the debate emerges even between theists.

The problem with Phillips's assessment of the rational arguments about the existence of God, however, is that it is these arguments that actually seem to belong to a "language-game," as properly understood, and it may be Phillips who does violence to its grammar—a grave offense for any Wittgensteinian. Somewhat less controversially, we can point out that Christianity has a long-standing historical practice of presenting rational cases for the existence of God. Likewise, whether a belief in God ought to be susceptible to proof or not, rational arguments for and against the existence of God have in fact historically influenced people's belief and disbelief throughout the centuries. Clearly, devising, defending, refuting, and refining such arguments involve a different "form of life" than worship and prayer, yet it is undeniable that this "form of life" has been practiced. If so, it seems to me that evidentialism cannot be so easily dismissed. Indeed, Phillips's overall position is also frequently critiqued in this manner; his position about the meaning and use of the word "God" purports to elucidate the logical grammar of the term in the context of how religious life is practiced, yet it seemingly is in conflict with how most actual believers use the term in practice.[82] After all, when believers state that they believe God exists, they usually mean to state something that is either true or false.

However, such critiques should still take note of his other two key points we have examined above: that a basic belief is "held fast" by that which surrounds it, and that this forms a world-picture, in which the basic belief is *in* one's thinking and reasoning. Even if we were to successfully dismiss Phillips's position because rational debate about the existence of God between the theist and the atheist has in fact been a historical practice—possibly a "language-game" of its own—we would not be warranted in dismissing his other points, namely, that a "basic" belief embedded in a comprehensive intellectual position may be such that it is "held fast" by the entire set of beliefs in the "world-picture," and that such a belief is made implicit in the very way such a position reasons. This observation could very well hold true even if we were to somehow prevail against Phillips that the existence of God is a proper subject of rational debate. It is these two points that will be of key interest for us in the next chapter.

INCOMMENSURABILITY IN THE CONTEMPORARY DEBATE

In our parable of the two explorers, their disagreement about the existence of the "benevolent ruler" was comprehensive and complex, because it stemmed from the difference between entirely different systems of sociopolitical organization. They differed not only on whether the "benevolent ruler" existed, but on how to define such a ruler, what ought to be considered as evidence for the ruler's existence, how to evaluate such evidences, and even what it was they were seeing before them—an election, or a superstitious ritual. Their differences extended far beyond the ruler, into areas of sociopolitical institutions, governance, jurisprudence, and values. The question I have explored in this chapter is simply this: does the debate between the theist and the atheist resemble that of the explorers?

The differences between the opposing positions in the contemporary debate about the existence of God, it turned out, are likewise comprehensive and complex. Underlying any answer to whether God exists is an array of positions on a multitude of issues, each with its disputes. There are disputes on whether the existence of God is even a proper subject of rational debate. There are disputes regarding the starting point of the debate, and on whether a belief is rational only if there is evidence for it, or until there is evidence against it. Differences here, in turn, imply different forms and purposes of rational argumentation. Even between those who seemingly debate from a common ground, there can be significant differences in the premises, assumptions, standards of justification, and usage of concepts. Nor are these levels of disputes separable from one another; to hold a particular position on one issue shapes the contour of one's position on the others. These considerations suggest that the differences between the opposing positions in this debate—theist and atheist, broadly conceived—are incommensurable.

It may be tempting at this point to reply that we can still formulate a grand argument that addresses all of the key disputes outlined so far. For example, an atheist evidentialist may imagine such an argument to simply be a long series of refutations of a particular theist position on each issue above—including the challenge against evidentialism itself—in order to conclude that there is no reason to believe that God exists.

God in the Age of Science?, by Herman Philipse, is a good recent example.[83] Indeed, there has been no shortage of works boldly arguing for a theist or an atheist position despite the kind of difficulties I have described. However, surveying the ongoing debate about God, I see no sign that such work has successfully brought about any decisive shift in the existing battle lines between the opposing positions. Part of this is due to the sheer number of relevant issues, premises, and concepts involved in such a sweeping argument for, or a critique against, the kind of *comprehensive* intellectual standpoints that characterize the opposing positions in this debate. That is, there are simply too many areas in which an opponent can contest an undefended premise or assumption, or find an overlooked relevant evidence, or disagree with the implication or the evaluation of a particular point, and so on.

However, even greater difficulties await such a task. Imagine an evidentialist critique against a set of theist positions. Let us suppose that it somehow decisively refuted a representative theist position in each of the levels of disputes I outlined, and did so despite resorting to contested premises or assumptions. Even if such an unlikely feat were accomplished, this would not be decisive in a debate between large-scale, comprehensive intellectual positions such as theism and atheism. First, when we categorize the answers to the question of whether God exists as a simple yes or a no—leaving aside the agnostic response—we find an immense number of vastly different possible ways that lead to the same answer to that question. Even the tiny fraction of that number that was surveyed in this chapter alone reveals a glimpse of this. That is, theists pose diverse answers regarding not only the issues we discussed so far but also many other relevant issues we have not, which together compose the same overall answer to the question—of course, this is likewise for the atheists.

Consider just the example of the issue of appropriate "evidence" in the debate. Swinburne's inductive, cumulative case assumes a particular position regarding what counts as evidence and how to evaluate it. However, in the last five years alone, as this book was being written, other theist philosophers have presented significant and radically different views regarding the kind of evidence we ought to expect in the debate, which flow from the views of the kind of God that existing monotheistic religions actually hold. Thus, C. Stephen Evans redefines evidence as "signs" from a personal God interested in forming a relationship with human beings, but also respecting their freedom to ignore the evidence.[84] Evidence for the existence of God is therefore intentionally given, and meant to be both suggestive and ambiguous. If so, we ought to expect that each sign would not be compelling by itself, but would form a cumulative, probabilistic case that can still be rejected. Paul Moser and John Cottingham critique what they call a "spectator" approach to philosophy of religion, which assumes that the body of evidence will primarily be impersonally accessible data—discussed from a detached, third-person perspective—from which one infers or deduces the existence of God, or fails to do so. However, if God is the God of Judeo-Christian beliefs, with whom we must interact personally, the primary form of "evidence" we ought to expect must be personal participation in the moral and spiritual transformation through divine grace, which is irreducible to mere propositional evidence.[85] Remarkably, none of the theist positions described above that emerged in the past five years subscribes to the view ascribed—albeit too simplistically—to Reformed epistemologists that belief in God is justified without evidence. That is, in terms of how I described the debate in this chapter, these recent theist positions are evidentialist, engaged in the dispute at the same level as Swinburne's.

Therefore, in our previous example of the evidentialist critique of theism, such a sweeping argument must not only address each of the numerous issues of disputes, but for each issue, choose which particular theist position among many it will refute. However, for large-scale, comprehensive standpoints that characterize the opposing positions in this debate, these issues of contention are interrelated. Moreover, each particular position regarding the overarching question about the existence of God relates its answer to each of the issues differently to its answer to each of the other issues. This allows for an immense number of possible variations not only in the answers to each issue, but in the *configuration* of the overall position and the reasons for such a position. That is, two particular positions may share the same answer on one issue, such as definition of causation in regard to the cosmological argument, yet depending on their answers to other relevant issues and how each has arranged them into its overall position on the existence of God, the significance and the meaning of their same answer to one issue will drastically differ.

Thus, a piecemeal approach, according to which one isolates each of the relevant issues of dispute that compose the question of whether God exists—such as the starting point of the debate—refutes one representative position on that issue, moves on to the next issue, and selects yet another position to refute (which is what Philipse tries to do in his book), faces the predicament that even if it is somehow successful in this task, each of these refutations will not necessarily apply beyond the very specific configuration of positions it has chosen to refute for that particular question.

This predicament is, finally, compounded by the enormous range of topics, drawing even from outside philosophy proper, which are, or may become, relevant to the debate. Consider how recent developments in cosmology or neuroscience contribute to the current debate, or how new arguments that draw from wide-ranging sources such as religious experience, history, beauty, and so on are always being proposed. All of the factors we have considered mean that new variations or configurations of existing positions, or even completely novel arguments, will likely continue to emerge. We may recall that earlier in this chapter, this is precisely how the rational debate about the existence of God, once thought closed, was historically revived.

We now return to the situation at hand, where the debate about the existence of God has come to an impasse, facing a predicament similar to that which the two explorers faced in the parable. The opposing positions in the debate, most broadly conceived as the theist and the atheist—each with numerous variations—are incommensurable, in the way MacIntyre defined. However, to understand this problem of incommensurability that we have explored in this chapter, we must now take a rather long detour to examine (1) some of the insights that emerged in the contemporary discourse about knowledge and (2) the philosophical concept of "worldview."

THREE

The Road

Rationality and Worldviews

The incommensurability of the different positions regarding the existence of God seems prominent now, largely due to the contemporary shift in epistemology. First, there was a widespread rejection of what Plantinga would critique, rightly, as the "classical foundationalist" position, which views knowledge as "built up" upon a kind of "foundation" that consists of "indubitable"—incorrigible, self-evident, or evident to the senses—beliefs. Thus a revised form of foundationalism, such as neopositivism, acknowledged that the epistemology of "verification" by means of incorrigible sense experience was untenable, and instead emphasized the "confirmation" through ordinary scientific data. Even contemporary arguments of evidentialists like Swinburne indicate some dissatisfaction with classical forms of foundationalism, by presenting a cumulative and probabilistic case for the "theistic hypothesis" as a "comprehensive philosophy," rather than presenting a definitive "proof," built from indubitable foundations.[1] However, some philosophers began to argue that foundationalist epistemology, as such, was an inadequate account of human knowledge and rationality. Phillips would be one recent example, as he criticizes the Reformed epistemologists for the fragment of foundationalism that remains in their position because they posit belief in God as a "properly basic belief."

What interests us here, however, is not this ongoing debate in epistemology regarding foundationalism. Rather, the question I wish to examine is, if all this is a shift *from*—though by no means wholesale rejection of—foundationalism, what is it a shift *to*? How does this affect our understanding of the debate about the existence of God? What seems to have emerged is a more holistic and historical conception of knowledge, rationality, and intellectual inquiry; in regard to the existence of God, this suggests that the debate about the existence of God is a competition between such comprehensive, historically conditioned networks of belief, which I will argue is exemplified in the philosophical concept of "worldviews." This, as we will see, has an important implication for the debate.

ENLIGHTENMENT FOUNDATIONALIST EPISTEMOLOGY AND ITS CRITIQUE

The Enlightenment View of Rationality and the Epistemological Project

A key recent development in Anglo-American philosophy is its critique of the Enlightenment and its epistemological project. The dissatisfaction with the classical foundationalist epistemology is largely a reaction against this Enlightenment view. What is this view? Firstly, it held that human reason is such that it is able to evaluate every knowledge claim from a "neutral" viewpoint, independent of any larger social, cultural, historical, or philosophical background or assumptions. Second, it held that there is one method by which this can be done in every field of inquiry, for any intellectual position, at all times, namely, by ensuring that each knowledge claim is supported adequately by a suitable foundation. Ideally this foundation would be composed solely of that which is indubitable, and thus any knowledge claim would likewise be certain, insofar as it was supported by demonstrative reasoning from it. Epistemology, which was the defining project of "modern" philosophy, was therefore the search for precisely this method and foundation of knowledge.[2]

In this view, it would be impossible to claim that the opposing positions in a philosophical debate—such as the question whether God exists—may be truly "incommensurable" with each other. This is because in the Enlightenment view, rationality is "neutral" and claims to adjudicate between these different positions, regardless of the larger philosophical context and issues that surround them, by examining whether each position arrives at its conclusions properly through the right method, and thus is adequately supported by the "foundation" of knowledge. Any difference is explained as one or both positions having erred by holding beliefs or premises that are inadequately supported by this "foundation." Indeed, the evidentialist critique of the theist from classical foundationalism is that he or she affirms a belief—namely the belief that God exists—without sufficient evidence, which is to say, unsupported by the foundation of all knowledge.

However, this view of rationality has become increasingly untenable because of the failure of the modern epistemological project. That is, no indubitable foundation of knowledge, nor a singular method by which to build knowledge from it, has been found. The modern epistemological project posited two possible foundations to knowledge, with the rationalists arguing for innate ideas, and the empiricists arguing for immediate experience. Nancey Murphy, in her account of Anglo-American postmodernity, describes the failure of both:

> If the story of modern philosophy has been that of a quest for certain and universal knowledge it is a sad story, for it has yielded a series of disappointments. Ideas that were clear and distinct to Descartes appear to others hopelessly vague or just plain false. . . . Empirical foundations have proved to be less troublesome in themselves, but here the problem of construction looms large. David Hume showed that from a foundation in immediate experience, no certain conclusions could be drawn regarding anything but immediate experience. So there appears to be an epistemological corollary of Murphy's law at work: whenever foundations are suitably indubitable, they will turn out to be useless for justifying any interesting claims; when we do find beliefs that are useful for justifying the rest of the structure, they always turn out to be questionable.[3]

Indeed, according to Murphy, it is precisely this failure which plays a significant role in the emergence of a "postmodern" philosophy.

Furthermore, a number of philosophers even argued that the episte-mological project itself was simply misguided to begin with. Again, the purpose here is not to reiterate the numerous critiques and arguments in contemporary philosophy regarding the Enlightenment view of ratio-nality and its epistemological project. Rather, I present here a historically significant exemplar of such comprehensive critique in recent times, found in Richard Rorty's *Philosophy and the Mirror of Nature*, to give a general account of this contemporary direction in philosophy.

Richard Rorty on Confusion of Justification and Causal Explanation

Rorty levels an extensive critique against the epistemological project. He outlines the object of his critique early in his book: "The aim of this book is to undermine the reader's confidence in "the mind" as something about which one should have a 'philosophical' view, in 'knowledge' as something about which there ought to be a 'theory' and which has 'foundations,' and in 'philosophy' as it has been conceived since Kant."[4] The three areas that Rorty seeks to undermine—"mind," "knowledge," and "philosophy"—are interrelated. "Philosophy," at least since Kant, is distinct from all other sciences, because its inquiry is directed to the "mind," in order to dis-cover the "foundation" of all possible "knowledge," namely, the task of epistemology.

However, these concepts make sense only in relation to each other, and each, in turn, depends on historical, contingent claims of past phi-losophers.

> The very idea of "philosophy" as something distinct from science would make little sense without the Cartesian claim that by turn-ing inward we could find ineluctable truth, and the Kantian claim that this truth imposes limits on the possible results of empirical in-quiry. The notion that there could be such a thing as "foundations of knowledge" (*all* knowledge—in every field, past, present, and fu-ture) or a "theory of representation" (*all* representation, in familiar vocabularies and those not yet dreamed of) depends on the assump-tion that there is some such a priori constraint.[5]

Thus, the notion that depends upon the claims of Descartes and Kant is that there is a foundation of all knowledge for philosophers to discover, and that there is a set of irrefutable truths concerning certain fixed structures of the "inner" mind, with which we represent the reality "out there." That is, it is the notion that there is a fixed mental process, which we must discover, with which we experience and reason in order to form representations of reality. What then is the problem?

The problem is that we would not find such an account relevant to our conception of knowledge if it were not for the confusion between justification and causal explanation. That is, a causal account of how representations are formed has been confused with justifications of our knowledge claims. How did this happen? First, Descartes distinguished between the "inner representations" of the "mind" and the "external world," and thus raised the issue of "veil-of-ideas" skepticism. That is, he raised the problem of whether the "mind" can know the world "external to it," which required "epistemology." Thus Rorty writes: "The idea of a discipline devoted to 'the nature, origin, and limits of human knowledge'—the textbook definition of 'epistemology'—required a field of study called 'the human mind,' and that field of study was what Descartes had created. The Cartesian mind simultaneously made possible veil-of-ideas skepticism and a discipline devoted to circumventing such skepticism."[6]

Once the question was raised regarding how the mind can represent external reality accurately, John Locke's account of experience as "sense-impressions" made upon the "wax-tablet" of our mind became the basis for an empiricist epistemology. Rorty asks, however, why should a causal account of how we come to belief become the basis of justification for that belief? He offers an answer. It is because Locke did not consider knowledge as propositional. He thought, as had Aristotle, of "knowledge of" as prior to "knowledge that" and thus of knowledge as a relationship between persons and objects rather than persons and propositions.[7]

The problem was then compounded by Kant's intuition-concept distinction. Kant realized that knowledge is propositional, and that what is presented to our senses cannot be identified with propositions about nature, or reality. That is, representations in our mind, in the form of sense experience or "impression," are not knowledge propositions. However, Kant's conclusion was the "Copernican Revolution" of philosophy, which states that the mind imposes its mental structures on reality, or more precisely, on its "pure" sense experience of reality, in order to make knowledge claims. Knowledge, for Kant, became putting representations of one kind—intuitions—together in the mind using another—concepts. Rorty points out that Kant confuses synthesis, which is putting together representations, with predication, which is saying something about an object. He then concludes:

> The notion of a "theory of knowledge" will not make sense unless we have confused causation and justification in the manner of Locke, and then it will seem fuzzy until we have isolated some entities in inner space whose causal relations seem puzzling. "Concepts" and "intuitions" are exactly the entities required. If Kant had gone straight from the insight that "the singular proposition" is not to be identified with "the singularity of a presentation to sense" (nor, for that matter, to intellect) to a view of knowledge as relation between persons and propositions, he would not have needed the notion of "synthesis." He might have viewed a person as a black box emitting sentences, the justification for these emissions being found in his relation to his environment (including the emissions of his fellow black boxes). The question "How is knowledge possible?" would then have resembled the question "How are telephones possible?"[8]

Simply put, without such confusion, "synthesis" of inner representations would have seemed irrelevant to what we claim to know and how we justify these claims of knowledge.

Knowledge as Relationship of Propositions vs. Knowledge as Privileged Representation

All this, however, reveals a particular conception of knowledge which underlies this history of confusion:

> We may think of both knowledge and justification as privileged relations to the objects those propositions are about. . . . If we think of knowledge [this] way, we will want to get behind reasons to causes, beyond argument to compulsion from object known, to a situation in which argument would be not just silly but impossible, for anyone gripped by the object in the required way will be *unable* to doubt or

to see an alternative. To reach that point is to reach the foundation of knowledge.[9]

Such conception seeks to discover a foundation of knowledge, which will be "privileged" in that it will simply be indubitable. It is only when knowledge is conceived this way that a causal account of how beliefs are formed becomes relevant to knowledge and its justification, for such an account may reveal what is foundational, or privileged, in such a process.

What underlies this conception of knowledge is an ocular metaphor, that is, one that conceives of knowledge as a kind of vision, and the mind as a "mirror of nature" that reflects reality. Rorty summarizes the historical development of this conception succinctly in this key passage:

It helps to think of the original dominating metaphor as being that of having our beliefs determined by being brought face-to-face with the object of the belief (the geometrical figure which proves the theorem, for example). The next stage is to think that to understand how to know better is to understand how to improve the activity of a quasi-visual faculty, the Mirror of Nature, and thus to think of knowledge as an assemblage of accurate representations. Then comes the idea that the way to have accurate representations is to find, within the Mirror, a special privileged class of representations so compelling that their accuracy cannot be doubted. These privileged foundations will be the foundations of knowledge, and the discipline, which directs us toward them—the theory of knowledge— will be the foundation of culture. The theory of knowledge will be the search for that which compels the mind to belief as soon as it is unveiled. Philosophy-as-epistemology will be the search for the immutable structures within which knowledge, life, and culture must be contained—structures set by the privileged representations which it studies.[10]

Hence, to know the truth is to represent reality in "the Mirror of Nature," and within the mirror are a kind of "privileged" representations which can never be denied and which thus compose the indubitable foundation of all knowledge and the standard to which every field and

all of culture are to be judged. This is the goal and the heart of the epistemological enterprise.

Rorty also turns this critique toward the contemporary analytic philosophy from the twentieth century onward, in which philosophers no
longer talk of the mind, or knowledge, but of meaning and language.
Rorty comments early in his book:

> As I see it, the kind of philosophy which stems from Russell and
> Frege is . . . simply one more attempt to put philosophy in the posi-
> tion which Kant wished it to have—that of judging other areas of
> culture on the basis of its special knowledge of the "foundations" of
> these areas. "Analytic" philosophy is one more variant of Kantian
> philosophy, a variant marked principally by thinking of representa-
> tion as linguistic rather than mental, and of philosophy of language
> rather than "transcendental critique" or psychology, as the discipline
> which exhibits the "foundations of knowledge."[11]

Rorty notes that analytic philosophy inherited Kant's intuitions-concepts
distinction, namely, the "distinction between what is 'given' and what is
'added by the mind,' or that between the 'contingent' (because influenced
by what is given) and the 'necessary' (because entirely 'within' the mind
and under its control)."[12] These distinctions are found in various forms:
in the analytic-synthetic distinction, or in particular as Rudolf Carnap's
appeal to the "given," or as Bertrand Russell's "knowledge by acquain-
tance," or as C. I. Lewis's "expressive language."

These distinctions have been attacked by Wittgenstein, J. L. Austin,
and others, but most notably by Wilfrid Sellars and W. V. O. Quine.
With their critiques it becomes impossible to distinguish the purely
"necessary" or "analytic" from the "empirical," nor can we distinguish
the "given," "pure" experience from what we say about it. That is, in our
analysis of language, we cannot find a set of privileged representations
that justify our belief. What we do find, Rorty argues, is this: "Nothing
counts as justification unless by reference to what we already accept,
and . . . there is no way to get outside our beliefs and our language so as
to find some test other than coherence."[13] Thus, Rorty concludes, "We
understand knowledge when we understand the social justification of
belief and . . . have no need to view it as accuracy of representation."[14]

What does this mean for philosophy? Rorty argues that the conception of knowledge based on the metaphor of the mirror of nature made philosophy "confrontational," in that it views itself as the judge of all knowledge claims.[15] Its belief in privileged representations has made philosophy, including its contemporary analytic variant, "committed to the construction of a permanent, neutral framework for inquiry, and thus for all of culture."[16] It is thus committed to the project of "discovering" a universal, nonhistorical—that is, noncontingent—and fixed method, or algorithm, with which we may arrive at knowledge. This philosophy, based on epistemology and its metaphor of the mirror of nature, Rorty calls "systematic philosophy," which is to be contrasted with what he calls "edifying philosophy."[17] Edifying philosophy engages in conversation rather than confrontation, aims for agreements, and seeks edification, without the pretensions of epistemology.

What does this mean for the debate about the existence of God? Rorty's critique of the Enlightenment project definitively closes one possible avenue of response to the problem of incommensurability. If he is correct, there is no neutral, universal standard of rationality—established by some causal account of how we form indubitable representations of reality—to which every position in the debate must conform. That is, there is no neutral standpoint from which we may adjudicate between the theist and the atheist, each with competing accounts of rationality, evidences, or standards of justification. We all must stand at a particular place to judge their arguments, and it need not be a same place! However, all this should be somewhat expected, considering what we have seen in the previous chapter regarding the kind of disputes that are ongoing in the debate.

HOLISTIC CONCEPTIONS OF RATIONALITY, KNOWLEDGE, AND INTELLECTUAL INQUIRY

Quine's Holistic Web of Beliefs

To abandon the epistemological project does not preclude the need for some kind of understanding of what it is to know, and what it is that we do when we know. That is, abandonment of the epistemological project and its form of epistemological foundationalism requires an alternative account of knowledge, rationality, and intellectual inquiry—"epistemology" as more broadly defined. We must go beyond the critiques of the Enlightenment notion of an "indubitable" foundation of knowledge, to propose what is a more adequate account of how we actually form, organize, and structure our knowledge claims. Many contemporary philosophers have proposed "moderate" or "modest" versions of foundationalism that avoid the difficulties of its classical form, and such a version of foundationalism is followed by most evidentialists as well as by the Reformed epistemologists, such as Plantinga.

Some others argued for the abandonment of foundationalism altogether. Rorty, for example, presents a "pragmatist" position on knowledge and truth, which is considerably more controversial than his critique of the epistemological project. There are, of course, many other significant theories in contemporary epistemology, including the internalist, externalist, and reliabilist forms of "moderate" foundationalism; coherentism, which abandons foundationalism altogether; and alternatives like constructivism, contextualism, and others.

However, the matters that concern us here are some very general, key features of human knowledge that emerged from these recent discussions that will explain the characteristic incommensurability in the debate about the existence of God. I speak here of the shift to a more holistic conception of rationality, knowledge, and intellectual inquiry. First, we will examine an earlier writing, by Quine, which has become a contemporary classic in philosophy.

If the imagery of foundationalist epistemology is of a building of knowledge claims, supported by a foundation, the new imagery that Quine proposes is that of a web of interconnected beliefs. He first presents this position in the article "Two Dogmas of Empiricism," where he critiques the two key tenets of logical positivism—the analytic-synthetic distinction and reductionism.[18] First, he argues that there is no clear distinction between analytic statements, which depend solely on a priori linguistic meanings, and synthetic statements, which depend on experience. That is, although it seems "natural" to suppose that the "truth of a statement is somehow analyzable into a linguistic component and a factual component," the distinction between the two cannot clearly be drawn.[19] Second, he then examines and rejects reductionism, which claims that each statement derives its meaning from a logical construction of terms that refer directly to immediate experience. With the rejection of these two tenets of logical positivism, no single statement may be reduced to its empirical content—that is, its "factual components"—and thus no single statement by itself holds empirical meaning and is subject to verification. Rather, every statement is interconnected, such that the meaning and confirmation of each depend on the others.

Quine therefore proposes that the "unit of empirical significance is the whole of science," which is to say, it is the whole of science, rather than single scientific statements, which is to be confirmed. He writes:

> The totality of our so-called knowledge or beliefs, from the most casual matters of geography and history to the profoundest laws of atomic physics or even of pure mathematics and logic, is a man-made fabric which impinges on experience only along the edges. Or, to change the figure, total science is like a field of force whose boundary conditions are experience. A conflict with experience at the periphery occasions readjustments in the interior of the field. . . . Re-evaluation of some statements entails re-evaluation of others, because of their logical interconnections—the logical laws being in turn simply certain further statements of the system. . . . Having re-evaluated one statement we must re-evaluate some others, whether they be statements logically connected with the first or whether they be the statements of logical connections themselves. But the total field is so undetermined by its boundary conditions, experience, that there is much latitude of choice as to what statements to re-evaluate in the light of any single contrary experience. No particular experiences are linked with any particular statements in the interior of the field, except indirectly through considerations of equilibrium affecting the field as a whole.
>
> If this view is right, it is misleading to speak of the empirical content of an individual statement—especially if it be a statement at all remote from the experiential periphery of the field.[20]

Thus, we may describe Quine's position this way. The web of beliefs encompasses the "totality of our so-called knowledge," or "total science," which is to say, every belief regarding the world. Quine is an empiricist and holds that it is experience that forms our beliefs. However, every belief is interconnected in the web, and thus experience is the "boundary condition," which is to say, experience forms and affects the web as a whole. However, some beliefs are more central to the web, and thus connected to a far greater number of beliefs, and less directly affected by experience, than those at the "periphery." When there is conflicting experience that requires "re-adjustments" to the web, the belief "at the periphery" may therefore be revised, rather than these core beliefs at the center of the web.[21] Furthermore, Quine argues that with no analytic-synthetic distinction, every statement in the web is revisable, and likewise, any statement may become "necessarily true"—that is, held true come what may—within the web, depending on the statement's logical relation to the other statements. Indeed, even logic may be revised, as Quine shows by the example of the development of quantum logic in modern physics.

Quine then outlines the implications of his argument. The first is that the distinction between metaphysics and natural science is blurred. The scientific theory of physical objects and the gods of Homer are epistemologically comparable. That is, although Quine considers it a *scientific* error to believe in the Homeric gods rather than physical objects, epistemologically the difference is in degree, not in kind, because both physical objects and the Homeric gods are "cultural posits" or "myths." The reason one ought to adopt the physicalist view is pragmatic, in that "the myth of physical objects is epistemologically superior to most in that it has proved *more efficacious* than other myths as a device for working a manageable structure into the flux of experience."[22]

It would be an understatement to say that Quine's position has been influential. Numerous philosophers, including Rorty, acknowledge the importance of Quine's work—especially from the arguments in his "Two Dogmas"—on their writings. Indeed, Quine's arguments have directly affected the contemporary discourse on whether God exists. Oppy, for example, comments that his own position on belief-revision, and thus his assessment of the arguments about the existence of God, is largely based on his "*neo*-Quinean" picture of the web of belief.[23] Neither the theist nor the atheist arguments are successful, because of the difference in the "priors," such as the premises in their position and bodies of evidence that each organizes and evaluates differently than the other, and this is precisely because they hold different webs of beliefs.

Gary Gutting provides one of the most recent assessments of this influence, placed within the context of other significant developments in contemporary analytic philosophy that includes, among others, the works of Plantinga, Rorty, and Kuhn. However, while acknowledging that the "Two Dogmas" definitely undermined the position of logical positivism, Gutting argues that this was not because of "cogent argumentation."[24] Quine's refutation of the synthetic-analytic distinction is "widely accepted," but inconclusive, although it has become the starting point for a new conception of analyticity.[25] His holistic conception of knowledge is almost entirely unargued, and resembles a philosophical manifesto or a program more than argumentation.[26] However, it is this unargued epistemological holism that has become an increasingly definitive, influential development in philosophy.

This was due, according to Gutting, to two factors. First, the logical positivist version of foundationalist epistemology was already "losing its grip," because "[even] by its own lights, it had failed to sustain . . . [its] verificationism and reductionism."[27] Second, what Quine did in proposing his holistic view with the web of interconnected statements that compose the "totality of knowledge" was to propose a "fruitful" and "imaginative" alternative, such that even those who defended the analytic-synthetic distinction against Quine found it attractive. For example, Gutting notes how Hilary Putnam considers Quine's "error" on the distinction to be of "little importance," instead identifying his holism as the "exceedingly important theoretical insight" regarding "the monolithic character of our conceptual system," which brought "philosophic progress" from the "sterility" of the alternative.[28] However, if Quine's holism was unargued, this is not so with Kuhn and his historical account of natural science.

Kuhn's Historical Account of the Paradigm Shifts in Natural Science

Modern science has served, for Western philosophy, as the exemplar par excellence of rationality and knowledge. Rorty observes, for example, "Since the Enlightenment, physical sciences had been viewed as a paradigm of knowledge, to which the rest of culture had to measure up."[29] If there is any form of inquiry that exemplifies the Enlightenment view of "neutral" rationality and its foundationalist epistemology, surely it would be science! However, this understanding was severely challenged in the twentieth century. This challenge signified a shift away from what was an idealized view of modern science to the realization of how science has actually, and historically, been practiced.

Michael Polanyi, a physical chemist as well as a philosopher, was one of the first significant figures who critiqued the established notion of science, arguing that all knowledge, including scientific knowledge, is personal knowledge. What he means in regard to science is as follows.[30] First, there is a "tacit" dimension to scientific knowledge in that all who practice science tacitly—even unconsciously—accept the background structure of concepts and theories within and from which they carry out their scientific inquiry. Second, this tacit dimension requires "faith," in that one must first believe this background knowledge that is passed down from earlier scientists in order to understand their scientific discipline and do further research. Third, because of these considerations, truth seeking is circular; knowledge is personal, dependent upon where one begins the inquiry; it is what is tacitly accepted and taken in faith, which is confirmed through further inquiry. There is no pure objectivity, although all knowledge enterprises refer to an independent reality. That is, an objective reality is approached subjectively. Lastly, because of these characteristics of personal knowledge, the pedagogy is that of master-apprentice, according to which the apprentice learns through accepting the authority of the master and "surrendering himself uncritically to the imitation of another," before developing the expertise to work on his own.[31]

Polanyi's critique was followed by a further challenge by Thomas Kuhn in *The Structure of Scientific Revolutions*. Kuhn argues through his historical account that science does not progress, and has not progressed, linearly through simple accumulation of knowledge. Rather, there are periodic scientific revolutions, which involve a "Gestalt shift"—that is, a holistic transformation of the nature of scientific inquiry of that entire field.[32] In what he calls "normal science," science operates within an overarching theoretical framework, which is the "reigning paradigm." The paradigm, rather like the tacit dimension of knowledge for Polanyi, is simply accepted. It is the paradigm that sets the methods of research, standards of justification, and the definition of relevant data, measurements, and errors. Experimental observation and results, according to Kuhn, are not "neutral," but "theory-laden," because such empirical data themselves are defined by, and measured through the standards of, the paradigm. The paradigm is, finally, a concrete and historical exemplar of how to conduct scientific investigation in that paradigm.[33] It is from within such a paradigm, and by commitment to it, that a particular field of science progresses and scientists are able to solve problems in the field.

In normal science, scientists engage in what Kuhn calls "puzzle-solving," which uses the method and standards prescribed by the paradigm to extend the scientific knowledge of the field.[34] Any data that do not conform to, or that even outright contradict, the reigning paradigm are explained as the error of the scientist or as an issue of instrumental imprecision, or understood as a puzzle yet to be solved from within the paradigm. However, when the number and the significance of these anomalous data become too extensive, "revolutionary science" may occur, but only when there is a competing, alternative paradigm to replace the existing one. This shift from one paradigm to a new one is a scientific revolution. The problem is that these paradigms, according to Kuhn, are "incommensurable" with each other.[35]

This notion of "incommensurability" raises the most controversial implication of Kuhn's account, which is the seeming relativism and irrationality in science. First, the competing paradigms are semantically incommensurable, because scientists in different paradigms use different vocabulary, or use the same terms in different ways, so that communication across paradigms is difficult. Second, the competing paradigms are epistemically incommensurable, because different paradigms have different standards of justification, with different sets of methods, measurements, and relevant data. That is, there is no way to resolve the competition between paradigms through experimentation, because the standards for what counts as experimental justification are defined by, and thus internal to, the particular paradigms. Kuhn even suggests that although there is an objective reality independent of paradigms, the scientists in different paradigms nevertheless live in "different worlds," suggesting a nearly antirealist conception of science.[36]

Kuhn did argue against the relativist implication to science in "Objectivity, Value Judgment, and Theory Choice," where he lists five "criteria" that guide the theory choice in scientific revolution.[37] Scientists choose the theory that is more (a) accurate in its description and prediction of observation and of experimental results, (b) internally consistent, and also externally consistent with other bodies of scientific knowledge,

(c) broad in scope, with its consequences extending beyond the data it is required to explain, (d) simple in its formulation and in its organization of data, and (e) fruitful for further research. However, Kuhn adds that these criteria cannot determine theory choice because they are imprecise; these are guidelines, not rules or algorithms. Thus, scientists who use these criteria may nevertheless reach different conclusions because they may disagree about the importance of each criterion over the others, or how these criteria are to be understood and applied to the choice between particular theories.

The influence of Kuhn has been enormous. His account is significant precisely because it is historical; it describes what actually seems to have occurred in science, for example, in the historical transition from Ptolemaic to Copernican astronomy, or from Aristotelian to Newtonian, and Newtonian to relativistic and quantum physics. The implications of his account of science for the concept and role of rationality—especially as envisioned by the Enlightenment—in large-scale philosophical debate and argumentation cannot be overestimated, as it called into question the notion that there is a completely neutral rationality which adjudicates between different positions. Aside from its implications for our conception of rationality, science, and intellectual inquiry, it also has affected our understanding of the rationality of religion. For example, Hans Küng uses Kuhn's concept of paradigm shifts to understand changes in Christian thought and theology. Likewise, Ian Barbour, who writes extensively on the relationship between religion and science, has argued for a structural similarity between their respective modes of reasoning in terms of Kuhnian paradigms and use of models.[38]

Gutting, however, presents a startling assessment of the current influence of Kuhn in contemporary philosophy. Although he writes that Kuhn's book "precipitated an intellectual revolution," he adds:

> The question remains of where . . . Kuhn's effect was deep enough to be judged truly revolutionary. Certainly not in the history of science, where Kuhn himself purported to be offering nothing that historians had not known. . . . Not even, it might seem, in philosophy of science, to which Kuhn intended his book to be a contribution. There he undeniably created a major stir, but . . . "by 1980, it is fair to say, Kuhn had become a marginal figure." More than twenty-five

years later the judgment of marginality seems reaffirmed. The grand Kuhnian issues of rationality and truth are no longer central to the discipline. Most of the best philosophy of science consists of highly specialized discussions in the conceptual foundations of specific disciplines, particularly physics, biology, and cognitive science. Nor is this because the big questions Kuhn raised have been decisively settled. The challenge to science's cognitive authority associated with his work continues to flourish in the new discipline of social studies of knowledge (SSK), where the *irrationality* of science is often taken as an unquestioned starting-point. Philosophers of science, however . . . no longer seem to view the challenge with urgency.[39]

How has this come to be? Gutting's subsequent explanation of the marginality of Kuhn in philosophy of science is, again unexpectedly, consistent with the account so far of the more holist shift in our conception of knowledge.

According to Gutting, the marginalization of Kuhn in philosophy of science did not happen because Kuhn's position was refuted. His historical account, in general terms at least, is widely accepted; no credible historical account that would refute Kuhn ever emerged. The debate, therefore, centered on whether Kuhn's description of science implied that science itself was relativistic and irrational. For example, semantic incommensurability raised the problem of how rival theories may share enough meaning to be rationally compared. This problem disappeared once philosophers developed an alternative account of meaning and reference that seemed to eliminate such a divide. Epistemic incommensurability raised the question whether theories or paradigms are accepted on the basis of irrational social factors. However, those who seriously questioned the rationality of science this way tended to assume the largely discredited logical positivist view of science as the only possible conception of rationality, with the only alternative being "global skeptical theses"—the latter being characterized as "self-refuting" by Gutting. Others who acknowledged the social factors at work did not, by and large, conclude that these were the "final determinants" of theory choice.

The final problem then was to formulate a new general theory or model of rational, scientific development, consistent with Kuhn's historical account. Gutting lists the work by Imre Lakatos, Stephen

Toulmin, and Larry Laudan as significant exemplars of such projects, improving on Kuhn's simplistic "paradigm-anomaly-crisis-revolution" model. However, this problem eventually "dissolved in the new view" that "Kuhn's paradigm model . . . operated at a level too far from actual scientific practice to pose a serious challenge to that practice."[40] That is, it was difficult to show how, specifically, Kuhn's large-scale account challenged the scientific rationality of, say, theoretical particle physics or evolutionary genetics or cognitive neuroscience. What Gutting seems to argue is that Kuhn's account was not rejected, but rather that that account was insufficient to pose a challenge to scientific rationality in actual practice in each particular field. Consequently, a new model of scientific rationality was no longer urgently needed.

Gutting then argues that this was because philosophers of science had a "pre-philosophical conviction" that science was rational, and had no need to abandon this without a decisive demonstration of the irrationality of science. That is, they eventually came to understand that there is no need to supply a philosophical justification or foundation for the belief that science is rational unless something concretely threatens the rationality of science in its actual practice—a point strikingly similar to the Reformed epistemologist position.[41]

Nevertheless, it is interesting how Gutting's account of the "marginalization" of Kuhn in philosophy remains consistent with our account so far of the shift in epistemology. On the one hand, philosophers since Kuhn seem to largely accept his more holistic account of scientific development, including the concept of "paradigms," while rejecting the notion that this somehow threatens the rationality of science. That is, as their understanding of rationality and intellectual inquiry has shifted to fit Kuhn's historical account, they have seen no need to propose a new epistemological foundation to justify science. On the other hand, if the notion that science is rational is a "conviction," it seems this "conviction" was not abandoned precisely because the relatively more "peripheral beliefs in the web," such as the theory of meaning and reference, or conception of rationality, were revised accordingly. That is, what the philosophers of science themselves did in response to Kuhn is itself an exemplar of the kind of belief-revision described by Quine's holistic conception of knowledge and the web of beliefs.

Quine and Kuhn and the Debate about the Existence of God

At the close of the previous chapter, I summarized a number of difficulties that underlie the debate between large-scale comprehensive positions that characterize the opposing standpoints regarding the existence of God. First, the matters in dispute are not only the arguments for or against the existence of God, or even the different sets of premises and concepts involved in such arguments, but also the opposing standards of justification, evaluation, and relevance of various kinds of evidence; the purpose of arguments; the conception of rationality; the starting point of the debate; and so forth. Not only are there a bewildering array of disputed issues, but one may arrive at the same answer on whether God exists through very different answers to these issues—or even through the same set of answers that relate to each other in very different ways—in varied configurations. This opens a seemingly limitless set of possible variations of the *whole* position on either side of the debate, and the applicability of a critique against one particular variation to the others is significantly limited. The insights of Quine and Kuhn we have examined so far explain why this is so and how these difficulties arise.

If we conceive of the two opposing positions in the debate, very broadly, as those of the theist and the atheist, we immediately encounter a difficulty in trying to group together the immensely diverse and different positions even within the same side. However, it is possible to understand at least a majority of the different positions within each side as holding a common set of core beliefs, though perhaps with differing emphases. For example, let us suppose that for the theist, such beliefs are as follows: God is a necessary being, personal, perfectly good, the Creator of all that exists, and so on, and it is rational to believe that God exists.[42]

However, according to Quine's account of the web of beliefs, such core beliefs may be connected to a large set of more peripheral beliefs, which may be revised to keep the core intact. That is, the core beliefs such as the rationality of the belief in God are placed in a complex network of other related, more peripheral beliefs, such as particular positions on the standard of justification, evaluation of different kinds of evidence, and so on. This even includes the exact meaning of the terms or concepts that compose a *core* belief, such as a particular conception of "rationality" and so forth.[43] Even if one or more such positions regarding these peripheral issues that surround the core are refuted, these positions can be revised as needed to keep the core belief that a belief in God is rational. It may even be possible to keep the particular peripheral belief in question intact, by revising yet another peripheral belief connected to it. In this way, a sufficiently comprehensive intellectual position, because of the immense scale of the web of beliefs involved, can have a staggering number of possible configurations of relevant peripheral beliefs and definitions at its disposal, but will nevertheless retain the same core belief at its center. The problem then is, what happens when two or more such comprehensive positions are placed into a debate against each other?

What Kuhn reveals is that this problem is not unique to the philosophical debate about the existence of God. It appears—though on a smaller scale—in the history of natural science in the forms of reigning paradigms, which have in place the kind of defenses against disproof that are present in a Quinean web of beliefs. Furthermore, the problem of incommensurability that I have outlined in the previous chapter is precisely the kind of difficulty described in Kuhn's account of choosing between competing paradigms whenever a reigning paradigm is called into question. Specifically, it is what Gutting calls the "epistemic incommensurability," which has been prominent in disputes between the rival positions in the debate about the existence of God. It is thus significant to note here that in a recent conference commemorating the fiftieth anniversary of the publication of Kuhn's book, Hasok Chang argued that rather than semantic incommensurability, it is this epistemic—he calls it "methodological"—incommensurability that was the most significant impediment of theory change and theory evaluation in the history of science, specifically in the chemical revolution.[44] Lastly, Kuhn's point that scientists who accept the same set of criteria to guide the choice between competing paradigms may nevertheless disagree about the comparative importance of each criterion, or how the criteria are to be understood or applied, closely parallels how and why Swinburne and Mackie largely shared a set of "scientific" criteria—similar to what Kuhn outlined, in fact—for assessing the rational case for the "theistic hypothesis," yet disagreed on the conclusions.

However, historically, scientists did choose between competing paradigms, and paradigms did change. Furthermore, according to Gutting, Kuhn's work did not cast serious doubt on the rationality of those choices, especially not in the actual practice of particular scientific disciplines. The reasons Gutting's account suggests for this reveal another important insight about the nature of intellectual inquiry, an insight further elucidated by Alasdair MacIntyre's work.

MACINTYRE AND SOCIOHISTORICAL CONCEPTIONS OF RATIONAL INQUIRY

MacIntyre's Account of the Historical Narrative Dimension in Intellectual Inquiry

If Kuhn presented a historical account of intellectual inquiry—namely, of natural science—MacIntyre presents an account of intellectual inquiry as historical. MacIntyre contends that any given form of rationality is historically contingent; any rational, intellectual inquiry, including science, is defined and shaped by the particular historical background from which it proceeds. The failure of modern philosophy is largely the failure to understand this, a trend that began with Descartes. MacIntyre describes Descartes as "having abjured history as a means to truth" and consequently fallen into an epistemological crisis. Concerning Descartes's project to answer the skeptical challenge of his day, he writes: "Descartes radically misdescribes his own [epistemological] crisis. . . . The agent who is plunged into an epistemological crisis knows something very important: that schema of interpretation which he has trusted so far has broken down irremediably, in certain highly specific ways."[45]

That is, we are able to understand where we are having problems in knowing, or even *that* we are having such problems, only from the context of some background knowledge inherited from our history of inquiry.

The problem is that Descartes begins with the misguided assumption that "he knows nothing whatsoever until he can discover a presuppositionless first principle on which all else can be founded."[46] MacIntyre adds that Descartes failed, and had to fail, because he rejected the background of his tradition and history of inquiry, and this blinded him, ironically, to his inherited presuppositions:

> Descartes' failure is complex. First of all he does not recognise that among the features of the universe which he is not putting in doubt is his own capacity not only to use the French and the Latin languages . . . and as a consequence . . . what he has inherited in and with these languages, namely, a way of ordering both thought and the world expressed in a set of meanings. These meanings have a history; seventeenth-century Latin bears the marks of having been the language of scholasticism.[47]

Thus, Descartes's formulation of his skeptical questions and his use of clear and distinct ideas to answer them depend on the language he used, a language inseparable from a particular philosophical position and its conceptual framework, and contingent on history. MacIntyre continues:

> He did not notice either what Gilson pointed out in detail: how much of what he took to be the spontaneous reflections of his own mind was in fact a repetition of sentences and phrases from his school textbooks. Even the *Cogito* is to be found in Saint Augustine.
> What goes unrecognised by Descartes is the presence not only of languages, but of a tradition—a tradition that he took himself to have successfully disowned. It was from this tradition that he inherited his epistemological ideals.[48]

That is, even the proposed foundation of Descartes's epistemology, including his presuppositionless first principle of the *cogito*, is from the historical, intellectual tradition he had inherited, and of which he was unaware.

MacIntyre's critique of Descartes is part of his response to Kuhn's historical account of the natural sciences, because when incommensurable paradigms compete, there is also an "epistemological crisis." However, MacIntyre argues that such crises may be resolved not through adjudication by some neutral, independent, and ahistorical form of rationality, such as that which Descartes sought, but precisely through the historicity of the inquiry. That is, it is resolved through the historical narrative with which one understands how one fell into the epistemological crisis. Thus, he writes: "When an epistemological crisis is resolved, it is by the construction of a new narrative, which enables the agent to understand *both* how he or she could have intelligibly held his or her original beliefs *and* how he or she could have been so drastically misled by them."[49] That is, if an agent understands through such a narrative why he or she intelligibly held the previous intellectual position—such as a scientific theory—and how this resulted in recognizable problems and difficulties, and how his or her new position resolved these problems, then the new position is rationally superior.

Thus MacIntyre writes regarding the succession of scientific paradigms:

> It is more rational to accept one theory or paradigm and to reject its predecessor when the later theory or paradigm provides a standpoint from which the acceptance, the life-story, and the rejection of the previous theory or paradigm can be recounted in a more intelligible historical narrative than previously. An understanding of the concept of the superiority of one physical theory to another requires a prior understanding of the concept of the superiority of one historical narrative to another.[50]

MacIntyre's argument thus explains Gutting's account of how Kuhn's work was eventually understood to pose little challenge to the rationality of the actual scientific practice. This is because of a feature of the scientific paradigm that Kuhn himself noted, which is a rewriting of the history of the science and its earlier achievements in the terms of the present paradigm, so that there is a sense among the scientists that they belong to a long-standing historical tradition. Kuhn rightly points out how such a narrative *mis*describes the nature of scientific development and past scientific positions, but it is also precisely this ability of the new paradigm to present such a narrative—in which past achievements and problems become more intelligible in the context of present inquiry— that makes it the reigning paradigm. This also explains the lack of urgent need to formulate a new model of "scientific rationality," because such "rationality" is already embedded in the existing historical narrative of each particular field of scientific inquiry.

Tradition-Constituted and Tradition-Constitutive Rational Inquiry

MacIntyre later applies his understanding of theoretical rationality to the area of practical reason in his now influential writings on ethics and, in doing so, further develops his account of rational inquiry.[51] In *After Virtue*, MacIntyre introduces several important concepts relevant to our purpose, as he argues how ethics is intelligible only in terms of a particular conception of the telos, or goal, of human beings.[52] The first concept is "practice," which MacIntyre describes as "any coherent and complex form of socially established cooperative human activity through which goods internal to that form of activity are realized in the course of trying to achieve those standards of excellence which are appropriate to, and partially definitive of, that form of activity, with the result that human powers to achieve excellence, and human conceptions of the ends and goods involved, are systematically extended."[53] Practices include activities such as playing chess, farming, and importantly, different forms of intellectual inquiry, such as scientific or philosophical disciplines. What is important here is that a practice is a "socially established" and "cooperative" activity that seeks to achieve "goods internal to that activity." The "internal goods" are goods particular to, and gained only through, the practice. For example, in chess, there may be "external" goods, such as money or fame, but these are not achievements inseparable from the activity of chess, such as strategic ingenuity, competitive sportsmanship, and so forth.

The next concept is his account of narrative, described in terms of a medieval view of a "quest." That is, it is not simply a narrative that is required for understanding a particular practice; it is a particular form of narrative—a narrative of a quest for, a journey toward, the goal—or the "goods"—of a practice. For example, in a particular intellectual inquiry, such as physics, the goal may be a perfect understanding of all physical motion, celestial and terrestrial. MacIntyre then writes: "It is in the course of the quest and only through encountering and coping with the various particular harms, dangers, temptations and distractions which provide any quest with its episodes and incidents that the goal of the quest is finally to be understood. A quest is always an education both as to the character of that which is sought and in self-knowledge."[54] Thus, what the goal is and what it is to have attained it are not precisely understood during the quest, and part of its narrative consists not only of the journey toward the goal, but of learning what it is that the journey seeks.

A practice, however, is also a socially established, cooperative activity and is historically extended, spanning across many generations. Thus, MacIntyre introduces the concept of tradition: "A living tradition . . . is a historically extended, socially embodied argument, and an argument precisely in part about the goods which constitute that tradition. Within a tradition the pursuit of goods extends through generations, sometimes through many generations."[55] It is within the larger context of a tradition that the narrative of a particular practice, as well as of an individual life, is placed. "The history of a practice in our time is generally and characteristically embedded in and made intelligible in terms of the larger and longer history of the tradition through which the practice in its present form was conveyed to us; the history of each of our own lives is generally and characteristically embedded in and made intelligible in terms of the larger and longer histories of a number of traditions."[56] Thus, in the context of ethics, as represented in *After Virtue*, the "rationality" of a particular intellectual inquiry is inseparable from the narrative of the larger tradition.

In his next book, *Whose Justice? Which Rationality?*, MacIntyre argues for what he describes as a tradition-constituted and tradition-constitutive rational inquiry. "Rationality" must be understood in the context of its tradition, with its particular conceptual schema, standards of justification, and mode of reasoning, which constitute a part of the historical narrative of how this form of rational inquiry has arrived at the current state of affairs, in its quest toward its goal.

What the Enlightenment made us for the most part blind to and what we now need to recover is . . . a conception of rational enquiry as embodied in a tradition, a conception according to which the standards of rational justification themselves emerge from and are part of a history in which they are vindicated by the way in which they transcend the limitations of and provide remedies for the defects of their predecessors within the history of that same tradition.[57]

To participate in a rational inquiry is to first understand the historical narrative of the tradition, of how its principles and theories for a given inquiry and its standard of reasoning that justifies them have been formed, challenged, revised, and changed. The "rationality" of the tradition is justified in the narrative of how it has remedied the problems and transcended limitations of the inquiry's predecessors.

MacIntyre thus reiterates and elaborates on his response to Kuhn as he defines progress in general in a rational inquiry, including that of natural science, in terms of the socially embodied, historically extended quest-narrative of a tradition:

> Rational enquiry is itself always tradition-dependent. The best established theories—those which it is rational to accept—in contemporary natural science are not worthy of acceptance because they conform to some timeless set of canons for scientific theories, positivist or otherwise. Rather they are worthy of acceptance because of their superiority to their immediate predecessors, in respect of providing resources for the solution of certain types of problem and remedying certain types of incoherence, in the light of some particular conception of what it would be to perfect theory in this or that area.[58]

Rational inquiry is therefore tradition constituted in that a given intellectual inquiry—along with its concepts, standards of justification, modes of reasoning, and goal—is inherited from and is practiced within a particular tradition, and understood only in the context of its narrative history. It is tradition constitutive in that the inquiry then solves what the tradition understands as its own problems and difficulties, advances it toward what it understands as the goal of its inquiry, and thus develops, revises, and transforms the tradition.

I have sought to distinguish "rational inquiry" from "tradition," because for MacIntyre, a tradition includes numerous forms of intellectual inquiry, including theoretical and practical reasoning, natural and social sciences, and philosophy. MacIntyre includes, for example, areas of biology and physics, metaphysics, morals, and politics in Aristotelianism, which he explicitly calls a tradition, and argues that though Aristotelianism has failed in key respects in terms of biology and physics, it has "succeeded in vindicating itself" in the others, and thus as a whole is the best theory so far—presumably with relevant corrections.[59] In other words, a tradition is truly comprehensive—at least insofar as the various areas of rational inquiry are concerned—and what a contemporary society would distinguish as natural and social sciences, humanities, philosophies, and even theology, to name a few, all form a coherent whole, in which success in one may even offset—note the striking parallel to Quine's account of the web of beliefs here—a failure in another, or vice versa.

There is a far older concept of such a holistic, comprehensive system of beliefs, to which Quine's, Kuhn's, and Macintyre's work may be understood as a contemporary extension and contribution. This is the concept of a worldview.

WORLDVIEW AND THE PROBLEM OF RATIONALITY AND RELATIVISM

The Concept of Worldview in Relation to Philosophy and Enlightenment Rationality

David Naugle, in a concise but thorough book on the concept of worldviews, comments that the definition, or the "ordinary meaning," of the term "worldview" is largely uncontested. It is the more nuanced features of this concept which raise various problems associated with it. He writes: "What [the term "worldview"] actually *denotes*—is reasonably straightforward and relatively noncontroversial, for *all* concerned. Roughly speaking, it refers to a person's interpretation of reality and a basic view of life. The controversies arise . . . when its *implications* or various *nuances* are considered—what it in fact *connotes*—and when its relationship to theoretical or scientific thought is explored."[60] Indeed, there seems to be an overall consensus on the general definition of the term itself as an overarching framework of beliefs that form a viewpoint on life and reality. The "controversy," however, consist of precisely the same issues that emerged in the contemporary challenge to the Enlightenment view of rationality. Therefore, I will briefly explore the history and the key features of this concept, including its relation with "theoretical or scientific thought."

The term "worldview," for the West at least, seems to have originated from Immanuel Kant as the German word *Weltanschauung*, which for Kant meant simply the sense perception of the world.[61] However, the word became a significant concept through its subsequent use in German Idealism and Romanticism, by authors such as Johann Gottlieb Fichte, F. W. J. Schelling, Friedrich Schleiermacher, Novalis, and G. W. F. Hegel. In their writings, the term came to denote what Albert Wolters calls a "global outlook on life and the world—akin to philosophy but without its rational pretensions."[62] When the term thus developed to denote a comprehensive framework of beliefs about reality and living, while being distinct from "philosophy" and its close association with rationality, the question regarding its exact relation to philosophy arose.

I need to digress and describe the five positions Wolters outlines regarding this relationship.[63] The first possibility is that a "worldview repels philosophy," which is a position held notably by Søren Kierkegaard and others. That is, philosophy, with its theoretical concerns, and a worldview, with its existential concerns, constitute equally legitimate and necessary poles in tension in human life. The second is that "worldview crowns philosophy," a position that characterizes the Roman Catholic position. It claims that the goal of philosophy is to address the ultimate questions of reality and meaning, and therefore philosophy must lead to a worldview. The third is that "worldview flanks philosophy," a position held notably by those such as Edmund Husserl and Martin Heidegger, who argue that worldview must be kept rigorously separate from what they propose as a value-free and neutral "scientific philosophy." The fourth is that "worldview yields philosophy," a position Wolters claims is held by those such as Wilhelm Dilthey and the Calvinists.[64] It claims that it is worldview that produces a particular philosophy, and not vice versa. The fifth is that "worldview equals philosophy," held by dialectical materialists and the logical positivists, for whom a particular worldview—that is, their own—is simply identified with a scientific philosophy, along with its claim to universal rationality and validity. Note that these five positions are simply models—a kind of typology—and as Jacob Klapwijk points out in the same collection of essays, the philosophical or theological positions Wolters uses as examples cannot be adequately captured or characterized entirely as any one type in the schema he proposes.[65]

What concerns us here, however, is the concept of worldviews that underlies this schema. Wolters observes that the concept of worldviews was developed during the period in which there was a reaction against the Enlightenment and its "intellectualism," a reaction where the particular, concrete, and temporal was favored above the Enlightenment ideals of the universal, abstract, and eternal.[66] This reaction formed the concept of worldview to be as follows. First, a worldview is "historically individual," that is, whether held by an individual or a collective—everyone in a nation, class, or a period—it is particular to them, and it is dependent upon, limited by, and relative to their history. Second, it is nonscientific, and thus "pretheoretical" and "for the masses."[67]

However, the issue of rationality may elucidate this distinction between "worldview" and "philosophy." To be precise, "philosophy" here is the Enlightenment view of rationality and its classical foundationalist epistemology, which Rorty, Quine, Kuhn, and MacIntyre challenged. That is, worldviews are historically contingent, and thus not "rational" in the sense that the Enlightenment defines "rational," since the primary task of the Enlightenment version of philosophy is to construct an *a*historical, neutral viewpoint from a presuppositionless, indubitable foundation of knowledge. If this is so, worldviews are distinct from philosophy and vice versa, such that the question of the relationship between the two becomes significant.[68] Indeed, the five types that Wolters outlines may also be distinguished precisely in terms of where each position would stand regarding this issue of Enlightenment rationality.

We have already examined how this construction of a neutral, rational viewpoint, which was the task of Enlightenment philosophy, has proven to be untenable. If so, what is the distinction between philosophy and worldviews? An even more significant question is, if the task of "philosophy" as envisioned by the Enlightenment fails, and if we are left only with worldviews, what of the issue of rationality, or truth? Thus, rather like Kuhn's account of science, the issue of relativism emerges from the concept of worldview. These are the questions that philosophers have struggled with as the concept of worldviews developed, and for this, we will return to Naugle's account. I can, of course, give only a cursory summary of Naugle's historical account here, which obviously cannot adequately describe the positions of the philosophers Naugle discusses; what I am aiming for here is a broad overview of the development of the concept of worldview, especially in regard to the theme of rationality and relativism.

History of the Development of the Concept of Worldview

Naugle describes how the concept of worldview developed in the nine-teenth century through the work of a few key figures. First, Hegel raised the point, contra Kant, that many different ways of living and looking at the universe are embodied in individual or national consciousness and express themselves aesthetically in the arts.[69] However, worldviews for Hegel are historical and cultural instances of the Absolute Spirit, and there are alternative frameworks and conceptual schemes only because these are instantiations of the dialectical process of the Spirit, and the "truth of the universe" will be realized at the end of time.[70] Dilthey de-veloped a systematic, comprehensive, and theoretical statement on world-views, but without Hegel's epistemological eschatology.[71] For Dilthey, there is no absolute, scientific or philosophical metaphysics that describes reality perfectly. We have worldviews, the formation of which are con-tingent upon individual, cultural, and historical experiences, events, and circumstances, yet somehow are rooted in human life—or "lifeworld"—and thus reflect some aspect of reality. Thus, every worldview—and Dil-they even devised a typology of different worldviews—has only a partial, incomplete, and historically contingent account of reality. Nietzsche de-veloped this issue of historical contingency and relativity of worldviews to its fullest. Rejecting the notion of objective truth, as well as good and evil, he espoused a radical perspectivism, where instead of truth or good-ness, there are only worldviews, or ways of seeing things—among a pos-sibly infinite number of different ways—which provide a horizon for thoughts, beliefs, and behaviors.[72] Nietzsche's declaration that "God is dead" was precisely to say that the West was awakening from the illusion that there is one absolute and universal perspective on truth and good-ness. Consequently, he remarked, Western civilization will be cast into a sea of "infinite horizon"—that is, it will face an infinite number of pos-sible views and values with nothing to judge nor guide their choices.[73]

In the twentieth century, a number of philosophers sought to re-spond to these relativistic features of worldviews. First, Husserl proposed that philosophy, in contrast to worldviews, is a rigorous science. This philosophy, his transcendental phenomenology, sought to bracket and set aside all metaphysical assumptions and simply describe, without any presupposition or interpretation, consciousness and its intentional objects. However, Naugle adds that Husserl's philosophy itself was also a world-view, and that Husserl himself seems to have realized later that world-view, rather than rigorous scientific philosophy, seems to be the "only intellectual apparatus human beings were constructing."[74] Husserl's solution was to propose an enigmatic concept, *Lebenswelt*, "lifeworld," which is phenomenologically pregiven to the consciousness as its object, prior to any conceptualization, but nevertheless has general structures; it is also the absolute, to which all objective science refers.[75] Simply put, "life-world" seems to denote reality itself, in which we live—as opposed to a *view* of reality—described in terms of phenomenology. However, only the intellectual apparatus with which each of us engages and knows the "lifeworld" is still a worldview.

Heidegger, who followed Husserl, acknowledged that historically, there is no distinction between "scientific" philosophy and worldviews.[76] However, he argued that whereas a worldview is concerned with beliefs and attitudes about particular beings, philosophy ought to be concerned solely with being itself and with the ways we encounter it. Thus, philosophy, as a "science of being as such," is the "prerequisite to worldview as interpretation of beings."[77] He also criticized modernity as the age of the world-picture, when the world is understood as an object to be pictured by a kind of Cartesian thinking subject, a duality which misunderstands the relation between human beings and reality, and thus has "obfuscated an encounter with being."[78] According to Naugle, the problem for Heidegger, as for Husserl, was that his philosophy did not seem to outstrip all worldviews, nor was it without its presuppositions—something which Heidegger himself acknowledged.[79] Naugle also lists numerous commentators who have stated that Heidegger's magnum opus, *Being and Time*, itself is a product of his "historical conditions" and "intellectual lineage."[80]

What does Naugle's account so far suggest? The early twentieth-century efforts to respond to the historical contingency and relativity of worldviews, by introducing a kind of a neutral, "worldview-less" system of philosophy, have failed. The next set of figures in Naugle's account seem to have abandoned such efforts altogether. Wittgenstein, for example, rejected the twentieth-century positivist notion that there is one proper, logical language, and argued that there are many different "language-games," with diverse uses of words, which are bounded up in what he calls a shared "form of life," or a way of living.[81] There are many forms of life, and rationality cannot go beyond a form of life, as he writes: "If I have exhausted the justifications, I have reached the bedrock, and my spade is turned. Then I am inclined to say: 'This is simply what I do.'"[82]

Others are far more radical. Jacques Derrida rejected what he called the "metaphysics of presence," which supposes that there is something "present" beyond language. That is, he rejected the notion that a worldview, and its linguistic account of the world, refers to, accesses, or is connected with reality. Rather, for Derrida, "worldviews, once deconstructed, are reduced to a self-referential system of linguistic signifiers, dispossessed of any authentic, metaphysical, epistemological, or moral import."[83] Perhaps Michel Foucault, more than others in Naugle's account, summarizes and exemplifies the eventual direction of the themes of truth, rationality, and relativity bound up in the concept of worldviews: "Foucault is essentially saying something like this: nothing exists; if anything exists, it cannot be thought about or apprehended by humanity; even if it can be apprehended, it cannot be communicated; even if it can be communicated . . . it is communicated in discursive practices that are always in the interest of the stronger party!"[84]

Finally, Naugle describes contemporary developments in science and philosophy and their interaction with the concept of worldview. Here, among others, he gives a detailed account of the work of Polanyi and Kuhn, arguing that the philosophical concept of worldview has "migrated" and impacted the area of the philosophy of science, especially in Kuhn's "understanding of the role worldview-like paradigms play in normal operation and extraordinary revolutions in the natural sciences."[85] He then identifies a number of significant figures that—at least philosophically—"deepen our understanding of the nature of a worldview and its influence on all things human."[86] Here he discusses, along with writings of figures such as Heidegger, Umberto Eco, Ninian Smart, Hans-Georg Gadamer, William Wainwright, and others, the importance of the epistemological issue raised by Rorty and of the social, historical, and narrative nature of rationality asserted by MacIntyre. In doing so, he integrates these significant contemporary developments in philosophy we have examined here so far into a larger historical narrative of the concept of worldview.[87]

WORLDVIEWS AND THE DEBATE ABOUT THE EXISTENCE OF GOD

The concept of worldview and its key features pose significant implications for the debate about the existence of God. This is because whether God exists seems to be primarily a question of worldview; indeed, the question is unanswerable solely in terms of any other, smaller-scale intellectual inquiry, such as a particular field of natural science—say, particle physics, or evolutionary biology. Thus, the different positions in the debate regarding whether God exists consist of different worldviews—a conclusion that, at first glance, seems rather banal. However, parallel to Naugle's introductory comment about worldviews, it is not what this statement says—namely, that theist, atheist, and other positions constitute different worldviews—but what it *implies* that is significant. That is, the implications of the concept of worldview and the contemporary shift in our understanding of intellectual inquiry and rationality, examined in this chapter, together with the seemingly uncontroversial observation that the different positions in the debate are different worldviews, inevitably raise the problem of relativism.

First, let us identify what seem to be the key features of interest in the concept of worldview in our account so far. Of course, one's view of worldview also depends on one's worldview. For example, many Christian writers have argued how the Christian perspective must transform or redefine the concept of worldview in terms of its commitment to the objective reality of God and its biblical ideas of creation and revelation, or sin and grace.[88] We do not require, for our purpose here, to present such a complete account of worldviews, itself integrated within the terms and framework particular to that worldview. We are concerned, rather, with three features in particular, which will be relevant to the debate on the existence of God and from which "incommensurability" of the opposing positions, discussed thus far, emerges.

Again, a sizable list of important features may be noted. Naugle, for example, proposes that a worldview is (a) a system of symbols and signs, (b) which consists not only of doctrines or propositions, but "world-interpreting narratives," which shape varieties of human practices, and (c) sets the standards and ways of reasoning, and (d) provides the background—or horizon—for interpretation and intellectual inquiry.[89] James Olthuis describes worldviews also from the perspective of a Christian, by presenting the following list. A worldview, he writes,

> grounds life in the confessed ultimate certainty;
> relates life to the universal order of existence;
> serves as the interpretative and integrative framework for all life;
> acts as the cohesive, motivating, and pervasive "mind" binding
>   [members] into a community;
> is expressed in symbols;
> is crucial in shaping personal identity;
> evokes and occasions deeply held emotional attitudes and moods of
>   deep . . . joy and peace;
> induces intellectual assent and deepened conceptual reflection;
> sanctions sacrifice on its behalf;
> once shaken, shakes it adherents to the very core;
> induces and invites incarnation in a way of life.[90]

To this, Olthuis adds that a worldview is also a process, with features of subjectivity, relativity, and continual development, open to justification, challenges, modification, and change, which echoes MacIntyre's description of a "living tradition."[91]

However, the first significant feature of our concern seems to be the comprehensiveness of worldviews. The recurring problem in the philosophical project of constructing a neutral—that is, a worldview-less—viewpoint, which is described partly in the brief account of philosophical history above, seems to be that the framework of worldview seems to be all-encompassing. Every human practice, including every form of intellectual inquiry and the standards that govern acts of reasoning, seems to be encompassed and ordered within a particular worldview.

Furthermore, the beliefs, concepts, practices, and attitudes that constitute a worldview are interconnected to form a whole, coherent web of beliefs, so that it seems impossible—at least, there has been no such case—to entirely separate any endeavor, including that of constructing a philosophical position or formulating or evaluating a scientific theory, from a particular worldview's overarching framework. Arthur Holmes, for example, describes how disciplines of theology, philosophy, and sciences contribute to the formation of worldview and in turn are affected by it. Sciences have an impact on worldview, but conversely, worldview also affects the sciences, acting as a "personal, tacit, background knowledge of the scientists themselves (Polanyi)," or as their "implicit metaphysical paradigm (Kuhn)."[92] Due to this comprehensive, holistic feature of worldviews, any given worldview has many strategies with which to respond to any experience, data, or argumentation that seems to refute its central claims. Such data or argument may simply be ignored or may be reconciled to the worldview's central claims by revising relatively unimportant beliefs in the web. The difficulty that arises in a debate between such interconnected systems is then compounded by the all-encompassing scale and comprehensiveness of worldviews, magnifying the range in which such refutation and revision happens. All this parallels what was described in the second chapter.

The second feature of a worldview is its historical contingency. Another recurring problem in the philosophical project of constructing a neutral, "worldview-less" viewpoint or intellectual inquiry was that every such position was eventually shown to be a product of the historical background and condition from which it was formulated. That is, a worldview is inseparable from the history of the conceptual and intellectual context within which it is situated. Yet if the beliefs, concepts, practices, and attitudes of a worldview depend on the particular historical experiences, circumstances, and inherited intellectual background of its adherents, then different worldviews will develop from different historical conditions.

The third feature of a worldview is its inescapability. If there is nothing beyond worldview—no neutral viewpoint or rationality—and the worldview is also the intellectual, historical background a person inherits, he or she inescapably thinks, reasons, and acts within that worldview. A worldview, in this sense, is in most cases invisible to the person who holds it and implicit in the way he or she thinks, reasons, and acts. Thus, the final recurring problem in the project of constructing a neutral viewpoint was that those who proposed such a viewpoint were "blind" to the premises, concepts, and standard of reasoning particular to the worldview they unconsciously inherited and held. The inescapability, and the invisibility, of a worldview also bring about a tendency in its adherents to regard their own worldview as "the norm," or at least as the "starting point," from and with which to rationally evaluate any alternative, comprehensive viewpoints—that is, other worldviews.

Again, these three features of worldviews are not to be contrasted with ahistorical, neutral—or even scientific!—philosophy. Rorty's critique of the epistemological project, Kuhn's historical account of natural science, and MacIntyre's conception of rationality, which are again exemplars of what seems to be the larger, contemporary philosophical shift away from the Enlightenment concept of rationality, have made a compelling case that rationality and intellectual inquiry as such share these very features of worldview—which is to be expected, as even these are part of, and thus inseparable from, a worldview.

However, I should clarify one key point here; in my discussion so far of the holist shift in our conception of knowledge, I am not committed to either side of the foundationalist-coherentist debate in epistemology. Rather, I am simply pointing out that (1) if a position regarding the existence of God is situated in a larger philosophical position, and (2) if such positions are composed of *interconnected* sets of beliefs, definitions, commitments, and theories—however epistemologically justified or founded—and (3) if classical foundationalism or the Enlightenment conception of rationality fails—that is, if there is no foundation, or if there can be different foundations, or different rational constructions and configurations of beliefs and reasons for beliefs even from the same foundation—then no debate about the existence of God, nor any arguments therein, can be isolated from the larger debate between the particular worldviews as a whole. If so, the predicament that arises in a debate between entire worldviews—the problem of relativism I outlined in the latter sections of this chapter, and the problem of incommensurability, quoted from MacIntyre in the first chapter—would characterize the debate about the existence of God. If these are the features of worldviews, and indeed rationality as such, what happens in a debate between different worldviews? If the existence of God is a *worldview* question, how would we go about answering such a question? Is it even possible to do so?

To this problem we now turn.

FOUR

At the Crossroads of Worldviews

A conundrum faces those who hold, as I have, that any rational case for or against the existence of God is inseparable from the comprehensive, holistic, and historically contingent belief-system—namely, the world-view—from which it reasons. How so? To hold that there is a rational answer to the question whether God exists, and that it is inseparable from the background of interconnected premises, beliefs, reasoning, and concepts that form its particular worldview, is to affirm two seemingly opposing points. On the one hand, it is to claim that such an answer rationally affirms the truth of a core belief in a particular worldview—namely, the belief that God exists—if not the whole worldview itself. On the other hand, it is to hold that the standards with which to evaluate the rationality—and to that extent, the truth—of this answer are internal to that particular worldview. That is, it is to hold that the question of whether God exists demands an answer that is objectively true, and that the means to do so are inescapably relativistic. How then shall we proceed? I discussed the importance of MacIntyre's account of the historical and narrative dimension of rationality in chapter 3. Here I will argue that among the different responses to the incommensurability and relativity of worldviews, MacIntyre's position seems to present the most promising solution, given that the question of the existence of God is situated in worldviews.

I chose the word "promising" rather deliberately. What I have argued so far is not intended to claim anything more than the simple observation I have presented in the opening of the first chapter: there is something odd about the way we argue about the existence of God, and it is odd for the same reason that we would find the way in which the explorers argued in the parable odd or awkward. Just as the difficulties in the debate between the explorers regarding the existence of the "benevolent ruler" arose from the comprehensive difference between the sociopolitical systems they inhabited, the difficulties in the debate between the theist and the atheist arise from the comprehensive and incommensurable difference between their worldviews. If so, what do I mean then by "promising"?

How would we argue if we were one of the explorers? That is, how would we, familiar with the workings of both feudal monarchy and liberal democracy, proceed to answer the question about the "benevolent ruler"? Rather than argue about whether the "benevolent ruler" exists, we would first begin by observing that both sides do agree that some kind of ruler—again, recall that we are drawing our terms only from feudal monarchy and liberal democracy—governs the natives. From there, we would examine the different aspects of native society to assess whether they resemble the aspects of a feudal monarchy or of a liberal democracy. Furthermore, we would do so by the terms of each position—for example, having inhabited a liberal democracy, we would recognize what the explorer from a democracy would acknowledge as evidence for or against the presence of equality or the institution of suffrage in the native society, and use the appropriate standard.

Ours would be primarily a comparative task, and because we began from the common agreement that there is some kind of ruler, we are, in a sense, sketching out *what* this ruler is, by forming an adequate understanding of what the native society is as a whole. Furthermore, in this task, it may turn out that the native society resembles both sociopolitical systems in some ways, and in others, neither. Thus, the positions of the two explorers would function as a set of conceptual or intellectual resources with which to understand the native society. That is, rather than a confrontational mode of discourse in which each refutes or argues against the other, we would engage in a cooperative inquiry. The "victor" of the debate would then be the explorer for whom the *core* of his or her position remained intact in the end.

However, I am not arguing that this is somehow the *correct* way to proceed in such a debate; I am suggesting that such a way seems more "promising" if we want to move past the existing disagreements and reach a better understanding of the native society. The task here then is fourfold. The first task is to give a brief account of how the concept of worldviews may clarify some of the disagreement in the debate, particularly in the examples I discussed in chapter 2. The second is to examine the last option we have that may avoid the kind of difficulties I have raised regarding the debate between worldviews, which is to define the atheist position as not asserting anything, including the proposition that God exists. I will argue that this option is unfortunately untenable, and thus it fails to dispel the problem of incommensurability and relativism in the debate. The third task is to examine the different responses and strategies to this problem of relativism, and the limitations of these positions. Finally, I will describe MacIntyre's account of how conflict between rival traditions—which, for our purpose, parallel the concept of worldviews—may be resolved, and in what ways this seems to solve the problems and difficulties of the other responses. MacIntyre's account of how rival intellectual traditions resolve their debate resembles the kind of cooperative inquiry I have outlined above for the debate between the explorers, and in that sense, his solution is the most "promising."

THE EXISTENCE OF GOD BETWEEN THE COMPETING WORLDVIEWS

Arguing about the Existence of God in an Inter-Worldview Discourse

The problem of incommensurability and relativity emerges because the arguments about the existence of God in our contemporary discourse are presented *from* particular worldviews, *to* rival worldviews. In this, I am using the concept of worldview to extend Oppy's position that the purpose of such argument is to bring about a belief-revision, presumably in those who hold different webs of beliefs. That is, the contemporary debate on whether God exists is such that these arguments are developed and formulated from a particular worldview, in order to convince those who adhere to different worldviews.[1] However, because different worldviews hold different interconnected webs of concepts, premises, and standards of reasoning, such arguments not only fail to convince, but fail for reasons that those who present them often would not acknowledge as good reasons. Furthermore, because each worldview is a coherent, self-contained, comprehensive position, and considered as the "norm," or the "starting point," of the debate by its adherents, the belief propositions from another worldview will be understood—and misunderstood—as unwarranted assertions. Likewise, because a worldview tends to be invisible to its adherents, this misunderstanding will tend to be invisible.

This, I suggest, is exemplified in the exchange between Swinburne and Mackie, as described in chapter 2. As we have seen, their differences are more complex than whether or not to postulate the existence of God. However, the concept of worldviews further clarifies the nature and implication of this difference and explains how each position—in this example, we will focus more on Mackie—has inadequately evaluated and characterized the rival viewpoint.

As we have seen, for Swinburne, God is the ultimate explanatory hypothesis, which explains everything that is. In this sense, his argument ironically supports D. Z. Phillips's contention that belief in God is "basic" to a worldview as the boundary of the world-picture, integral to all its beliefs and *in* how one reasons and thinks within it. That is, the existence of God is "basic," in Phillips's use of the word, to Swinburne's presentation of the theistic worldview as a comprehensive, ultimate explanation.[2] Why then is Swinburne's argument probabilistic in form? Swinburne is arguing for the probability of the worldview *as a whole*, in comparison against its rival. That is, what is being argued is the probability of a worldview—what he calls the "theistic hypothesis"—with its particular, comprehensive set of concepts, beliefs, narratives, and practices, and its account of rationality and intellectual inquiry, *to which* the existence of God is integral.

In contrast, for Mackie's worldview, belief in God is not basic in this way, but an unwarranted addition. To Mackie, who holds a rival worldview—in this case, naturalism—the existence of God has no explanatory function, because the explanatory schema of this worldview, with its own comprehensive set of concepts, beliefs, standard of reasoning, and notion of rational inquiry that includes what kinds of things require explanation, is already complete without God's existence. Thus, there would be no reason to affirm that God exists unless belief in God explains what Mackie's worldview cannot explain in its own terms—that is, unless it explains what a naturalist would acknowledge as needing an explanation yet is unable to explain. Thus, Mackie's particular wording in his conclusion is not simply that God does not exist, but that "we have no need for that hypothesis."[3] Likewise, regarding Hans Küng's argument that a belief in God is required to meet the challenge of nihilism, Mackie concedes that Küng's notion of fundamental trust about "truth," "unity," and "critical rationality" does answer the problems posed by nihilism, but criticizes Küng for relating such fundamental trust to faith in God: "Ironically Küng himself supplied all the materials for showing that the challenge of both intellectual and moral or practical nihilism can be met purely on human terms. . . . The further postulation of a god, even as indeterminate and mysterious a god as Küng's, is a gratuitous addition to this solution, an attempted underpinning which is as needless as it is incomprehensible."[4] Again, for Küng's position, the concept of God is integral to truth, unity, rationality as such. However, in Mackie's worldview this is an "incomprehensible" and "gratuitous addition" to concepts he defines—unknowingly—in different terms.

Thus, Mackie's critique of Swinburne and Küng is such that his argument is both a miscomprehension of their positions and an adequate intellectual response from an atheist standpoint. This is because the existence of God, as Swinburne presents it, is unwarranted for the already-comprehensive, explanatory schema that constitutes Mackie's naturalist worldview, but he does not grasp the way in which belief in God functions differently in a rival worldview. His critique that theism has no answer to "Why is there a God at all?" without the support of the ontological argument again exemplifies his difficulty. Many theists, such as Swinburne himself, pointedly omit the ontological argument, yet emphasize the existence of God as that which enables intellectual inquiry to "postulate the smallest number of brute facts," to explain all existence, even if God's existence itself remains unexplained.[5] Thus, Mackie does not account for the differences in the conceptions of intellectual inquiry and the role of ultimate explanation in their respective positions, from which they presented their arguments. His argument establishes that given his conception of intellectual inquiry, explanation, and so forth, which constitutes his worldview, there is no need to postulate the existence of God; but it establishes no more than that.

A similar problem arises when Mackie argues that the existence of suffering and evil in the world counts against the existence of God, and that the free will defense is inadequate because God could have created human beings to have free will and always choose the good. This seemingly straightforward argument turns out to be one that requires a very particular philosophical position—namely, that determinism and free will are compatible. This would then be a puzzling argument, since a theist need not accept such a position, which remains, despite Mackie's extensive arguments, highly controversial. However, the thrust of this argument becomes intelligible when we reconstruct it as arguing that belief in the existence of God is not only unneeded in the naturalist worldview, but can be made untenable in certain formulations of it. But, then again, it can do no more than that.

Thus, the concept of worldviews presents a background in which the efficacy of an argument for each of the opposing positions becomes more intelligible. With this background, we can characterize Mackie in this debate as posing the question whether his worldview has adequate intellectual resources to explain what the rival, theist worldview purports to explain. If not—if, for example, it cannot explain the existence of the universe, its order, experience of consciousness, and so forth, which Mackie mentions—the question then becomes whether such supposed failure is sufficient to require him to abandon his worldview, and whether the explanation of the rival worldview is superior in this regard. Another significant question then would be whether the rival worldview lacks problems of its own, at least from Mackie's standpoint, and thus justifies a switch. His conclusion for all these questions is that such a switch is not justified.

Obviously, this is not what Mackie understands himself to be doing. This is because for him the conclusion that the existence of God is an unwarranted addition in *his* worldview is the same as the conclusion that it is an unwarranted addition as such. That is, he views the reasons for stating that there is no need to believe that God exists for his worldview as reasons valid for all rational persons, for all positions, for all time. Because of this conflation, which I suggest comes about because of the tendency of a worldview to be invisible to its adherents, Mackie seems incognizant of how he is reasoning from his particular worldview, using its standard and terms to understand or critique a philosophical position from another, and it is because of this that he fails in significant ways to understand theist positions.[6]

This difficulty, of recognizing the significance of the fact that arguments about the existence of God are conducted from and to different worldviews, is likely due to the assumption that the worldviews of the theist and the atheist are sufficiently similar that the only significant difference seems to be that the theist is positing an additional being, namely, God. It is only when the rival worldview is seen to be obviously different in many ways that the participants in the debate present their cases differently. Consider, for example, how the philosophical debate may be conducted between two obviously different worldviews such as Buddhism and Christianity. In most schools of Buddhism, there is no "God." Would the participants then argue for and against the existence of God? Has this been the case in the actual interaction between the two? Or, in a less obvious example, when Mackie himself argues against Berkeley's Idealism, he recognizes it as not an "addition" of God to the universe, but a proposed substitution of materialism.[7] Consequently, his argument against Berkeley does not ask whether the hypothesis of God is needed, but rather critiques Berkeley's argument against materialism.

The Presumption of Atheism and the Notion of Common Ground

To answer the question whether God exists, is a debate between worldviews, along with the accompanying problem of relativism, unavoidable? If so, then how is a rational debate about the existence of God even possible? Is there some way to sidestep this predicament?

The last option is to propose a kind of "default" position, a common ground from which the debate between worldviews may begin. Furthermore, such a proposal may argue that an atheist position, such as Mackie's, is the appropriate starting point, and that it is still the theist who bears the burden of proof. Or, to put it differently, it is the theist that must convince the atheist. How so? As we have seen, one of the most significant exemplars of this proposition is Flew's argument for the "presumption of atheism." He argues that he is proposing atheism not as a metaphysical assumption, but as a procedural presumption of the debate. In such a debate, it is the theist that affirms a positive, knowledge-claiming assertion, while the atheist simply does not affirm it. The atheist in this case makes no assertion at all, but merely "opposes" the theist. Thus, the debate is to proceed by means of the theists justifying their claims from a procedurally atheist starting point. However, it is again the concept of worldview that makes Flew's position largely untenable.

What Flew misses is that an atheist who "simply" does not affirm the existence of God, or any other philosophical proposition, may do so intelligibly only from a background of other knowledge-claiming assertions he or she already holds. It is only from a standpoint of an existing web of beliefs, extensive enough that he or she is able to form a coherent and workable understanding of the world, of the self, and of others, and even of rationality, evidence, and intellectual inquiry as such, that one may even understand the proposition that God exists, evaluate the arguments regarding it, and "simply not affirm it" until there is "sufficient evidence." Yet, such a sufficiently extensive standpoint is invariably a worldview of its own. That is, an atheist who "simply" does not affirm that God exists can do so only from a large array of positive knowledge-claiming assertions that constitute his or her particular worldview, and thus the atheist is far from merely "opposing" or "not affirming" the theist claim—as we saw with Mackie. The debate does not consist simply of the theist making an assertion and the atheist opposing the assertion, because both positions are, in fact, *asserting* a competing worldview, to which the question about God is posed. If so, no justification remains for even a "procedural" presumption of atheism in the debate.

However, perhaps the "presumption of atheism" may be reformulated further in terms of worldviews. What if the debate begins from a "worldview" that affirms only what is known scientifically? It may be argued that a such starting point would be, in most cases, the common ground for supposedly different worldviews in the debate, for few would deny the extraordinary accomplishments of modern science. This may even be presented as a response against Reformed epistemologists, as a kind of "default" position with a set of knowledge claims that opposing positions ought to hold in common. Thus, such a position ought to be the starting point, from which a nonscientific claim, such as the existence of God, is proposed and debated. Indeed, is not this what Mackie and Swinburne are actually doing in their debate, and is it not I who misdescribe their differences in terms of incommensurable worldviews? Though I doubt either Mackie or Swinburne himself would view his common ground in the debate in such a simplistic way, as affirming only what is known scientifically, let us examine this possibility briefly.

A worldview that claims to affirm "only" what is known scientifically is commonly called "scientism" and is one of the significant intellectual positions today. It is difficult to contest that most participants in the contemporary debate on whether God exists would share in common their affirmation of science. The question, however, is whether scientism affirms only scientific knowledge. That is, is there a worldview that affirms only scientific knowledge that could serve as a common ground or a starting point? Again, to justify the presumption of atheism, this "default atheist" starting position needs to be such that it is only the theist who asserts.

Does scientism meet this requirements? The proponents of scientism generally demand all claims to be proven or supported "scientifically." Mikael Stenmark, however, levels a devastating critique of such forms of scientism actually held by those such as Richard Dawkins. He notes how this form of scientism makes the following claims: that only things that exist in the world are the ones that science can discover, or that the only kind of knowledge we have is scientific knowledge.[8] However, both claims are self-referentially incoherent, since neither claim is a scientific statement. Likewise, there is no conceivable scientific experiment or method to demonstrate either claim in a "non-question-begging way," because to attempt to do so would be to use "methods whose scope is in question to determine the scope of these very same methods."[9] Furthermore, there clearly are nonscientific kinds of knowledge—such as beliefs of memory, observational and self-reflective knowledge, intentional knowledge, and knowledge of linguistic meaning—that are required for scientific knowledge. Thus, the central tenets of such a naturalist worldview do not meet their own standards of justification.

However, perhaps we can propose a merely procedural form of scientism that parallels Flew's presumption of atheism, a form of scientism that does not preclude a priori the existence of things beyond science. It merely begins from affirming only scientific knowledge. Yet is even this possible? According to Quine's conception of the web of beliefs and Kuhn's account of scientific paradigms, described in chapter 3, scientific theories are not entirely separable from metaphysics. This point is made much more forcefully by those like Michael Hanby, who argues that modern science holds latent a priori metaphysical and even theological positions—or rather distortions of such positions—on the meaning and nature of being, reason, truth, creation, and even God.[10] Thus, a position that claims to be composed only of scientific knowledge—even if it eschews the self-referentially incoherent claim that this is the only possible knowledge ever—would nevertheless implicitly hold metaphysical beliefs.

Let us examine this further. If we are to affirm scientific knowledge "only," what will such "knowledge" constitute? If by "scientific knowledge" we mean a set of established scientific theories that describe the laws of nature, how are we to understand what these "laws" are? Are these laws merely "descriptive summaries" of the regular occurrences in nature, or do they describe universal, objective principles of reality that tell us "how things must behave"? Do the laws even describe reality, at least in approximation, or are our minds merely projecting order into our experience?[11] Similarly, mathematics has been indispensible for scientific inquiry, but what sort of things are mathematical entities? Do they exist objectively?[12] Are they real? Indeed, what do we mean when we say an object "exists" or is "real"? Can we limit the definition of existence to "physical" objects without question-begging claims? Again, a similar set of questions may likewise be asked of key concepts of "causation," "matter," "energy," "force," "chance," "process of evolution," and so forth.

Furthermore, there are many scientific disciplines, from the main disciplines of, say, physics, chemistry, biology, psychology, and sociology to the vast array of their respective subdisciplinary and interdisciplinary studies. How are we to organize the knowledge of these disciplines? That is, how are we to understand the different scientific disciplines—which use different terms, concepts, and methods—in relation to each other, so that all scientific knowledge forms a coherent whole?[13] This issue becomes even more problematic in cases in which the subject matters of two disciplines overlap. For instance, in describing the same event (speaking simplistically), cognitive neuroscience speaks of physiological brain-states, whereas cognitive psychology speaks of internal mental states. How are we to relate these different scientific accounts of the same event? I am not asking how these disciplines interact—a question that can be answered rather simply, by the historical narrative of how these forms of inquiry have interacted—but what such interaction implies. For example, are we to understand that psychology, with its talk of mental processes and states, is a product of our insufficient knowledge, which will eventually be reduced completely to neuroscience, because the mind is, in the end, reducible to the brain? Or is such reductionism untenable?

How are we to answer these numerous questions above without appealing to nonscientific premises? Indeed, these are not scientific questions, nor are they required for the practice of actual science—at least, so far. Yet once one claims to affirm "only" scientific knowledge, even as a starting point, questions such as these become unavoidable. This is because scientific theories are intelligible only within the context of that particular form of scientific inquiry, with its set of concepts and method, which constitutes that discipline. Furthermore, as Kuhn and MacIntyre argued, the rationality of such inquiry is defined by its overarching paradigm, which is justified by the historical narrative of that particular inquiry. Thus, to affirm "only" the whole body of scientific knowledge collected from very different scientific disciplines, taken out of such particular contexts and without answering the above questions, inevitably raises the question what such a position can claim intelligibly. That is, it asks, can such a position provide a sufficiently coherent, intelligible background against which the question of the existence of God can even be asked, let alone its answer be evaluated?

Again, I am arguing that the context of worldviews—worldviews which make nonscientific, metaphysical claims—in the debate on whether God exists is inescapable. This, in turn, makes any notion of a neutral or even a common ground of the debate as a starting point untenable. It had become untenable ever since the failure of the Enlightenment epistemological project to build knowledge from indubitable foundations. It is simply a consequence of this failure and of the subsequent shift in our contemporary conception of knowledge and rationality that just as knowledge cannot be built from indubitable foundations alone, a worldview cannot be "built" out of scientific knowledge alone.

Starting Points of the Debate and the Problem of Relativism

The different positions in the debate on whether God exists therefore begin their debate from a different starting point, which depends on their respective worldviews. That is, proponents of each position are justified in beginning the debate—and moreover, cannot but do so—from the worldview they already hold. In this sense, the Reformed epistemologists, such as Plantinga, rightly critique the evidentialist position. However, an argument about the existence of God does not argue only *from* a particular worldview, but also *to* or *against* another worldview. This is what Plantinga calls presenting a "defeater," or "defeater-defeater," and so on.

Yet, precisely because of this, when an argument is presented to those who hold other worldviews in order to convince them, there *is* a "presumption" in the debate, namely of the one to whom the argument is being presented. To quote Wolterstorff again, a Reformed epistemologist himself whom we considered in chapter 2, "A person is rationally justified in believing a certain proposition which he does believe unless he has adequate reason to cease from believing it."[14] That is, Flew's presumption of atheism is justified so long as a theistic argument is being presented *to* an atheist. However, if such arguments fail, the conclusion is not atheism, but merely the justification of an atheist in continuing to hold his or her worldview. Furthermore, as we have seen, because of the incommensurable differences in worldviews, these arguments do tend to fail, and because there is neither a neutral nor common starting point, there is no way to judge which worldview is true.

Thus we return to the issue of relativity. It is precisely this problem of relativity that Plantinga's position does not adequately resolve; if one begins from a different "properly basic belief," and if the standards of rationality and knowledge between opposing positions are different, as was the case with Plantinga's own epistemological theories of "warrant" and *sensus divinitatis*, is it possible for there to be an adequate rational argument for or against the existence of God that works across different worldviews? If so, how? Plantinga's conception of using defeaters drawn from the body of knowledge that the opposing position accepts may be a beginning of an answer. However, such defeaters still face the problem of their limited applicability to a variation or a revision of the defeated position—a kind of defeater-defeater. Thus, when defeaters are conceived as combative tools to defeat a comprehensive intellectual position that underlies an entire worldview, this contest of defeaters seem destined to end in the kind of stalemate that does in fact characterize our contemporary debate about God.

Again, as we have seen, MacIntyre responded to the implication of relativism in Kuhn's account of scientific paradigms by arguing that the competitions between paradigms may be resolved through a construction of narrative history. However, this is possible because in this account the different paradigms sequentially follow each other. A new scientific paradigm emerges from the historical circumstances of the older paradigm, and thus it is possible to construct a coherent narrative of a *single* history of sciences, albeit punctuated with revolutions. This is not so with worldviews, because competing worldviews, so to speak, are presented side-by-side, and each worldview has its own, largely independent historical narrative.

How then are we to proceed?

RELATIVITY OF WORLDVIEWS AND THE PROBLEM
OF TRUTH AND REALITY

Affirmation of Truth and Objective Reality over Relativity of Worldviews

Perhaps the most unnerving problem that the relativity of worldviews poses is that of subjectivity and truth. That is, a worldview is relative insofar as it is a "subjective" view of reality, which raises the question of "objectivity" and, more precisely, of "objective reality." Hence, the first way to address the problem of the relativity of worldviews is to affirm that there is a "reality out there." Naugle, for example, argues that the "affirmation of objectivity rooted in God is the antidote" to the problematic concept of "worldview, [which has been tainted] for over two centuries with the hues of relativism," which states that "there are no universal truths" nor "intrinsic characteristics" of reality.[15] With this theological affirmation, he advocates a "critical realism" in epistemology, over the extremes of "naive realism" or "creative antirealism."[16] Critical realism affirms the existence of independent, objective reality and its fixed characteristics, and asserts that human beings have trustworthy capacities to apprehend and know this reality. However, it acknowledges that this knowledge has cognitive and epistemological limits and that the frameworks through which this knowledge is formed have parameters, such as worldviews. Thus though we can know truths about reality, these truths are in that sense and to that extent constructed and relative.

Naugle's response seems to have a number of precedents in the other philosophers who struggled with the concept of worldviews. For example, we have seen in his account how Dilthey asserted that all worldviews are rooted in "life itself" and thus reflect reality, and how Husserl responded to the relativity of worldviews with the concept of *Lebenswelt*, the "lifeworld." Likewise, critical realism regarding science was the response to the implication of relativism in Kuhn's account of the incommensurability between scientific paradigms.[17] Contemporary arguments for scientific realism acknowledge the difficulties regarding scientific knowledge raised by works like Kuhn, but nevertheless assert that science does give adequate and approximate descriptions of reality, though through the medium of concepts, metaphors, analogies, and models.

Rorty's Critique of the Notion of Truth as Correspondence to Reality

What is at issue here, however, is not whether there is an objective reality, but whether our worldview somehow corresponds to it. That is, the response of realism is not merely that there is a reality independent of our beliefs, but that our beliefs are true because they somehow correspond to this reality. It is again Rorty who raises, through his critique of the Enlightenment epistemological project, one of the most notable challenges to this view. He does not deny that there is an objective reality but that, in addition, there is something called "the truth" about that reality. He argues that he cannot make sense of this notion, adding: "When the realist tries to explain [the notion of the truth about the world] with [the notion that the] truth about the world consists in a relation of 'correspondence' between certain sentences (many of which, no doubt, have yet to be formulated) and the world itself the pragmatist can only fall back on saying, once again, that many centuries of attempts to explain what 'correspondence' is have failed."[18] That is, the notion that truth consists in the correspondence of some sort of representation to an objective reality remains unintelligible.[19] How so?

Rorty's position on truth is implied in his critique of the epistemological project in his *Philosophy and the Mirror of Nature*. If knowledge is not a matter of "representations" in the mind that have a "privileged relation" to the objects that knowledge-claims are about, then there is no viable connection between our beliefs and reality. That is, if our belief propositions are justified by other belief propositions, rather than by those propositions' relations to a set of indubitable foundations of knowledge, foundations that have a "privileged relation" to the reality "out there," then our beliefs are not justified as "true" because of their correspondence to such reality. The failure of the Enlightenment epistemological project is consequently the failure to give an intelligible account of the correspondence theory of truth.

What then does Rorty say about truth, if it is not correspondence to reality? We call something true when those involved in the conversation agree that it is and endorse it. This is not to say that truth is merely agreement, but unlike correspondence, this is a substantive description of what happens when we call a proposition true. He anticipates the question of how one can explain the success of natural science without the correspondence view, and argues that saying science corresponds to reality presents no further explanation of its success than saying opium has "dormitive power" to explain why opium puts people to sleep.[20] Nevertheless, he acknowledges that the actions based on "true" beliefs tend to be successful, and presents a pragmatist position, writing: "[The pragmatist] shares . . . the notion that knowledge is power, a tool for coping with reality. But . . . he drops the notion of truth as correspondence with reality altogether, and says that modern science does not enable us to cope because it corresponds, it just plain enables us to cope."[21] Thus, truth also refers to properties of belief propositions that work, or more precisely, help us cope with reality.

The implication of Rorty's position on truth for understanding worldviews is found in his view of the use of language in describing reality. His position is that there is nothing to be said beyond language; this emerges in his argument against those he calls "intuitive realists." These realists argue that there is something to perennial philosophical questions about truth, goodness, reality, and so forth that, despite our failure to answer or even make sense of them, is nevertheless important. Rorty states that the debate between the pragmatists and the intuitive realists leads to the question of whether language "goes all the way down." "[The intuitive realist] might say either that language does not go all the way down—that there is a kind of awareness of facts which is not expressible in language and which no argument could render dubious—or, more mildly, that there is a core language which is common to all traditions and which needs to be isolated."[22] This means the failure to answer the perennial questions may be explained in two ways. The first is the pragmatist position that there is nothing significant to be said about them. The second is that our language is still, or perhaps forever will be, inadequate to talk about them.

If we take the second position, then there are mainly two possibilities. The first is that as we struggle to talk about what was previously inexpressible, our language may become adequate to answer questions of truth, goodness, reality, and so on. The second is that we may never be able to answer these questions, for these issues are ineffable and beyond language, but that asking these questions is important nevertheless. Rorty comments:

> Here we hit a bedrock metaphilosophical issue: can we ever appeal to non-linguistic knowledge in philosophical argument? This is the question of whether a dialectical impasse is the mark of philosophical depth or of a bad language, one which needs to be replaced with one which will not lead to such impasses. *That* is just the issue about the status of intuitions, which I said above was the real issue between the pragmatist and the realist.[23]

Rorty's pragmatist position is clear, however; it is language "all the way down." "The intuitive realist thinks that beneath all the texts, there is something which is not just one more text but that to which various texts are trying to be 'adequate.' The pragmatist does not think that there is anything like that."[24] Thus, in terms of worldview, what Rorty is arguing resembles what Naugle describes Derrida as saying, which is that there is no reality that a worldview somehow accesses or to which it connects; there is nothing beyond its linguistic account of reality but its interconnected set of belief propositions.

Truth as Correspondence to Reality in Charles Taylor

In contrast to Rorty's view is the position of Charles Taylor, who largely accepts Rorty's account in *Philosophy and the Mirror of Nature*, which he characterizes as a critique of the "foundational enterprise" of epistemology.[25] Epistemology sought the foundations—what Rorty called "privileged representations"—of all knowledge, a search that, as Rorty argued, was exemplified in natural science. Taylor comments: "In practice, epistemologists took their cues from what they identified as the successful sciences of their day, all the way from Descartes's infatuation with mathematics to the contemporary vogue for reduction to physics."[26] However, what the epistemologists sought were the foundations that such sciences may reveal—foundations, independent of these sciences, without which no knowledge is possible. It is this that Rorty successfully critiqued.

However, Taylor argues that there is a wider conception of knowledge in epistemology that this critique of foundationalism does not address, namely the conception of "knowledge as correct representations of an independent reality."[27] The key word here is "independent," meaning independent *from us*. Taylor explains: "[This conception] is bound up with very influential and often not fully articulated notions about science and about the nature of human agency. Through these it connects with certain moral and spiritual ideas of the modern age."[28] That is, epistemology assumes a particular conception of reality and ourselves, often idealized in moral or spiritual terms.

Specifically, the epistemological project is linked with three related, distinct notions, connected with the ideal of individual freedom:

> The first is the picture of the subject as ideally disengaged, that is free and rational to the extent that he has fully distinguished himself from the natural and social worlds, so that his identity is no longer to be defined in terms of what lies outside him and these worlds. The second, which flows from this, is a punctual view of the self, ideally ready as free and rational to treat these worlds—and even some of the features of his own character—instrumentally, as subject to change and reorganizing in order the better to secure the welfare

of himself and others. The third is the social consequence of the first two: an atomistic construal of society as constituted by, or ultimately to be explained in terms of, individual purposes.[29]

Such a self is independent of the society and the world, thus both able to and needing to form objective "representations" of the world. To elaborate on Taylor, this conception of the self would raise the problem of "how to accurately represent" reality or, say, "the inner states of other people," which are after all independent—and separated!—from the self. This is what makes the question of whether there is an "external reality" or "other people" possible. Thus, to challenge epistemology is to challenge not simply foundationalism, but also these notions.

First, Taylor argues that the notion of a disengaged self is rendered impossible by Heidegger's work: "[Heidegger's] analysis of being-in-the-world shows that the condition of our forming disengaged representations of reality is that we must be already engaged in coping with our world, dealing with things in it, at grips with them. Disengaged description is a special possibility, realizable only intermittently of a being (*Dasein*) who is always 'in' the world in another way, as an agent engaged in realizing a certain form of life."[30] Even to form "disengaged" theories about the world, we must be agents; we must investigate, set ourselves to observe, experiment, control variables, and so forth. That is, the supposed disengaged human knower is not "disengaged" at all, but engaged in the midst of the world.

Taylor argues that if there is a kind of "foundation" to knowledge, it is this engaged form of life: "This shows the whole epistemological construal of knowledge to be mistaken. It doesn't just consist of inner pictures of outer reality, but grounds in something quite other. And in this 'foundation,' the crucial move of the epistemological construal—distinguishing states of the subject (our 'ideas') from features of external world—can't be effected."[31] It is this sort of "foundation" which forms a background to any knowledge—indeed, background assumptions that are embodied in the way of living, with which even the so-called "disinterested" theories are made possible. This means that the task of reason is not representing reality or foundations of knowledge, but "articulating the background" of knowledge claims and "'disclosing' what it involves."[32]

Taylor then argues that, likewise, the punctual notion of the self is rendered impossible. Both Heidegger and Maurice Merleau-Ponty have shown the inescapability of this background: "Heidegger shows how *Dasein*'s world is defined by the related purposes of a certain way of life shared with others. Merleau-Ponty shows how our agency is essentially embodied and how this lived body is the locus of directions of actions and desires that we never fully grasp or control by personal decision."[33] Hence, the self can never fully disengage from its surroundings, the world it is engaged in, to be free to act upon it in an instrumental way. Likewise, the atomistic understanding of the self and society is dismantled in turn. Taylor notes how Heidegger's and Merleau-Ponty's critiques reveal the priority of society as the locus of the self's identity. Furthermore, theories of language have indicated that language is essential to human thought, and place capacity for language not simply in the individual, but primarily in the language community.[34]

However, it is precisely this critique of the notion of the self as independent from reality that brings Taylor to argue against Rorty to affirm that truth is indeed a correspondence to reality, though in a very different sense. According to Taylor, the correspondence theory of truth that Rorty criticizes is that which claims we are unable to directly access the thing-in-itself and thus our knowledge of a thing is mediated by our representation of it. If that is what Rorty criticizes, he is right to ask in what sense we can say there is a correspondence. However, Taylor responds in "Rorty in the Epistemological Tradition" that such "absurdity" is not what he, Taylor, means by "correspondence to reality."[35] He argues that there is no "mediated knowledge," because we, as agents, are engaged and interacting with the world, and therefore are aware that there are things that are independent of what we believe about them. This is what "truth as correspondence" means. However, Taylor charges, Rorty does not realize that there are such alternative conceptions of truth as correspondence, and this is an indication that Rorty is still "a prisoner of the epistemological world-view."[36]

The debate between Rorty and Taylor continues, but what is important for our purpose is the implication of Taylor's conception of truth regarding the problem of relativity, subjectivity, and truth of worldviews.[37] Taylor's argument is a critique not only of "antirealists," who deny that "truth corresponds to reality," but also of the "realists." This is because for Taylor, the debate addresses a question that is already fundamentally misguided. Its concern regarding subjectivity and objectivity, or independent reality, and whether there are "trustworthy" cognitive faculties to access or describe objective reality is a question that is possible only because of a defective conception of the self in the world. This, in fact, was the critique, briefly mentioned in chapter 3, that Heidegger leveled against the modern concept of worldview as obfuscating the encounter with being in his "Age of the World-Picture," and it was the point of his concept of *Dasein*, the human knower already "being there" in the midst of the world. It is a point Naugle himself recognizes.[38] For Taylor, human constructions of historically contingent conceptual schemes, categorical frameworks, languages, and, indeed, worldviews are not some veil or a medium that separates us from reality as it truly is; rather, such constructions are merely *how we engage with reality* in the midst of which we find ourselves. The realist-antirealist debate regarding worldviews thus depends also on a particular worldview, and a confused one at that.

However, this is not sufficient to resolve the problem of the relativity of worldviews. Whether there is an objective reality, and whether we have the means to access it or are already engaged in the midst of it, are significant issues raised by the concept of worldview. But these issues do not address the relativity of worldviews. A simple point illustrates why. Theism and atheism in the debate about the existence of God are incommensurable worldviews, each of which would nevertheless affirm—rightly, Taylor would argue—the correspondence of its position to reality. Both sides would affirm that their worldviews are more than merely incommensurable sets of belief propositions; each would claim, on the contrary, to present—at the very least—a more adequate account of reality. The problem is more adequately. How are we to determine this?

THE PROBLEM OF THE RELATIVITY OF WORLDVIEWS AND ITS RESPONSES

The Winch-MacIntyre Debate

It would be helpful to first describe the debate between MacIntyre and Peter Winch in order to address the issue of relativity in worldviews. This debate, in which MacIntyre criticizes Winch's anthropologically informed relativism, is significant because it indicates how MacIntyre began to face the problem of relativism.[39] The debate, however, took place in a period—that is, before 1971—when his current position began to be formed. He describes this period as one during which his position was characterized by "disparate, and sometimes conflicting sets of concerns and beliefs," when he was "unable to move decisively to any resolution."[40] Thus, the debate itself shows a glimpse of how MacIntyre himself advanced from this position, which will become important for our discussion later on.

Winch's position can be succinctly put in the following words: "Criteria of logic are not a direct gift from God but arise out of and are only intelligible in the context of ways of living and modes of social life."[41] He then gives an example of how science and religion would have different criteria, and how it is likewise with modern, scientific, Western societies and primitive cultures, such as the Azandes, with their beliefs in witches and magic. This excludes the possibility of judging which is "more rational." He thus adds that if a sociologist or anthropologist—say Lucien Lévy-Bruhl—perceives a belief or a concept in a primitive culture to be irrational, or "pre-logical," it is not the case that the culture is irrational, but that he is confused, unable to understand the criteria of rationality or intelligibility different from his own.

MacIntyre argues against this in "Is Understanding Religion Compatible with Believing?" He argues that even when we understand the primitive culture's standards of intelligibility, or why they believe what they believe is true, this does not answer whether they are right.[42] This is because to "make a belief and the concepts which it embodies intelligible, [we] cannot avoid invoking our own criteria," criteria of rationality.[43] Thus, it is unavoidable to raise the objection that there are data that would falsify, or at least pose a problem for, the beliefs of the Azande—such as there being no rain even if proper rites were done—even if the Azande themselves do not recognize these as problems.[44] Furthermore, he points out that concepts and criteria of intelligibility have a history in which they change through criticism.[45] For example, there is a historical reason why beliefs in witches were abandoned in the West. In Winch's position it would be impossible to explain the transition from a medieval, Christian belief-system to that of the secular, modern West.

Winch argues back, stating that he already stated that criteria of intelligibility of a given society are "open" and change in history.[46] What MacIntyre misses is that criticism of the criteria also has a history—but then the question is, history of which society?[47] Simply put, rationality has a history, but it is contingent on a particular society, and we cannot judge the rationality of other societies, such as the Azande, except by their own terms. This does not mean that we may approach the other culture without our criteria, but that we must somehow "extend our understanding" to fit their criteria.[48] Thus, it is inappropriate to use the standards of Western science, and its notion of evidence and falsifiability, to judge the Azande. Winch argues that in their own terms, the belief system of the Azande seems more concerned about being in tune with the world than about gaining technological control over, or predicting, rain.

Charles Taylor agrees with Winch in the debate, but raises one objection: "Now the difficult thing about the relation of ritual magic in primitive societies to some of the practices of our society is that it is clearly not identical with any of our practices, nor is it simply different, as others of their practices—their games, for instance—might be. Rather they are incommensurable. They are different, yet they somehow occupy the same space."[49] That is, it is true that criteria of intelligibility and rationality depend on societies—or for our purpose, worldviews of such societies—such that each worldview must be understood and judged in its own terms and by its own standards. However, each worldview is not merely different, but incommensurable, and by this, Taylor introduces a new dimension to the meaning of the term, namely that both occupy the "same space." Simply put, comparing them is inevitable, which raises the unavoidable question of which worldview is more true, or rational, and so forth.

Thus, we return to the same problem with which this chapter began. Different worldviews have—or at least claim to have—trustworthy means to engage or know objective reality. However, the standards with which to do so are internal—that is, relative—to each worldview. Furthermore, each "occupies the same space," that is, each describes what it purports to be the same reality, with intrinsic, fixed characteristics, which exist independently of what we may believe, making the comparison between them unavoidable. It is precisely this, I suggest, that Phillips, whose position draws from Winch extensively in *Faith after Foundationalism*, either misses or ignores. Taylor's assessment of the Winch-MacIntyre debate implies that even if Phillips's view that different worldviews are radically different language-games is true—which I have suggested is problematical—nevertheless, because they occupy the same space, their difference merely adds to the problem of relativity.

Judging Each Worldview by Its Own Standards

One response to the problem of relativism is to compare how each worldview fares by its own standards. This is what Holmes prefers. He rejects fideism, which he describes as a "refusal to take seriously the plurality of alternatives, the problem of subjectivism, and the question of truth," and therefore as a "[refusal] to weigh conflicting claims."[50] He argues against the kind of epistemological foundationalism that seeks to find indubitable and incorrigible foundations of knowledge with which to judge worldviews, stating that all such attempts "fail to be presuppositionless as they claim," because "philosophy is always to some extent 'perspectival.'"[51] Rather, he argues that a worldview is "justified by virtue of its coherence within the entire body of what one knows and believes."[52]

Ninian Smart, whose writings on worldviews have become influential in the study of world religions, presents a similar position. First, he proposes a kind of philosophy that goes beyond standard "philosophy of religion"—a philosophy of worldview, which analyzes, describes, and evaluates radically different worldviews, east and west, religious and secular.[53] However, he rejects "methodological rationalism," which he describes as "the attitude that one may understand the way other cultures work partly in terms of a universal model of rationality: roughly MacIntyre's rather than Winch's position in that famous debate."[54] He believes this view of rationality is still dominant in Western philosophy, along with a particular worldview associated with it, namely scientific humanism. However, he notes that there have been significant challenges to it from Rorty, Kuhn, Feyerabend, Putnam, and later MacIntyre in his works from *After Virtue* onward.[55]

However, to evaluate the truth of worldviews is not a simple task for Smart. He does not hold a simple coherentist position. He rejects the notion that only within a worldview can a given worldview be understood, because in numerous cases people have successfully studied and understood alternative worldviews to their own.[56] He rejects as too simplistic the claim that there is no neutral arena where competing truth claims may ever be settled, because there have been facts or data outside the framework of a particular set of competing worldviews—such as natural sciences for two competing religions—which affected both positions; however, he argues that there is no absolutely neutral arena. Likewise, Smart argues that there are no "public" or empirical "facts" that verify or falsify a worldview as a whole, but such facts do make a worldview more or less plausible. What Smart seems to be saying here is this: a worldview as a system—rather like Kuhn's paradigm—is not something that may be proven or falsified by facts in some neutral ground; rather, such facts, "neutral" to the extent that they are accepted by the opposing worldviews in a given dispute, can affect these worldviews as a whole in unspecified ways. However, Smart cautions that each worldview weighs such evidence differently, again making comparison and adjudication difficult.

This position seems similar to what Taylor argues regarding the Winch-MacIntyre debate when he suggests that it is possible to make transcultural judgments, such as between "theoretical" and "atheoretical" societies.[57] For example, each worldview may hold different standards to justify itself, such as technological control versus being in tune with nature, but historically, evidences of technological control from Galilean science had a profound impact on the position of a Renaissance sage with a very different standard, namely, the standard of being in tune with nature.[58] To elaborate on Taylor, when worldviews are actually compared, each leaves an impact on the other, despite the different criteria and standards they hold. However, Taylor also raises the problem that, nevertheless, such evidences or strengths are weighed differently depending on the worldview. That is, there is no set algorithm or rules that determine how these different factors and evidences are to be calculated when one is evaluating the two worldviews or judging between them.

This conclusion is repeated thoroughly in Wilko van Holten's *Explanation within the Bounds of Religion*, which will nicely reiterate some of the points we have discussed so far regarding the characteristics of a debate between worldviews, especially as it relates to religious belief in God. Van Holten argues that a central function of religious belief is to explain, and thus make sense of, the experiences of life. That is, religious belief, such as theism, is a cognitive and explanatory account of reality, rather than, say, merely an expression of religious sentiment.[59] He first examines whether there is a single, authoritative account of explanation in contemporary philosophy of science. That is, he examines whether there is a consensus on a definition, or a model, of what makes a scientific theory an explanatory account of reality. He concludes that there is no such consensus, and so a religious belief need not comply with some external—and nonexisting—standard from science in order to claim itself as an explanatory account of reality.

Religious belief, such as theism, is therefore a "metaphysical hypothesis or a system" and, as such, a "worldview," which claims to be the inference to the best explanation.[60] However, van Holten describes how in the case of large-scale theories or paradigms in natural science, there is no "magic algorithm" to mechanically infer to best explanation, and theory choice is based on "rationality of judgment" rather than "rationality of rules."[61] That is, there are no formal rules nor method to *calculate*, so to speak, which large-scale theory is the best explanation. This poses a serious challenge to the notion that it is possible to determine the truth of a theistic worldview by somehow measuring the explanatory power of the theistic hypothesis through some formal argument, exemplified by Swinburne's cumulative, probabilistic argument.

Van Holten therefore argues for an "informal reasoning" in assessing the explanatory power of a worldview. He lists a number of criteria—which, he adds, is not exhaustive—for such an assessment.[62] First is the internal coherence and consistency of the worldview and its external consistency with other, established scientific facts and theories, such as the theory of evolution. There is also the question of factual objectivity, which is whether the facts that a worldview purports to explain—such as the order in nature—refer to what objectively exists. Another important criterion is the scope and comprehensiveness of the worldview in its ability to account for all aspects of reality and human experience, and the simplicity of this explanation. Last is the pragmatic usefulness of the worldview—that is, it should also help people cope with living.

However, van Holten emphasizes that these criteria cannot determine which worldview is the best explanation:

> Does the application of the criteria enable us to *decide* between metaphysical theories; do they enable one to infer from many possible theories to a theory or a hypothesis that is true or most probably true? The emphasis on the person-relativity of most of these criteria already suggests that no such thing is possible. But, we now know that this is not peculiar to religion or metaphysics. . . . The analysis of scientific decision-making in earlier sections of the chapter showed in detail why this is so.[63]

That is, there are again no formal rules on how to apply these criteria to judge between competing worldviews. Thus, the criteria of assessing worldviews that van Holten proposes have the same functions and limitations as Kuhn's proposed criteria for theory choice regarding scientific paradigms. Van Holten thus concludes that "the claim that theism is the best explanation appears to be intelligible only from the standpoint of faith," by those who already "adopt a theist framework."[64]

Thus, we are faced again with the problem of relativism. Different worldviews may claim to be true or the "best explanatory" accounts of reality, yet the standards for judging any given worldview's claims are internal to that worldview. Nor can we understand or evaluate a worldview solely on its own terms, because different worldviews inevitably compete—and have historically competed—against each other. In doing so, each worldview does affect the other, but it is difficult to specify how. Furthermore, comparing how one worldview fares by its own standard with how another fares by its standard is problematic, because of the complexities of weighing evidences or assessing the coherence in each given worldview. There seem to be some general criteria or considerations when comparing different worldviews, but these do not enable us to decide between worldviews. To sum, none of the responses to relativity of worldviews examined so far proposes a workable resolution to this relativity; rather, together they merely raise the following dilemma. Worldviews compete, but there is no set of rules for winning this competition.

MACINTYRE AND THE CROSSROADS OF WORLDVIEWS

The Narrative and Telos of Rational Inquiry

Where are we to place MacIntyre's account of tradition and rationality (which we examined in chapter 3) in regard to the problem of relativism? It seems at first glance that his position resembles the other views described so far. He argues that the rationality and the justification of an intellectual tradition are to be measured in terms of how it has solved the problems and difficulties in its own history. The criteria of success and justification are internal to the tradition, which raises the problem of what happens when traditions are competing, each with its own set of concepts, standard of rationality, and history of its intellectual inquiry. However, his account adds a new dimension to this solution. To understand it, we will need to first examine his concept of the telos of intellectual inquiry.

MacIntyre's response to the relativism implied in Kuhn's account was not to present a set of criteria to determine or even guide theory choice. Rather, for MacIntyre, what resolves the conflict between paradigms is found within the actual, historical practice—or more precisely the narrative of this practice—of the particular scientific inquiry. That is, to understand why a new scientific paradigm was chosen over its predecessor, we do not examine which paradigm satisfied some generalized criteria of theory choice, but rather the actual, historical narrative of that particular form of intellectual inquiry. For example, rather than propose some general criteria that scientists followed to justify the choice of Einsteinian theory over Newtonian theory in physics, we would need to examine the actual narrative of physics and its account of how this particular conflict in paradigm was resolved.

What gives direction to such narrative, however, is the conception of the end, a telos, toward which that particular inquiry progressed. That is, insofar as rational inquiry itself is an activity (what MacIntyre calls a practice), it has a general conception of the intellectual goal toward which it aims—however vaguely the goal is conceived—and in terms of which the "progress" of an inquiry is understood. MacIntyre thus writes:

To engage in intellectual enquiry is then not to simply advance theses and to give one's rational allegiance to those theses which so far
withstand refutation; it is to understand the movement from thesis
to thesis as a movement toward a kind of *logos* which will disclose
how things are, not relative to some point of view, but as such. The
conception of what each kind of thing is as such not only gives a direction to the enquiry that it would otherwise lack but also provides
a resource for correcting and reformulating our successive theses as
we aspire to move from hypothesis to unconditional assertion.[65]

MacIntyre elaborates on how this notion of the progress toward the telos
makes the narrative of an intellectual inquiry intelligible. First, the later
stage of the inquiry would be based on the findings of the former—not
in that it would confirm them, but in that it has progressed *from* them.
Second, if there is progress toward the goal of inquiry, the later stages
will be better able to account for errors and inadequacies of the earlier
stages. Third, the later stages, being close to the goal, will have more adequate conceptions of the goal, or the "good of the enquiry." Last, and
most important, the conception of the telos of the inquiry, as it becomes
more adequate in successive stages, will also be the conception of "what
it would be to have a completed enquiry."[66]

Thus, the successes and failures of a particular set of concepts, beliefs, or standards of reasoning in such an inquiry will be measured by
how the inquiry progresses toward its goal.[67] However, in a rational inquiry, certain limitations, incoherences, inadequacies, or defects in a tradition's concepts, beliefs, standard of reasoning, or even its particular
conception of the goal or telos of its inquiry may impede the tradition
from any further progress toward the goal of its inquiry, namely, what it
understands so far as "what it would be to have a completed enquiry." To
describe how these limitations, incoherences, and so on were overcome—
assuming the tradition did overcome them—requires a narrative account
of how the tradition's conception of the telos, its standard of reasoning,
and so forth were revised in order to do so. Their formation and revision
constitute the narrative of the progress or decline of an intellectual tradition, and in fact, this defines what it is for the tradition to be "true."

Therefore, MacIntyre, in contrast to Rorty, also affirms a substantive
notion of "Truth." In his account, "Truth" is the telos of a socially em-

bodied, historically extended practice of intellectual inquiry. That is, "Truth" is what makes the narrative of a tradition of intellectual inquiry, as a whole, intelligible, and in this sense, what "corresponds" to reality is not a particular belief proposition in isolation, but the intellectual tradition itself.

MacIntyre's Account of the Rival Traditions in Conflict

What happens if there are rival intellectual traditions? Again, with no neutral standpoint from which to judge between conflicting traditions, each tradition, with its respective standards of reasoning, will disagree regarding what evidence is to be counted, what argument is rational, or even how each characterizes their disagreement.[68] At this point, both traditions may fall into an epistemological crisis, because neither can resolve the conflict of knowledge claims between them, and consequently neither can progress toward its telos, which involves, in MacIntyre's words cited above, understanding "how things are, not relative to some point of view, but as such." In such a case, MacIntyre argues that resolution begins only by understanding the other tradition in its own terms, namely by understanding the particular, historical narrative that constitutes each rival intellectual position. That is, understanding each other as a tradition brings more conceptual and explanatory resources with which to resolve the conflict than excluding such an understanding brings to the task.

When two traditions begin to seek such understanding, initially each tradition understands—or more to the point, misunderstands—the other through its own terms. However, the protagonists of each intellectual tradition may eventually and successfully understand the rival position on the rival's terms. This occurs when a protagonist of one intellectual tradition is able (1) to give an account of how the rival tradition could intelligibly hold its concepts or beliefs and (2) to employ the rival's standard of reasoning as adeptly as that of his or her own tradition. Such a protagonist has become a participant of both traditions. This is when

> the protagonists of each tradition, having considered in what ways their own tradition has by its own standards of achievement in enquiry found it difficult to develop its enquiries beyond a certain

point, or has produced in some area insoluble antinomies, ask whether the alternative and rival tradition may not be able to provide resources to characterize and to explain the failings and defects of their own tradition more adequately than they, using the resources of that tradition, have been able to do.[69]

Such a protagonist is able to advance a tradition's intellectual inquiry and solve the problems internal to it, but do so through the resources of the other tradition. What this suggests is that if the resources of one tradition clearly solve what its rival recognizes as its own problems, but not vice versa, then the tradition providing the solution is to be deemed superior. However, this requires not a neutral position in which to compare two opposing worldviews, but particular individuals who belong, in some sense, to both worldviews and are able to advance the goals and solve the problems internal to each position.

If there is no clear superiority, a protagonist of one tradition may construct a new standpoint in which the problems, limitations, incoherencies, or inadequacies of each intellectual tradition may be overcome, or transcended, by the resources of its rival, or through the synthesis of the two.[70] This new intellectual tradition that emerges from the two rival traditions will then possess its own narrative of rational inquiry, and one of the significant events within it will be precisely how its standpoint was formed. That is, the new standpoint will have constructed a narrative of the history of its rational inquiry in which *both* its old standpoint and its rival tradition will be properly understood as its *predecessors*. This, MacIntyre argues, is what historically happened when Aquinas synthesized the competing Augustinian and Aristotelian traditions.

Thus, MacIntyre's solution to the problem of relativity in worldviews is to describe what actually happens or has happened when two rival worldviews come together. Worldviews are incommensurable and historically contingent, yet it is precisely this historicity of worldviews that enables a comparison of competing worldviews. Previous solutions to the problem of relativity seemed to have understood the comparison of worldviews as an ahistorical process, despite repeatedly noting the historical nature of worldviews. That is, the things being compared were comprehensive systems or frameworks of beliefs, concepts, and rational criteria as they are in the present. Those making the comparisons were comparing worldviews in terms of how each justified itself, or how coherent it was, or how it fared by its own standards in a *fixed state* of *now*. What MacIntyre does is to extend each worldview to its past and its future and describe how the two rivals may interact. That is, it is the historical narrative of the intellectual inquiry of a given worldview, regarding where it has come from and where it seeks to go, that enables a protagonist to construct a narrative in which one worldview successfully defeats its rival worldview on the latter's own terms—that is, in terms of the latter's narrative. Such a narrative successfully retells the rival's quest for its telos in ways that bring the rival closer to its telos than the rival could get on its own.

At this point, it may be more helpful to use a different metaphor for worldviews, considering them as different paths on a journey. It is difficult to compare two journeys when they are taken out of the context of where each comes from and where each is headed. Comparing worldviews is analogous to coming to a crossing of two journeys: only when standing upon such a crossroad, gazing afar to where each path has come from and where each is heading, can we compare the two.

THE EXISTENCE OF GOD AT THE CROSSROADS

The different positions regarding the existence of God argue from different, incommensurable worldviews and, rather like the explorers in our parable, are largely incognizant of such differences or are arguing for or against each other in a debate that poses the same kind of difficulties the explorers faced in their disagreement. There is, furthermore, no indubitable foundation of knowledge or neutral standpoint or completely independent standard of justification which can adequately adjudicate between these positions. Nor is there a kind of default position, composed solely of a commonly agreed-on set of beliefs—such as established scientific facts—on which we may somehow fall back. Instead, for the question of whether God exists, a debate between worldviews in which each argues for itself and against the other is inescapable. Yet when this nature of the problem is revealed, we face the problem of relativism.

In the parable of the explorers, however, the resolution of their conflict seems rather simple for us, precisely because we inhabit a standpoint where both forms of government are part of the historical narrative that constitutes our understanding of society. That is, we are at a standpoint from which both positions—including their competing conceptions of the shared idea of the "ruler"—are intelligible, a standpoint from which we can understand the predicament of their disagreement and see a "promising" way to proceed. From such a standpoint, we can see ways to bring the two positions in the debate together so that they contribute to the final answer on the society of the natives.

MacIntyre's work thus presents a novel way to resolve conflicts between worldviews: construction of what I call a crossroad of worldviews. How then are we to understand the arguments about the existence of God? A rational case for or against the existence of God would be that which exists only in the context of the crossroads of worldviews. It would argue from one historically extended tradition, or worldview, to the other, at a point where rival worldviews encounter each other. However, for such an argument to be not only rational but successful, it must be a part of the process in which the conflict between intellectual traditions is resolved. That is, such an argument would be inseparable from the MacIntyrean project of constructing a narrative of a worldview in which the worldview's rival becomes its predecessor. Indeed, arguments for the existence of God from a given worldview may be understood as a significant first step in this project of integrating the rival worldview and its journey into one's own. In a sense, it is rather like the explorers first agreeing that a ruler of some kind must govern the natives. I suggest that this is indeed the case with Thomas Aquinas's classic arguments for the existence of God.

FIVE

The Crossroad We Have Passed

The Project of Thomas Aquinas

Antony Flew, in his argument for the "presumption of atheism" as the neutral starting point of the debate about the existence of God, claims that Thomas Aquinas also began from this presumption, and that Aquinas's Five Ways are "an attempt to defeat the presumption of atheism" by presenting "proofs" that God exists.[1] What Flew is doing is presenting Aquinas as a historical exemplar, against whom any particular understanding of what it is to argue about the existence of God may be tested. Thus, any rival position to Flew faces an additional task of giving a rival account of the Five Ways. I have argued, in contrast to Flew, that rational debate regarding the existence of God is inseparable from the context of the encounter between rival worldviews, each a comprehensive, historically contingent, and inescapable framework of beliefs and concepts from which the participants of the debate reason. There is no completely neutral rationality or standard of justification that can adjudicate between these rival worldviews, nor is there a default position, starting point, or onus of proof.

Rather, I have argued in chapter 4 that arguments about the existence of God may be understood as arguments at a "crossroad of worldviews"—that is, as a first step in constructing a particular worldview in which both rival worldviews are brought together as its predecessors. Of course, this is just one possibility that MacIntyre outlines; it may be that from such a crossroad, one worldview will be proved superior because of its ability to solve the problems and extend the intellectual inquiry of its rival by the rival's own terms, while the rival is unable to do the same. This, however, was not the case for the two competing worldviews in the time of Aquinas. Neither position was proved superior in the way outlined above, and thus the project Aquinas undertook was to synthesize the two worldviews in such a way that his new position would prove superior to both rivals. Therefore, what I will propose, in contrast to Flew, is an understanding of the Five Ways as situated within, and inseparable from, just such a project.

It is not my purpose to become involved in the ongoing debate about the Five Ways or the related issues in the current scholarship concerning Aquinas; my primary interest is to propose a different understanding of what it is to argue about the existence of God, especially for the contemporary debate between the theist and atheist positions. Specifically, I am arguing against a general position, exemplified by Flew, that understands the Five Ways as philosophical proofs presented from a presumption of atheism and in a neutral rationality independent of the context of worldviews. That is, I am arguing against a position prevalent not among Thomistic scholars, but among the current participants in the debate about the existence of God, for whom the Five Ways are just one historical exemplar of theistic proofs. My purpose here parallels Flew's attempt to argue that his particular position is supported by a significant historical exemplar in Aquinas; I will likewise argue, based on MacIntyre and others, that my position regarding what it is to argue about the existence of God is supported by what Aquinas does in his Five Ways. Moreover, my rival account of Aquinas is a more adequate understanding of his position as a whole, situated in his historical and intellectual background. In this chapter, we will examine the background in which the arguments in the Five Ways are set, namely, the context of the *Summa Theologiae*, and the historical setting in which it was written.

THE FIVE WAYS OF AQUINAS IN THE *SUMMA THEOLOGIAE*

The Significance of Aquinas in Contemporary Discourse

Aquinas has been a central figure in Catholic philosophy and theology, especially since the encyclical *Aeterni Patris* in 1879, which called for a restoration of a Christian, and specifically scholastic, philosophy in Catholic teachings. Since then, Aquinas has been considered as the "model of how to deal with modern philosophy" since Descartes, and with that philosophy's preoccupation with epistemology.[2] His stature was very different in secular English-speaking philosophy, however, as exemplified by Bertrand Russell's comment in *A History of Western Philosophy*: "There is little of the true philosophic spirit in Aquinas. He does not, like the Platonic Socrates, set out to follow wherever the argument may lead. He is not engaged in inquiry. . . . Before he begins to philosophize, he already knows the truth; it is declared in the Catholic faith. . . . I cannot, therefore, feel that he deserves to be put on a level with the best philosophers either of Greece or of modern times."[3] This dismissive assessment of Aquinas is all the more significant because, as we will see, his account of what Aquinas accomplishes is surprisingly similar to that of MacIntyre, who expresses the opposite assessment. This is because Russell is the main proponent of logical atomism and thus holds a classical foundationalist epistemology and the Enlightenment notion of a neutral rationality independent of any social, historical, or philosophical background or assumptions. Thus, for Russell, to begin from the presuppositions of a particular position—religious, and even more, Catholic!—is a severe flaw for Aquinas as a "philosopher."

However, that which damns Aquinas in one particular view of rationality redeems him in another. That is, in a conception of rationality as inseparable from particular comprehensive philosophical positions, for Aquinas to be a religious philosopher or a Roman Catholic theologian is not an immediate reason for dismissal. Indeed, the evaluation of Aquinas has shifted significantly in analytic philosophy since Russell. Anthony Kenny, for example, rightly recognizes that the writings of Aquinas must be understood as a whole, and from within a different framework.

He thus begins his analysis of the Five Ways by arguing that none of the modern, standard critiques of theism, such as the incoherence of the notion of a logically necessary being, the problem of the nonfalsifiability of God's existence, or the older refutations of theistic arguments by Kant, are effective against Aquinas when we take into account his position as a whole.[4] In a sense, it is ironically because of this strength that Aquinas's arguments "fail." Kenny writes in a remarkable passage: "The Five Ways fail, I shall argue, principally because it is much more difficult than at first appears to separate them from their background in medieval cosmology. Any contemporary cosmological argument would have to be much more different from the arguments of Aquinas than scholastic modernizations customarily are."[5] Nevertheless, Kenny writes in an introductory commentary on Aquinas's *Summa Theologiae* that though Aquinas's philosophy of nature and logic "has been antiquated," his "metaphysics, philosophical theology, his philosophy of mind and his moral philosophy entitle him to rank with Plato and Aristotle, with Descartes and Leibniz, with Locke and Hume and Kant."[6]

This increasing philosophical stature of Aquinas is noted by Brian Davies, who quotes both Russell and Kenny above and suggests a few reasons for Aquinas's growing influence. First is that *Aeterni Patris* prompted an extensive, careful, and critical examination of Aquinas, which led to a proper understanding of his whole position in its historical context. Second is that Aquinas's "logical rigor" and "detailed attention to linguistic usage" fit well with analytical philosophers. Lastly, he writes: "For many twentieth-century philosophers, Wittgenstein brilliantly showed that European philosophy from the time of Descartes was riddled with a large number of confusions and positive errors. Were these confusions and errors absent in earlier writers? Several contemporary thinkers (Kenny is a notable example) have concluded . . . that they were notably absent in the writings of Aquinas, and that [he] is therefore someone with whom it is currently worth engaging."[7] That is, the contemporary shift in philosophy led to the critique of the Enlightenment notions of philosophy and rationality from the time of Descartes, notions absent in prior figures such as Aquinas. MacIntyre's assessment of Aquinas (based on his critique of the modern conception of rationality) and his conception of tradition-based rational inquiry would be one such example.

This growing interest in and influence of Aquinas means, however, that it is not feasible to give even an adequate survey of the sheer amount of contemporary philosophical literature on Aquinas, even on one particular topic such as the Five Ways. The following account will therefore largely be concerned with very general characterizations of and positions regarding the Five Ways and the surrounding, relevant issues, as exemplified by a few key writers. However, let us first examine the general position that Aquinas presents in his Five Ways.

The Structure of the *Summa Theologiae* and the Preceding Questions

The Five Ways are found in *Summa Theologiae*, the most famous—although unfinished—work by Aquinas, written to be a "summary," or compendium, of all the main theological teachings of his time, to be read by beginning students of theology.[8] The *Summa* is divided into *quaestiones*, or "questions," each of which addresses a particular topic or an issue in the subject of theology, each question being subdivided into *articuli*, or "articles."[9] Each article is given in the form of a yes/no question and follows a fixed pattern, which resembles an actual debate in medieval universities. Davies describes those debates in this way:

> [The university's] educational strategy reached a peak in the disputed question (*quaestio disputata*) which was very much a feature of university life in Aquinas's time. It took the form of an extended debate presided over by a *Magister* (a Master, i.e., a senior professor) and frequently took place over several days. A particular question (along the lines of "is it the case that . . . ?") would be chosen for discussion. Participants would then offer a variety of reasons for favoring one conclusion or another. Finally, the Master would adjudicate, defend his own answer to the question, and reply at length to all cases made against his position.[10]

Masters, Aquinas included, often published accounts of such disputations, which are lengthy and thorough discussions of particular issues. The *Summa* is not such an account, but each of its articles conforms to the basic pattern of such a disputation.

Each article follows this pattern with a fixed formula of Latin phrases. For example, let us examine the article that presents the Five Ways to address the question whether God exists.[11] It begins with the formulaic "it seems it is not so" (*videtur quod non*) to introduce a number of arguments supporting the negative reply, namely, the argument from evil and the argument that "nature" and "human reason or will" can account for all things without supposing God. Aquinas then follows this section with "on the contrary" (*sed contra*), which introduces arguments or authoritative pronouncements for the opposite reply, which he favors and will later expound on. In this case, Aquinas cites Exodus 3:14, where God says of himself, "I am who I am." This is followed by the main body of the article, beginning with "I reply that it must be said that . . ." (*repondeo dicendum quod . . .*), where Aquinas explains his position, and this is where he presents "five ways" that demonstrate the existence of God. Finally, the objections in the beginning are addressed and answered.

The Five Ways, however, compose an extremely small fragment of the *Summa Theologiae*.[12] There are three parts—the second part is twice as large as the first—to the *Summa*, and the first part, which discusses God, eternal law, creation, and the nature of humanity, all together contains 119 questions, each with a number of articles. The existence of God is the second question, immediately following the question on the nature and possibility of theological doctrines. That is, the very first theological question Aquinas addresses once he establishes what theology is, is whether God exists, well before other theological issues such as creation, salvation, Trinity, and the incarnation. The question of the existence of God is in turn divided into three different articles: whether the existence of God is self-evident, whether the existence of God is demonstrable, and whether God exists. It is only in the main body of the third article of a single question—the second in the *Summa*—that the Five Ways are found.

In the first article, Aquinas argues that the existence of God is not self-evident, by first citing Aristotle, who states that no one can hold the opposite of (*cogitare oppositum*)—that is, deny—what is self-evident, and then citing Psalm 53:1, where the "fool said in his heart, 'There is no God,'" to argue that God's existence is in fact denied.[13] He then argues that the existence of God *is* self-evident, but not to us, because we do not know the what God is (*Deus quid est*). That is, we do not know the essence, or the nature, of God. Aquinas argues that for a proposition about a thing to be self-evident, what a thing is must logically imply that proposition. Thus, the statement that a human being is an animal is self-evident because the nature of a human being includes being an animal. However, we may not see certain self-evident truths as self-evident, precisely because we do not know the essence of certain things. To use a simple example to elaborate on Aquinas, that "human being is an animal" would not be self-evident to those who do not know the essence of "human" or "animal." Likewise, if we do not know what God is, then obviously we cannot know that the existence of God is self-evident.[14] This precisely is the problem, Aquinas argues, for no human being can know God as he truly is. The existence of God is self-evident truth, but not to human beings who do not know what God is and are thus unable to know the necessary implications of this.

He then replies to the previous objections he raised against his own position, namely that it is self-evident that God exists because (a) the knowledge of God is naturally implanted in all human beings, (b) the very concept of God as that thing than which nothing greater can be conceived implies that God exists, and (c) everyone agrees that truth exists, and according to the scriptures, God is Truth itself. To the first objection, he replies that human beings are implanted with a confused knowledge of God, which allows them to desire something like perfect "good" and "happiness," but not know that this is God. The second objection he rejects, drawing from his main argument that people do not truly understand or accept this concept of God that would lead them to conclude that God exists. For the third objection, Aquinas argues it is self-evident to us that "truth in general exists" (*veritatem esse in communis*), but not that the "first truth exists" (*primam veritatem esse*).

In the second article, Aquinas answers whether reason can demonstrate the existence of God, since that existence is not self-evident. We cannot know what God is, and therefore cannot demonstrate that God exists by expounding what God is. How then can we discuss whether something exists or not, when we cannot even determine what that something is? However, Aquinas points out that although we do not know what God is, we do know and understand his effects, his creation. It is through these effects that we can demonstrate that God exists. That is, every effect has a cause, and by examining the universe, the creation, we can conclude that there is a cause of all things. He then deals with the two related objections; we cannot demonstrate that God exists because we do not know what God is, nor can the finite effects—the creation— truly reveal the essence of their infinite cause, the creator. Aquinas replies that although the effects are inadequate to reveal the essence of the cause, it is adequate to demonstrate *that* there is a first cause.

What the Five Ways Argue

In the third article, Aquinas presents "five ways" that demonstrates that God exists.[15] None of these five ways, however, demonstrates the existence of "God" as understood by Christians, or even by theists in general. That is, the existence of "God," as one eternal, omnipotent, omnipresent, omniscient, personal, loving being—a general concept of God similar to, for example, what Swinburne defines *before* he presents his probabilistic theistic argument—is not what the Five Ways claim to demonstrate. Rather, the Five Ways argue simply that there is (a) a first cause of motion, or of the process of change, (b) a first efficient cause, (c) a necessary being that does not owe its existence to anything else, (d) a cause of things being and having goodness or perfection, and (e) something beyond nature that directs things that lack awareness and goals.[16] Indeed, the Latin word "deus" in the Five Ways, translated as "God" in English, is actually ambiguous—it can also mean a common singular noun for divine beings in general.

Another important repeated caveat is that Aquinas is not arguing for the "existence" of God, as we normally understand the term. The word "existence" is used for created beings. The phrase that Aquinas uses for his theistic arguments is "that God *is*" (*Deum esse* or *Deum est*). Davies writes:

> To be strictly faithful to [Aquinas's] manner of putting things . . . we should recognize that the Ways are concerned to make clear, not God's existence exactly, but that "God exists" (that *Deus est*) is true. To know God's existence is, for Aquinas, to know what God is in himself. But, he thinks, such is not the case when it comes to "God

exists." One can know that there is *something* stopping the door from opening without knowing *what* it is. By the same token, so Aquinas holds (both in [*ST* I.2.3] and elsewhere), one can know that God exists without knowing what his existence amounts to.[17]

That is, to exist is to be a thing with a particular nature, a set of defined qualities, whereas God transcends all humanly knowable categories! An older writing by Victor White is even more forceful on this distinction:

> The *Oxford Concise Dictionary* may be taken to indicate to us the meanings of the verb *to exist* in current English: "have place in the domain of reality, have being under specified conditions, occur, be found." In not one of these senses can the verb *to exist* be accurately used of God. If the Five Ways lead anywhere, it is to the affirmation of that which has *no* place in the domain of reality, but which contrariwise will be found both to transcend and to include it. . . . The Ways lead, not to what 'has being under specified conditions,' but precisely to what *has not* being, but *is* being and with no specified condition whatsoever. . . . The God to which the Five Ways lead precisely does not exist in any one of these accepted senses of the word.[18]

Thus, again what Aquinas argues is not that God, as clearly defined being, exists, but that there is that which *is* being, rather than merely "*has* being," and thus is radically different from anything we can conceive to exist. It is with this caveat in mind that we are to use the term "existence of God."

The first way, which Aquinas calls a "more obvious way" (*manifestior via*), is the argument from "motion" (*motus*). This argument, which is a concise summary of the argument found in Aquinas's earlier work *Summa Contra Gentiles*, begins with the observation that things in the world are moved, that is, in contemporary terms, undergo change. However, Aquinas argues that there is a first cause to all that is moved, which itself is not moved—that is, is not changed. This, Aquinas concludes, "everyone understands as God" (*hoc omnes intelligunt Deum*). In the second way, Aquinas uses the Aristotelian concept of efficient cause. He argues that because without cause, there is no effect, and the chain of efficient cause cannot go on to infinity, there must be a first efficient cause, which "everyone names as God" (*quam omnes Deum nominant*).

In the third way, Aquinas observes that it is possible for the things that exist to also not exist. What Aquinas means here is not that there are logically contingent beings—a contemporary notion—but simply that things come into existence or cease to exist or, more literally, are "found to be generated or corrupted" (*inveniantur generari et corrumpi*). Aquinas argues that there must be something that exists necessarily—again, not a logical necessity, but simply that it always exists—because otherwise there would be a point when nothing exists, and nothing can come from nothing. However, if something is "necessary" in this way, then the cause of this necessity—that is, the reason why it always exists—must be found in itself or in something else that is necessary. That which is the first, necessary cause, whose necessity is not caused by anything else, "everyone speaks of as God" (*quod omnes dicunt Deum*).

The last two ways are typically understood to be different from an argument to the first cause. In the fourth way, Aquinas observes that there are degrees of goodness and perfection, which enables us to say "more or less good, or true, or noble" (*magis et minus bonum, et verum, et nobile*) and so forth. This leads us to that which is the "maximum" (*maxime*) of goodness and perfection—note that this therefore does not mean maximum of every quality, such as hot, cold, and so on—which for Aquinas is the cause of truth, goodness, and other perfections. This "we call God" (*hoc dicimus Deum*). In the fifth way, Aquinas argues from the governance of things, according to which things that "lack intelligence" (*cognitione carent*), such as natural bodies, act for an end. What Aquinas seems to be arguing is that things that lack intelligence do not operate randomly, but intelligibly. However, things that lack intelligence do not move toward an end of themselves, and thus the intelligent being that directs such things "we call God" (*hoc dicimus Deum*).

What seems clear so far is that what Aquinas argues in the Five Ways is somewhat different from theistic arguments in our own time. The third way, for example, makes it clear that it does not argue, as does the *kalam* cosmological argument, that the universe is finite in time, nor argue, in terms used nowadays, of logically contingent or necessary being. The fifth way seems different from today's arguments from design in that it does not argue that there is "design" in living organisms, or even that the laws of physics are fine-tuned, but that nonintelligent things act "by intention" (*ex intentione*) for specific ends—that is, they act in an orderly manner. Nor do some of the core assumptions in his arguments make sense to contemporary readers. For example, why would we suppose, as Aquinas does in the fourth way, that what is most good is the cause of goodness in others? Finally, as we have noted, even the notion of the "existence of God" is to be understood differently. It is such differences of premises and concepts between Aquinas's positions and ours, and the problems that arise from these differences, that Anthony Kenny seems to have observed in his work mentioned above.

However, it still seems that the Five Ways are philosophical proofs, and we may still understand them as such, albeit argued with an outdated mode of reasoning. That is, we may still understand what Aquinas *does* through the Five Ways as presenting a philosophical argumentation that God exists from a neutral rationality, independent of "worldviews," and with the presumption of atheism. The question remains, is this an adequate understanding of the Five Ways?

AQUINAS, THE *SUMMA THEOLOGIAE*, AND THE CHRISTIAN WORLDVIEW

The Five Ways as Philosophical Proofs vs. the Five Ways as Theology

Philosophers who actively participate in the contemporary debate about the existence of God tend to understand the Five Ways of Aquinas differently from those who are scholars of Aquinas. Whereas the latter tend to regard Aquinas presenting the Five Ways as an inseparable part of the theology of the *Summa*, the former tend to discuss the Five Ways as philosophical proofs, in isolation from the overall theological position of the *Summa*. This difference seems pronounced, for example, also between Anglo-American and the Continental European readers, the latter tending to view Aquinas's position as a philosophical theology and studying his doctrines on "Trinity, creation, Christology, and so on," and the former tending to have "read little or nothing more than the Five Ways."[19]

Thus, it is not only Flew who understands Aquinas as presenting "proofs" to defeat the "presumption of atheism." Plantinga, who argues that the existence of God is "a properly basic belief" and thus would be completely opposed to Flew's position, nevertheless agrees with Flew regarding Aquinas. In "Reason and Belief in God," he also understands Aquinas as presenting proofs, thereby being a primary example of a theistic evidentialist, and a foundationalist.[20] He writes: "Aquinas and the evidentialist objector concur, then, in holding that belief in God is rationally acceptable only if there is evidence for it—only if, that is, it is probable with respect to some body of propositions that constitutes the evidence. And here we can get a better understanding of Aquinas and the evidentialist objector if we see them as accepting some version of *classical foundationalism*."[21] As discussed in chapter 2, this is precisely part of Kretzmann's critique of Plantinga when he argues that Plantinga fails to understand that "classical foundationalism" depends on evidentialism, not vice versa. Aquinas is an "evidentialist" in that he presents rational evidence that God exists, but this does not make his arguments dependent upon some form of classical foundationalism.[22] Everitt also understands Aquinas as presenting proofs when he dismisses a number of arguments in the Five Ways as poorly stated cosmological arguments for the first cause or a necessary being.[23] He also calls Aquinas's appeal against infinity of regression "worthless" as an "argument" because "the whole point of an infinite sequence is that it does not have to *start* . . . in order to *continue*."[24]

At first glance, Aquinas does seem to be presenting proofs, precisely because he has argued that the existence of God is not self-evident, but rationally demonstrable, and because he presents philosophical arguments, namely the Five Ways, to do so, rather than theology. Again, Flew's argument for this view is a good example. He is quite aware that his position on Aquinas is frequently denied, and he retorts:

[The Five Ways] were offered there originally, without any inhibition or equivocation, as proofs, period: "I reply that we must say that God can be proved in five ways"; and the previous second Article, raising the question "Whether the existence of God can be demonstrated?," gives the categorical affirmative answer that "the existence of God . . . can be demonstrated" [*ST* I.2.3]. It is worth stressing this point, since it is frequently denied. Thus, for instance, in an article in *Philosophy* for 1968, Dr L. C. Velecky asserts, without, citation or compunction: "He did not prove here the existence of God, nor indeed, did he prove it anywhere else, for a very good reason. According to Thomas, God's existence is unknowable and, hence, cannot be proved" (p. 226). The quotations just made from Aquinas ought to be decisive. Yet there seems to be quite a school of devout interpretation which waves aside what Aquinas straightforwardly said as almost irrelevant to the question of what he really meant.[25]

Thus, for Flew, it is those who deny that the Five Ways are philosophical proofs who misread Aquinas.

Flew points out further that an objection that Aquinas himself composed against his position that God exists, and which the Five Ways answer, is "a presumption of (an Aristotelian) atheist naturalism."[26] Again, this seems to be a compelling case, because this objection—the second one that Aquinas introduces against the belief that God exists, before presenting the Five Ways—argues that "everything we can see in the world" (*omnia quae apparent in mundo*) can be accounted for by "nature" (*naturem*), or by "human reason or will" (*ratio humana vel voluntas*), so that "there is no need to posit that God exists" (*Nulla igitur necessitas est ponere Deum esse*).[27] As it is, this seems to be a very standard description of the contemporary scientific atheist position, and Flew himself identifies this as a position of "Strato," who was "next but one in succession to Aristotle as head of the Lyceum, and was regarded by Bayle and Hume as the archetypal ancient spokesman for an atheist scientific naturalism."[28]

However, if the Five Ways are simply philosophical proofs that God exists, presented from the presumption of atheism, then this fact raises several unresolved puzzles. First is what Flew himself discusses at the end of his argument:

(ii) What is perhaps slightly awkward for present purposes is the formulation of the first Objection: "It seems that God does not exist. For if of two contrary things one were to exist without limit the other would be totally eliminated. But what is meant by this word 'God' is something good without limit. So if God were to have existed no evil would have been encountered. But evil is encountered in the world. Therefore, God does not exist."

It would from my point of view have been better had this first Objection referred to possible difficulties and incoherencies in the meaning proposed for the word "God." Unfortunately it does not, although Aquinas is elsewhere acutely aware of such problems.[29]

That Aquinas presented the objection regarding God and evil *before* presenting Strato's position, which Flew characterizes as the presumption of atheism from which the debate ought to start, is itself indeed "slightly awkward." This is so especially because, as Flew notes, Aquinas is "elsewhere acutely aware" of the way one may formulate the objection that would better fit Flew's reading—referring instead "to possible difficulties and incoherencies in the meaning" of the word "God"—yet chose not to do so. This already indicates that Flew's reading is inadequate.

Second, to read the Five Ways as Flew does seem somewhat inconsistent with what Aquinas writes in the prologue and the first question of the *Summa*, where he depicts this work as a study of theology, of sacred doctrines, intended for the instruction of the "teacher of the Catholic truth" (*catholicae veritatis doctor*). Third, if Aquinas is starting from a "presumption of atheism," then his philosophical argument in the prior article to the Five Ways, *ST* I.2.2, in which he argues that the existence of God is rationally demonstrable through God's effects, seems to beg the question. How so? Aquinas seems to assume what he is yet to prove, namely that the universe—I use the modern term here—is an effect, of which God is the cause. Lastly, the arguments of the Five Ways, even if successful, do not demonstrate the existence of "God" in any sense of the word that a theist, let alone a Christian like Aquinas, would use. This is in sharp contrast to how Flew envisions typical theistic arguments, where the concept of the theist "God" is first clearly and thoroughly defined and defended from possible "incoherencies," and then God is proved to exist.

White therefore explains, citing the prologue and the first question of the *Summa*, that the Five Ways are inseparable from the whole of the *Summa* as a work of Christian theology, but a part of the task of such theology is to equip theologians to teach those who do not accept Christian revelation.[30] That is, to put it in our terms, the Five Ways do not begin from a presumption of atheism, but are set in the context of a Christian worldview, which nevertheless has a concern for convincing those who do hold a presumption of atheism.[31] Thus, White notes that the arguments prior to the Five Ways already hold what Aquinas will argue philosophically later, that the universe is an effect, for which the first cause is what we call God.

What then is the role of philosophical argument, such as the Five Ways? To answer, White argues that Aquinas's position on the first question of the *Summa*, regarding the nature and extent of theology, is important. In the second objection to the *Summa's* first article, Aquinas addresses the question why theology is needed if there already is a philosophical "divine science," according to Aristotle's sixth book of *Metaphysics*. Aquinas answers that philosophers and Christian theologians may reach the same conclusions through different means, the former by natural reason, and the latter by divine revelation. White then emphasizes that this possibility, of the Christian theologian and pagan philosopher reaching the same conclusions on some general questions regarding God, is the basis for Aquinas to hold that the "God of Reason" and the "God of Revelation" are one and the same. "[Such a possibility] is a vitally important preliminary to understanding his identification of the 'God of Reason' and the 'God of Revelation.' It will enable him to maintain that reason can establish the reality of the selfsame God who reveals, though it cannot establish *that* he reveals or *what* he reveals. On this account only have the [Five Ways] any place in a *theological* work."[32] Thus, Aquinas's argument that Christian theology of "sacred doctrines" is distinct from philosophical "divine science" is simultaneously an argument for the two pursuits having shared subject-matter and even, in some cases, shared conclusions. This, in turn, justifies the role of philosophical argumentation in the work of theology based on revelation.

White observes again that part of the task of the "teacher of the Catholic truth," or theologians, is to teach those who do not accept revelation. There are limits to what natural reason can say of God, but insofar as "faulty reasoning constitutes [an atheist argument] against faith," philosophical argument may be used to argue what divine revelation reveals.[33] However, this places the Five Ways inseparably within the context and task of Christian theology:

The *Summa Theologiae* is not, as is sometimes supposed, a *potpourri* of theology and philosophy; it is wholly a *Summa* of Theology concerned with the *Sacra Doctrina*, the Holy Teaching of salvation given by God's revelation. But because it is that, it can *use* philosophical argument for its own end—which is *hominis salus*—the health or salvation of man [*ST* I.1.1]. It in no way substitutes a "natural theology" for revelation, nor does it appeal to reason for what only revelation can impart. But it is part of its own task to teach those who acknowledge no revelation at all—not indeed about the "God of Revelation" *as such*, but at least about such presuppositions (*praeambula*), doubt or denial of which is an intellectual obstacle to faith. Such supremely is the answer to the question, *An Deus sit?*—whether there is a God at all.[34]

That is, to borrow Wolterstorff's words, the Five Ways argue from "within the bounds of religion"[35] to those outside such bounds, not to prove that the God of the Christian revelation exists per se, but to clear some of the intellectual obstacles to faith. This also explains what Aquinas is doing when he presents the objections against the existence of God prior to the Five Ways—including the first objection, which seemed "slightly awkward" to Flew. What Aquinas may be doing is—to use Plantinga's words—listing potential "defeaters" to respond to, rather than setting up a presumption of atheism from which to begin his argument.

The Five Ways as Situated in a Christian Worldview of the *Summa Theologiae*

Kerr presents an even more compelling case for understanding the Five Ways as Christian theology rather than simply philosophical proofs. Aquinas argues that the existence of God is not self-evident, which is why he rationally demonstrates that God exists in the Five Ways. This again seems to support the position that Aquinas begins from the presumption of atheism, until Kerr raises an important point that the key reason why Aquinas argues against the view that the statement "God exists" is self-evident is biblical. Aquinas does present philosophical reasons—or at least, concise summaries of them—as he examines and refutes a form of ontological argument and an argument from existence of truth, both of which argue that the existence of God is self-evident. However, the main reason he expounds in the *sed contra* is that what is self-evident cannot be denied, but that in the scriptures, the fool denies that there is God.

> Here, again, we need to pause and consider how strange it is that Thomas needs to—anyway in fact does—cite Scriptures in evidence that God's existence has been—not just may be—denied. For us, of course, atheism is an entirely familiar intellectual position. Thomas, on the other hand, turns to the revealed word of God to hear of someone denying the existence of God. From the outset, then, atheism, for Thomas, is a properly theological concept. It will be many pages before he introduces the concept of sin, but what he assumes is that atheism is in effect a sin: it is the fool who says in his heart: "there is no God."[36]

Thus, what seems to be the most definitive case for the presumption of atheism in Aquinas is in fact a theological presumption of human sin and limitation. The Five Ways that rationally demonstrate the existence of God are presented from, and presented because of, the Christian worldview's perspective regarding the human condition.

Flew, however, has argued that the Five Ways begin from the presumption of atheism since Aquinas holds that the existence of God is rationally demonstrable through effects. Nevertheless, Kerr's argument applies here also, since Aquinas again cites a scripture for this position, namely Romans 1:20, which says: "The hidden things of God can be clearly understood from the things that He has made." That is, what seems to be an example of the presumption of atheism, leading to a philosophical argument based on some neutral rationality, independent of particular worldviews, turns out to be rooted in a worldview-specific theological position on God's relation to his creation and, even more to the point, in a particular scriptural understanding of divine revelation. Thus, Kerr concludes that for Aquinas it is "Christian revelation itself" that "allows us to entertain the possibility of making God's existence evident 'from things that have been made' (*per ea quae facta sunt*)."[37]

Furthermore, Kerr argues that even the arguments in the questions prior to the Five Ways, arguments that we understand as pretheological and philosophical, are "pervaded by theological assumptions."[38] Again, when Aquinas argues that the existence of God is rationally demonstrable through effects, and thus argues from effects to the cause in the Five Ways, he assumes—in a way a philosophical argument starting from a presumption of atheism would never do—that the world is an "effect": "From the outset, however, Thomas sees the world in a cause/effects perspective. More properly, perhaps, he is relying, tacitly, on the doctrine that the world is created. The demonstrations that 'God exists' which he will offer are articulations of the already accepted presuppositions that the world has a creator—not arguments that start from features of a world that are not yet identified as 'effects.'"[39] Likewise, even within the theistic arguments that Aquinas presents, Kerr notes, a "great deal of metaphysics is in place," such as the "traditional doctrine of the convertibility of transcendental concepts: unity, truth, goodness, beauty, and being."[40] This observation is especially important since, according to Jan A. Aertsen, these transcendental concepts, and the position that such concepts are convertible, constitute one of the most significant medieval philosophical developments from classical philosophy, and Aquinas is one of its most important contributors.[41] Thus, seemingly "neutral" rational argumentation is in fact situated within a particular, comprehensive theological and philosophical position—a worldview—and, moreover, as the example of the transcendentals suggests, such a position is situated in a particular stage of its historical development.

Even the *purpose* of philosophical argumentation of the Five Ways and the prior questions is not only philosophical but theological. Kerr reminds the readers of Aquinas that the questions prior to the Five Ways do not address atheists, but theists. That is, Aquinas argues against the view that "argument for God's existence is unnecessary because God's existence is so manifest in the natural world" and against the view that "argument is impossible because God's existence is solely a matter of supernatural revelation," both of which are Christian, *theological* positions.[42] In the case of the former, Aquinas presents a form of argumentation in the Five Ways that demonstrates the existence of God only through his effects, and not through what God is. Thus, for Kerr, the Five Ways are not "an exercise in rationalistic apologetics," to "open-minded atheists," but a "first lesson in [his] negative theology," the purpose of which is to "protect God's transcendence."[43]

Here, Kerr is reminding readers of Aquinas that the Five Ways are immediately followed by a long series of arguments, demonstrating that God is "simple"—that is, divine attributes are not distinct from God, but are God, and the related position that to be God is to be, so that the essence of God *is* his existence (*esse*)—good, perfect, eternal, omnipresent, and so forth, and that these arguments proceed by the ways of negation. That is, the Five Ways demonstrate that God exists only through his effects, which implies that God is radically different from all existence, and thus the arguments that follow argue from what God is not, namely, that God is not dependent, individual, finite, changing, composed of different parts, and so forth.[44]

Eugene Rogers, whose work Kerr mentions as importantly relevant to understanding the Five Ways as situated in Christian theology, argues further that this feature of negation in the Five Ways reflects a Pauline theology. That is, the Five Ways lead to a God who is radically different from all that exists, who is unknown in that he is known through negation, and thus the Five Ways "throw all human beings upon the mercy of *evangelica gratia*," that is, the gospel of grace.[45] Far from Karl Barth's view, then, that the Five Ways present an example of natural theology that claims to know God solely by human reason without the need of divine revelation, the Five Ways function within the context of Aquinas's overall position, as a key argument *for* the need of divine revelation through Christ.

Jean-Pierre Torrell, who has written an influential biography of Aquinas, presents an account of Aquinas's work that raises another important dimension of understanding the Five Ways as inseparable from a particular worldview:[46]

> The religious or spiritual meaning of this approach [of establishing the existence of God through the Five Ways] is quite clear. Thomas's attempt to establish the existence of God is not rationalist pretension but a confession of humility. Man cannot fully grasp God. . . . He knows himself incapable of arriving at a final knowledge of God. He constantly repeats the same leitmotiv: we cannot know "what He is" (*quid est*), only "what He is not" (*quid non est*). Still, Thomas does not give up the effort; he will have to confess that God *is known as unknown.* And if he dares to say something of God, it will be "like someone who stutters."[47]

What Torrell argues is that Aquinas's writings, including the example of the Five Ways, are inseparable from the spiritual attitude and the life he led as a Christian. That is, his case for the existence of God is inseparable not only from a conceptual and rational framework of belief that composes his worldview, but also from the form of life and practice that embodies it.

However, if from these accounts we were to understand the *Summa Theologiae* as simply a work of theology that presents a Christian worldview, it would be, though not an incorrect understanding, still an inadequate one. Flew's argument that the Five Ways respond to a presumption of "Aristotelian atheist naturalism" reaches at an important aspect of the *Summa*. The historical setting in which Aquinas wrote his works, culminating in the *Summa*, was a time when two rival intellectual traditions—two rival, incommensurable worldviews—were in conflict. The *Summa* and the Five Ways are to be understood in the context of the project Aquinas undertook in response to this conflict.

WORLDVIEW CONSTRUCTION AND TRADITIONS IN CONFLICT

The Project of Aquinas as Worldview Construction

It is evident that the *Summa Theologiae* presents what we would now call a worldview. Firstly, it is comprehensive. Even incomplete, the *Summa* covers an exhaustive range of topics. Aquinas addresses not only the question of the "existence" and the nature of God, but of creation, the cosmos, order in nature, humanity, angelic beings, good and evil, ethics, laws, politics, incarnation, revelation, grace, salvation, sacraments, and church practices. He even includes an account of human knowledge and the sciences, and thus of rationality as such. Secondly, the entire *Summa* is a single, holistic system, where each part is interconnected and supports the others. We have examined how even the earlier arguments, such as the Five Ways, are understood adequately only in terms of other, and often later, sections. Thus MacIntyre, as he explains the rationality of Aquinas's position, characterizes the *Summa* as follows: "First, Aquinas was engaged in an overall work of dialectical construction in the

Summa in which every elementary part finds its place within some larger structure, which in turn contributes to the order of the whole. Thus, the conclusions in one part of the structure may and do confirm conclusions reached elsewhere."[48] That is, not only is the *Summa* a presentation of a holistic system; it is a dialectical construction of such. What does MacIntyre mean? We will examine "dialectical" and "construction" separately.

"Construction" may be better understood using the example of a similar, earlier work by Aquinas, the *Summa Contra Gentiles*, in which we find the expanded form of the "first, and also more obvious way" of the Five Ways. Kretzmann, in *Metaphysics of Theism*, describes what he believes is the project of natural theology in *Contra Gentiles* as the "Grandest Unified Theory."[49] He argues that philosophy, and metaphysics in particular, is a rational investigation of the most fundamental aspects of reality and its first principles, and if such principles turn out to be divine, then God is indeed the subject matter of the Grandest Unified Theory. Thus, arguments for the existence of God in *Contra Gentiles* are for Kretzmann a part of the project for constructing and arguing for a metaphysical system as a whole, namely, the "metaphysics of theism." Indeed, in examining the case for the existence of God—note that this is the expanded form of the argument in the Five Ways—in the beginning chapters of *Contra Gentiles*, Kretzmann argues that Aquinas does not prove the existence of God, nor are such proofs required. What this part of *Contra Gentiles* does is to provide a "working hypothesis" about what Kretzmann calls the "Alpha," which he describes as a "broadly characterized sort of explanatory being, which needn't be identified as God, and in the absence of more detailed characterization, really shouldn't be identified as God."[50] From this hypothesis of Alpha as the first principle of reality, *Contra Gentiles* makes further arguments regarding the nature of Alpha, eventually concluding that this principle is indeed what Christians would understand as God.

Thomas Hibbs presents a reading of *Contra Gentiles* that differs significantly from that of Kretzmann, who views it as a work of "natural theology" and, to that extent, apologetics. Hibbs argues that the structure of *Contra Gentiles* is such that the narrative of Christian redemption and revelation in the fourth book informs the order, the arguments, and the conclusion of the topics of discourse in the first three, which Kretzmann assumed were purely philosophical.[51] Thus, Hibbs seems to argue for a point similar to Kerr's, that Aquina's Christian theological position is inseparable from his philosophical argumentation. However, Hibbs and Kretzmann would agree that *Contra Gentiles* is to be understood as constructing a comprehensive theist—or, more precisely, Christian—worldview. That is, Aquinas is engaged in a project in which he brings together and addresses a different, diverse, and comprehensive list of questions—although nowhere near as comprehensive as the *Summa Theologiae*—such that all the responses, including the argument for the existence of God, are inseparably interconnected and ordered to form a holistic viewpoint. What they disagree on is *how* Aquinas constructs this position.

"Dialectics" is an Aristotelian conception of intellectual inquiry according to which a tradition of inquiry progresses by means of engaging conflicting views, present and past, and refuting rival positions. Thus, for each article, Aquinas cites numerous authors to present different and rival positions on each issue, then proceeds to either support, explain, expound, or refute them. The very nature of the practice of this dialectics, as understood by Aristotle and Aquinas themselves, leaves their respective positions "essentially incomplete," since the very process implies that there may be better answers further along in the history of inquiry.[52] Yet this very practice defines the rational superiority, and indeed the "best answer so far." Hibbs also remarks on the importance of this Aristotelian dialectical inquiry for Aquinas: "[Philosophical argumentation in *Contra Gentiles*] takes its starting point from the received opinions of [Aristotle] and his commentators. What is striking about the method of this segment of the text is how closely it adheres to Aristotle's conception of dialectical inquiry. This is crucial for a number of reasons. . . . The prominence of dialectic in Aristotle's own texts makes it possible for Thomas to go beyond Aristotle without opening himself to the charge of infidelity."[53] Thus, Aquinas's use of dialectics is precisely what justifies him in reaching conclusions different from those of Aristotle and his followers yet allows him to remain, in the terms of MacIntyre's account, a legitimate *successor* to the Aristotelian tradition.

This brings us to the place of the *Summa Theologiae* as situated in what MacIntyre calls a tradition-constituted and tradition-constitutive intellectual inquiry. That is, the *Summa* evinces the historicity of both worldviews and their rationality. MacIntyre describes the dialectical process in the *Summa*: "Aquinas was careful in each discussion to summon up all the relevant contributions to argument and interpretation, which had been preserved and transmitted within the two major traditions. So biblical sources are brought into conversation with Socrates, Plato, Aristotle, and Cicero, and all of them with Arab and Jewish thinkers, as well as patristic writers and later Christian theologians."[54] Thus, Aquinas engages the significant historical figures, who in turn, engaged the writers before them. In so doing, Aquinas recounts the history of intellectual inquiry so far. That is, by engaging and bringing together the significant positions of the past, from biblical sources to classical philosophers to Christian patristic writers to Arab and Jewish thinkers to later medieval theologians, Aquinas is narrating the history of the intellectual inquiry to his time, including its achievements, difficulties, and obstacles. Furthermore, by supporting, explaining, expounding, or refuting such positions, he is advancing the inquiry. Simply put, throughout the *Summa*, Aquinas is arguing from a specific historical tradition and extending it.

However, MacIntyre does not say Aquinas argues from one tradition, but that he is bringing together the positions of two traditions. The *Summa* is not only a construction of a worldview, but a construction of a worldview from two different rival worldview-traditions.

The *Summa Theologiae* and the Traditions in Conflict

MacIntyre writes that before the time of Aquinas, the main intellectual tradition for Christian theology in Western Europe was Augustianism, which followed Platonic and Neoplatonic philosophy. This tradition came in conflict with Aristotelian philosophy, which seemed to be in irreconcilable conflict with Christian doctrines.[55] However, Aristotelian positions quickly came to dominate the sciences of the time, including metaphysics, physics, biology, politics, social science, and others, a dominance that in turn led to an increasing autonomy and thus separation of science from theology.[56] According to an often cited comment from a student of that time, "The above [Aristotelian] propositions are true in the Faculty of Arts, but not in the Faculty of Divinity."[57]

Jan Aertsen uses the term "Philosophical Revolution" to describe this impact of Aristotle in thirteenth-century Europe and its universities, and describes how Aristotelian forms of intellectual inquiry and conceptual frameworks came to dominate Europe's theoretical discussions, especially in the Faculty of Arts.[58] This contrasted with the reaction of the ecclesiastics, who issued a number of partial prohibitions against Aristotle's natural philosophy for its naturalistic conclusions. Despite this, the study of Aristotle spread widely, until what was "once primarily preparatory arts faculty," which merely prepared the students for other faculties, especially theology, developed into an independent "philosophy faculty."[59] Thus, during the thirteenth century, at least prior to Aquinas, the "philosophical" position on a number of issues, and the form of argumentation employed by each such position, were to a significant extent Aristotelian and non-Christian.

Aertsen describes three of the significant differences between Christian doctrines and Aristotelian philosophy. First was the Platonic theory of Forms, as separate from particular things, which Aristotle rejected. For the Christians, on the other hand, the language of the Forms was closely associated with the way of speaking of God in terms of transcendental concepts, such as "the Good." Second, the Arabic philosopher Averroes, who was regarded as the authoritative interpreter of Aristotle and given the title "the Commentator," had read Aristotle as arguing that there was only one and the same intellect for all human beings. This was incompatible with the Christian doctrine of individual immortality and moral responsibility. Third, Aristotle had concluded in *Physics* that the world was beginningless and eternal, because otherwise there would be no beginning of motion, or change. This seemed to contradict the scriptural position that "in the beginning, God created the heavens and the earth."

For MacIntyre, such incompatibilities constituted only the first level of the differences between these two traditions.[60] The two traditions differed not only in particular beliefs regarding the world, or human nature, but also in regard to their respective conception of intellectual inquiry, truth, and rationality. First, Aristotelian sciences were independent from theology, with its own ordered hierarchy of sciences. Second, a large number of questions that were hitherto the "exclusive province of theology," such as metaphysics, psychology, ethics, and politics, fell within the purview of Aristotelian sciences. Thus, in each tradition, different intellectual disciplines, ordered and organized differently in regard to other such disciplines, with different scopes of knowledge, posed different answers to the same questions.

Furthermore, such differences could not be brought to a constructive debate because the "standard of truth and rationality" with which to argue was not the same for both traditions. This is because in the Aristotelian conception of knowledge, the human intellect moves from potentiality toward actuality, by becoming adequate to the object of its knowledge. For Augustinian Christians, the human intellect is inadequate for knowledge, and requires divine illumination.

> For Aristotle an adequate characterization of the mind is of the mind as achieving knowledge; for Augustine it is of the mind as by itself incapable of knowledge but for some external source supplying what the mind cannot itself supply. Withdraw divine illumination from the Augustinian scheme and you have the mind in the predicament to be characterized by that late, solipsized Augustinian, Descartes, whereas from the Aristotelian point of view Descartes's questions do not and cannot arise.[61]

Thus, Augustinians and Aristotelians held very different "epistemology" —or at least, what we may term today loosely as such.

A related area of conflict was the conception of truth. For Aristotle, truth is characterized in terms of the relationship of the human mind to its objects and the adequacy of that mind to those objects. For Augustine, however, truth is *Veritas*, a "noun naming a substance," which is more fundamental than *verum*, or "true," an "attribute of things," which in turn is more fundamental than truth or falsity of statements. MacIntyre comments that for Augustinians, "to speak truly is to speak of things as they really and truly are; and things really and truly are in virtue only of their relationship to *veritas*," and this *veritas* is God.[62] Lastly, conceptions of defect and error differed for the Augustinian and Aristotelian traditions. For Augustine, intellectual error is caused by the will, and thus rooted in moral defect, especially in moral inquiry. Aristotle, however, had no concept of the will, and thus explained error and defect without reference to such notions, in terms of education and intellect.[63]

With such differences, the Augustinian and Aristotelian traditions were incommensurable, and rational debate between the two positions regarding most questions was increasingly considered impossible. There was no neutral nor even shared standard, precisely because the conceptions of knowledge, truth, human intellect, and errors with which to form such standards were different. MacIntyre argues, further, that such differences extend to the account of perception and imagination, so that an appeal to "how things *in fact* are in the human *psyche*" in order to adjudicate between their rival theories of knowledge—here, MacIntyre seems to be making a veiled reference to the Enlightenment epistemological project, so criticized by Rorty—would also fail.[64]

It is against this intellectual background that Aquinas writes. According to MacIntyre, what is remarkable about Aquinas is that under the influence of Albertus Magnus, he was "uniquely trained" to understand the two rival traditions of Augustinian theology and Aristotelian philosophy, "each from within."[65] Regarding this, Aertsen also remarks: "One of the most striking aspects of Aquinas's work is that a considerable part of his writings consists of commentaries on [Aristotle]. This is the more remarkable because such work did not belong to his proper academic duty: he was never a master in the arts faculty. Yet he apparently recognized in the reception of Aristotle a tremendous challenge to Christian thought and therefore considered it worth the effort to analyze Aristotelian philosophy thoroughly."[66] Aquinas's understanding of Aristotle seems to have been thorough. Ralph McInerny responds to the contemporary criticisms that Aquinas distorts Aristotle in his commentaries: "No one can read [Aquinas's commentary on Aristotle, *De unitate intellectus*], with its painstaking textual analysis and rejection of alternate readings, and fail to see that it was Thomas's intention to understand what Aristotle himself meant."[67] Thus, in MacIntyre's terms, Aquinas consciously sought to become a participant in the Aristotelian tradition, and was apparently successful, as he was widely respected among the Aristotelians of his time; in his biography of Aquinas, Torrell recounts occasions when, despite the conflict between the Faculty of Arts and the Faculty of Theology in a number of universities, the former actively sought after Aquinas's writings on Aristotle.[68]

As a participant in both traditions, Aquinas then began a project of synthesis, which would become the successor to both the Christian-Augustinian and the Aristotelian traditions. For MacIntyre, Aquinas is the paradigm example of his account, discussed in the previous chapters, of the ways in which the conflict between incommensurable traditions may be resolved and the problem of relativism of worldviews be answered. Such is what Aquinas's work, especially the *Summa Theologiae* and the *Summa Contra Gentiles*, accomplishes. C. F. Martin writes:

> [Aquinas] attempted to establish the framework for, or to make the first step in, creating a new complete synthesis, a synthesis of the Augustinian tradition and the wisdom of Aristotle. The joint importance of these two authors to Aquinas can be brought out in a crude but effective way: in the index of a recent edition of the *Summa Theologiae*, references to both run to over thirty columns, while references to their nearest rival, St Leo, run to only ten.[69]

That is to say, because Aquinas begins from two particular traditions, one based on Augustine—and the Christian scriptures—and the other based on Aristotle, his position referred most extensively to these authorities. As for the *Summa Contra Gentiles*, Hibbs describes the work as a "unified presentation of the two traditions of wisdom," of Aristotle and Christian theology, which is precisely his reason for rejecting the claim that it is simply a work of apologetics.[70]

Nor was the position of Aquinas a simple continuation of the Aristotelian or Augustinian tradition. Aertsen shows how Aquinas's position contains both Aristotelian and Platonic—the philosophical dimension of the Augustinian tradition—elements, but extends beyond them.[71] For example, following Aristotle, Aquinas rejects the Platonist theory of the Forms and participation in knowing concrete, material things, because it is a method that wrongly "projects our abstract mode of knowing onto the mode of being of things."[72] However, he goes beyond Aristotle by arguing that this method is legitimate in knowing the most general principles of metaphysics, such as being, one, and goodness, which are "transcendentals," and are important terms with which to describe God.[73] Aquinas's position is also distinct from both traditions in his theses that "all creatures are marked by the non-identity of their essence and their *esse*," and that only God's *esse* is identical to his essence.[74]

Likewise, in his reading of *Contra Gentiles*, Hibbs describes how Aquinas sometimes accepts Aristotle's position over the existing medieval position, such as adopting his method of inquiry, and at other times resolves several problems of the Aristotelian tradition by using the conceptual resources of theology. That is, the conflict between the two traditions raised problems for both traditions, and *Contra Gentiles* works a synthesis of the two through solving problems, through refutations and revision, and through dialectics. In doing this, however, Aquinas is not simply "picking and choosing" different positions in Aristotelianism and Augustinianism. Aquinas is addressing the problems of each tradition from within, and refuting what each tradition would recognize— or ought to recognize—from its standpoint and by its own standards as errors.

More importantly, through this process of dialectics, Aquinas is doing what MacIntyre describes in the following:

> [Aquinas] invite[d] [the rival Augustinians and the Aristotelians] to understand the point of view which he had constructed, one into which both the achievements of Augustinianism and Aristotelianism had been integrated in such a way that what were, or should have been, recognized as the defects and limitations of Augustinianism as judged from an Augustinian standpoint and the defects and limitations of Aristotelianism as judged from an Aristotelian standpoint had both been first more adequately characterized and then corrected or transcended.[75]

That is, Aquinas integrates the intellectual positions of both rival worldviews in such a way that he forms a single comprehensive and coherent standpoint—and one in which the intellectual inquiry of each worldview can more adequately understand its own positions and limitations, resolve its problems, and thereby progress further in its inquiry in its own terms. I will discuss in greater detail in chapter 6 how this is the case with Aquinas's position on the Platonic theory of the Forms regarding the knowledge of concrete things and the "transcendentals." Here, I will briefly outline how this also seems to be the case for a number of examples where he addresses the differences between Aristotelianism and Augustinianism.

Aertsen describes how Aquinas refuted a seemingly Aristotelian position, expounded by Averroes, that the intellect is the same in all human beings, which was in conflict with the Christian position, which affirmed individual human intellect, and therefore, individual souls. Aquinas first argues, through an extensive exegesis of *De anima*, by Aristotle, that this is not the position of Aristotle himself, and that thus on this issue, Averroes was a "corrupter" of Aristotelian philosophy. Secondly, Aquinas argues that such a position is untenable because there clearly is "an individual human being who understands."[76] Thus, he argues for what is initially a Christian, Augustinian position, but the reason he does so is to correct and extend Aristotelian intellectual inquiry; he corrects the Aristotelians from a misreading of their own central text, and observes how their position becomes unintelligible in terms of their own everyday experience.

Likewise, Aquinas addresses the question of the beginningless eternal world, and argues that although revelation reveals that the world had a beginning, reason cannot demonstrate whether the world is eternal or had a beginning in time. However, his main argument in this position, according to Aertsen, is against Christian theologians; he argues that there is no contradiction in the "concepts *created by God* and *eternal* (*beginningless*)." This consequently led to a "metaphysical deepening of the concept of creation," by a redefining of "beginning" not in terms of time but as "dependence of being."[77] That is, from the Aristotelian position regarding the beginningless world, Aquinas constructs a position that can transcend the limitation in the Christian position regarding its own doctrine of creation, and consequently expand its theological understanding of God as the Creator.

MacIntyre also summarizes how Aquinas resolves the key differences between the two traditions:

> In the three major areas in which the Augustinian tradition had confronted its central problems Aquinas developed new positions by both interpretation and argumentative means. Where Aristotle and Augustine had characterized one and the same relationship of particular individuals to those universal concepts by which essence and kind are identified, in two not only different but incompatible ways, Aquinas uses Augustine's Platonic account to characterize one set of relationships—those of particulars to the exemplars in the divine creating mind which are their formal causes—and Aristotle's account to characterize another set of relationships, those involved in the mind's apprehension of the *quidditas rei materialis* which is that mind's initial object of knowledge and enquiry. Where Aristotle's

psychology excluded the possibility of accounting for the phenomenon of the will, while Augustine lacked what Aristotle provided in his findings about the mind's powers and their theoretical and practical embodiments in enquiry, Aquinas was able to show how the will, conceived in Augustinian fashion, could both serve and yet mislead the mind, as conceived in Aristotelian fashion. And all this was achieved in a way not merely concordant with but supporting and illuminating the specific Christian dogmas.[78]

Thus, Aquinas was able to not only identify the incommensurable differences between the Augustinian and Aristotelian traditions regarding knowledge, truth, and error; he also constructed a comprehensive philosophical, and Christian, position in which the accounts of both traditions regarding these issues are brought together to support, supplement, and correct each other, and in so doing, advance the respective intellectual inquiries of both traditions in their own terms.

AQUINAS, CROSSROADS OF WORLDVIEWS, AND THE FIVE WAYS

The Five Ways are therefore not an argument from a neutral rationality from a presumption of atheism, isolated from the larger Christian standpoint, but a part of an overall project of constructing a comprehensive intellectual position. What Aquinas presents in the *Summa* and his other writings is what MacIntyre proposes as a solution to the relativism of worldviews—or in his words, "traditions of enquiry." Again, the *Summa* is a massive work, and the brief account above, with a survey of some significant recent work regarding it, is not adequate to describe how the two incommensurable traditions were integrated together. What I have argued so far is simply that such is the intellectual background in which the arguments about the existence of God in Aquinas, such as the Five Ways, are situated.

A possible objection to my account so far is that it is anachronistic to describe what Aquinas is doing in terms of "worldview construction," along with related contemporary concepts of incommensurability, paradigms, traditions of inquiry, and so forth. This is true. However, what I am arguing is that he was confronted with the type of problem, and undertook in response a type of intellectual project, which, as MacIntyre puts it, "we now understand much better" because of contemporary developments in philosophy—developments in which MacIntyre himself has played a significant role—that I have previously described.[79] This, in turn, is consistent with MacIntyre's conception of rational inquiry, in which those who are further along the intellectual tradition have better understanding of the problems, difficulties, and achievements of their predecessors, which have become part of their tradition's narrative.

Another objection may be that the characterization of Aquinas so far depends upon a particular philosophical position, or tradition of intellectual inquiry, within which one writes. This is a point MacIntyre again acknowledges.[80] Likewise, I also acknowledge that I have, and will be speaking from within, a particular "worldview," which historically extends in part from Aquinas, and recently, from MacIntyre. Yet, of course, I have argued already that there is no neutral rationality with which we present our case, nor is there a neutral narrative of our intellectual inquiry.

However, it is interesting that Russell, who clearly writes from a rival position, describes the works of Aquinas as follows:

> In its general outlines, the philosophy of Aquinas agrees with that of Aristotle, and will be accepted or rejected by a reader in the measure in which he accepts or rejects the philosophy of [Aristotle]. The originality of Aquinas is shown in his adaptation of Aristotle to Christian dogma, with minimum of alteration. . . . He was even more remarkable for systematizing than for originality. Even if every one of his doctrines were mistaken, the *Summa* would remain an imposing intellectual edifice. When he wishes to refute some doctrine, he states it first, often with great force, and almost always with an attempt at fairness. The sharpness and clarity with which he distinguishes arguments derived from reason and arguments derived from revelation are admirable. He knows Aristotle well, and understands him thoroughly, which cannot be said of any earlier Catholic philosopher.[81]

Thus Russell, whose negative assessment of Aquinas has become somewhat infamous, describes Aquinas's achievements in terms and words that are nearly identical to MacIntyre's.

Russell's words here are important for two reasons. First, the agreement on what Aquinas accomplishes between MacIntyre, a Thomist—or at least, an atheist turned Thomist—and Russell, who would be "hostile" to such position, is strong evidence for concluding that Aquinas was able to achieve what MacIntyre argues he has achieved—that is, a successful synthesis of two incommensurable traditions of inquiry. Second, the fact that despite this agreement, MacIntyre and Russell reach such different conclusions as to the importance of Aquinas as a philosopher is itself an impressive demonstration of the incommensurability of the standards of justification and reasoning between two rival traditions, or worldviews. Furthermore, that we can recognize the possibility of reaching such different conclusions with the same account, a possibility which could not have been envisioned by Russell himself, precisely because the relevant contemporary philosophical insights were unavailable to him, is another reason for claiming that my position has transcended his limitations.

Nevertheless, the question still remains: if the Five Ways are situated in the construction of a standpoint that brings rival worldviews together, what do they *do*? That is, if arguments about the existence of God are situated on the crossroads of worldviews, what do the arguments do at such a crossroad?

SIX

God at the Crossroads

What the Five Ways Do

How are we to understand the Five Ways of Aquinas, if his arguments are situated in the project to construct a worldview in which the conflict between two incommensurable, rival worldviews—or traditions—is resolved? The question being asked here is not what the Five Ways argue, but what they *do*. That is, in the narrative of the previous chapter on how Aquinas integrates the rival Augustinian and Aristotelian traditions, what part does the argument of the Five Ways play? Thus, I do not intend to present a detailed account of the content of the Five Ways, or the *Summa Theologiae*, beyond the general characterization I have already presented. Such content, for our question, simply provides clues to what the Five Ways do in Aquinas's project. Note then how this objective will yield a subtle difference in how we understand the significance of the Five Ways for the contemporary debate about the existence of God. In an account of what the Five Ways argue, the significance would lie in whether the arguments of Aquinas, situated as they are in a different worldview, are to some degree translatable or applicable to our own, or in whether there are reasons to adopt or inhabit his worldview. For an account of what the Five Ways do, however, the significance will lie in whether what Aquinas has done in his day is doable in our own. What do the Five Ways do? Simply put, what Aquinas does in the Five Ways is to identify and construct that which is necessary for the intellectual inquiry of both worldviews, which is then understood as "God."

It is difficult, however, to answer precisely what the Five Ways do, because the *Summa* represents a completed project of worldview construction—that is, although the *Summa* itself remains unfinished, it is the *result* of this project. Thus, what part the philosophical arguments, such as the Five Ways, play in the project itself is a very complex question. A complete answer would include an account of the intellectual development of Aquinas's position over his lifetime, beginning from his earliest work and culminating in the *Summa Theologiae*. Such an extensive account, suitable for a scholarly study focused primarily on Aquinas, is, again, not our purpose here. Instead, we will make do with a general, if less complete, understanding—namely, how the Five Ways function within the context of Aquinas's overall philosophical position. This will be sufficient to answer our primary question, which is, using the Five Ways as an important historical exemplar, how are we to understand what it is to argue about the existence of God, if such arguments are presented in the context of the crossroads of worldviews?

What the Five Ways do is inseparable from how Aquinas understands intellectual inquiry as such. This particular understanding, in turn, is derived from the concept of the ultimate end of intellectual inquiry that is held by both the Augustinian and Aristotelian traditions because of their shared philosophical root from Plato. What Aquinas does is therefore to present a new understanding of Christian theology as the highest Aristotelian science, which is based on the knowledge of God himself, which in turn is identified with the notion of perfect knowledge—a perfected or completed understanding of all things, in regard to the ultimate and most general level of reality, the level of "being," "truth," and the "good"—which is understood by both positions as the ultimate end of inquiry. What is significant here is that these notions were developed from both the Augustinian and Aristotelian philosophy. From this Aquinas will *identify*, rather than "prove," *that* without which the Aristotelian intellectual inquiry would be rendered unintelligible—that is, the notion of the ultimate end of the inquiry—which in turn the Christian would "call God." This, in turn, forms the *starting* point, not the end, of the

project in which the two worldviews are brought together and synthesized, and from which other differences in the two positions may be addressed dialectically. It is only at the *end of such project* that what Aquinas
has identified *as* "God" does turn out to be the Christian God.

THE CHALLENGE OF ARISTOTELIAN NATURALISM
TO CHRISTIAN THEISM

What difficulty did Aristotelian philosophy pose, specifically, for the
Christian belief that God exists? In the last chapter, we surveyed some
of the key points of conflict that Aquinas addressed. Among these, two
points that MacIntyre raised seem directly relevant to the question of
whether God exists.[1] First, the hierarchy and organization of Aristotelian
sciences conflicted with that of the Christian, Augustinian tradition; furthermore, within this differently ordered hierarchy, Aristotelian philosophy presented rival positions on topics hitherto considered to be exclusive
to theology and divine revelation in the Christian worldview. Second,
the Aristotelian conception of knowledge and truth, in which human
beings are capable of knowing what is "true" by their minds becoming
adequate to the objects of their knowledge, contradicted that of the Augustinian position, where human beings are incapable of knowing without divine illumination from the "Truth," which is God. Furthermore,
Aertsen presents yet another crucial difference between the two traditions, which seems to be closely related to, if not the basis of, the differences MacIntyre describes. He argues that there were two rival views on
how to understand existence in general. For the Aristotelian philosophy,
it is "nature," whereas for the Christian, it is "creature."

According to Aertsen, "philosophy," or human knowing as such, especially in Aristotle, is understood as an inquiry toward the "origin."
This "origin" is the *arche*, the principle from whence things originate, and
their end.[2] For the Greeks, and especially Aristotle, this "origin" is "nature." Aertsen writes regarding this concept:

> "Nature" is the Greek answer to the problem of being. The "physis"
> [that is, nature] is the "ousia," the essence of things (*Phys.* II, 1).
> "What is by nature," so Aristotle says in his *Ethic. Nic.* V, c. 10, "is

unvariable and has everywhere the same power." "Physis" is the notion that was developed in the Hellenic world during the transition from mythos to logos. It is a conception "that in one way or another lies at the foundation of the whole of Greek philosophical thought," a conception that as no other, is distinctively and essentially Greek.[3]

That is, for Aristotelian philosophy, the concept of "nature" is the primary term with which to understand the world. It was a concept developed to explain and understand how and why things are through rational inquiry, that is, "*logos*," rather than through mythological narrative, that is, "*mythos*."

How does the concept of "nature" enable rational inquiry to do so? Aertsen answers through Aristotle:

> In response to the question "What is nature?" (*quid sit natura*) . . . Aristotle concludes the definition of nature: it is a principle and cause of motion in that in which it is "per se." Nature is an intrinsic principle of movement. This can be twofold, namely matter and form. . . . The form, to be sure, is the nature "more" than matter is, for every thing is more what it is when it is in act than when it is in potency. Nature is also "end."[4]

Thus, simply put, "nature" answers the question of what the thing is intrinsically, or essentially, such that it explains why the thing is the way it is, behaves the way it does, and undergoes the kind of changes it undergoes. This "nature" is more "form" than "matter" because for Aristotle, it is the "form" that defines what the thing is, and "matter" is only potentially something—that is, it is not anything in particular without the "form" that makes it actually something. "Nature is also end," because Aristotle writes in the opening sentence of *Metaphysics*, "All men by nature desire to know," and to know what a thing is is to know its nature.

This, however, was in conflict with the Christian worldview. Aertsen describes the reaction of the ecclesiastical leaders in Aquinas's time:

> At the beginning of Thomas's era, the "auctoritas" of the Philosopher was suspect. "Lecturing" on precisely the writings on natural philosophy from the corpus Aristotelicum was forbidden on the ec-

clesiastical side on the pain of excommunication. As late as 1228, Pope Gregory IX sent a warning to the University of Paris. Let theologians not deviate "to the doctrine of the natural philosophers" and not falsify the Word of God with "the fictions of philosophers." Obviously, the Aristotelian concept of nature was considered a threat to a Christian understanding of reality from the Origin.[5]

Thus, the "philosophy" of the Aristotelian tradition was an intellectual inquiry that seemed to explain and understand things in terms that preclude what we would call the "supernatural," that is, God. However, the Christian understanding of "origin" is that of God, the Creator, and it is this view that would define Aquinas's position as a theologian. Aertsen continues: "Already by the first sentence in the Bible, in the book of Genesis, it is revealed that the world is *creature*, a term which means 'all that is by God' (*De pot. 3, 3 ad 2*). The Judeo-Christian idea of creation plays a central role in Thomas's thought."[6] The key difference then is that in Aristotelian intellectual inquiry, to be a particular being is to have a particular, intrinsic nature, whereas for Christian theology, to be a particular being is to be a creature.

It is through understanding this radical difference in worldviews—indeed, the Augustinian and Aristotelian traditions are quite literally different ways of viewing the world—that we may better comprehend what MacIntyre described as their incommensurable differences regarding knowledge, truth, and the conception of sciences. For Aristotelian philosophy, things have their own nature, and thus to know what is true is for the human mind to become adequate to the form, or the nature, of the thing. However, for Augustinian theology, what things are is defined in their relation as creature to God, and thus to know the truth of things, is to know the Truth, which is God, and this necessarily requires divine illumination, especially for human beings, whose intellect is impaired by sin. With such differences, the respective conceptions of sciences with which we are to understand the world, and indeed, what such sciences are capable of knowing, were radically different for Aristotelian and Augustinian traditions. Thus, Aertsen concludes: "How to connect the Christian interpretation of the meaning of reality with Greek philosophical rationality was the epochal task thought through by Thomas Aquinas."[7]

It is therefore no accident that the first question in the *Summa*, which Aquinas addresses prior to the question on the existence of God, is that of the status of theology as a science.

ARISTOTELIAN PHILOSOPHY OF NATURE AND CHRISTIAN THEOLOGY OF GOD

Understanding of Theology in the *Summa Theologiae* in Response to Aristotle

In the time of Aquinas, Aristotelian philosophy became the dominant mode of inquiry for other philosophical sciences in the Faculty of the Arts. That is, the Aristotelian tradition presented a conception of science as an inquiry into the intrinsic nature of things, which seemed, in MacIntyre's terms, to overcome the problems, difficulties, and obstacles that were unresolvable in the existing forms of intellectual inquiry of its rival Augustinian tradition. Why this was so will be examined later. However, these were natural sciences belonging to human reason, whereas theology, understood itself as based on divine revelation, was less susceptible to the challenges posed by the natural philosophy of Aristotle— hence arose the kind of incommensurable differences described so far. The question for the Augustinian tradition then was whether to sever its theology from the other sciences that now followed its rival tradition in their conception of intellectual inquiry. However, for the Augustinian tradition, other sciences were understood not as independent of, but rather as prologues to, theology. Thus, MacIntyre summarizes the problem: "And hence arose and continued the underlying Augustinian dilemma: to refuse to integrate the Aristotelian corpus and its teaching into the curriculum would have been to seem to abandon the claim that theology can indeed order and direct the other secular sciences and arts; yet it seemed that to accept the Aristotelian corpus into the curriculum would be to produce incoherence in the structures of teaching and knowledge."[8] Thus, a key task for Aquinas was to construct a position in which two rival conceptions of intellectual inquiry and related notions, such as truth, knowledge, and hierarchy of sciences, may be brought together.

The very first question Aquinas addresses in the *Summa Theologiae* is therefore the status of theology as an intellectual inquiry, and its relation to the other sciences. Furthermore, the Aristotelian challenge to Augustinian theology is found in the very first article of the first question, in the second objection, which cites Aristotle's sixth book of *Metaphysics* to argue that "everything that is, even God, is treated in philosophical science" (*de omnibus entibus tractatur in philosophicis disciplinis, et etiam de Deo*). In chapter 5, we briefly saw how White uses the response to this objection to understand the role of philosophical argumentation in Aquinas's theology. What is of interest here, however, is that in this response, Aquinas claims that both the philosopher and the theologian may reach the same conclusion, or more precisely, that "there is nothing to prevent" (*nihil prohibet*) the things learned by philosophical science through the "light of natural reason" (*lumine naturalis rationis*) from being taught by theology through the "light of divine revelation" (*lumine divinae revelationis*). This, however, is a bold claim, since a key point of the conflict between the two traditions is precisely that the conclusions of this "natural reason" do contradict, in many significant places, what is taught through "divine revelation." It is a claim that can be vindicated only from the successful synthesis of the two traditions presented by the *Summa* as a whole. That is, at the first question of the *Summa*, it is no more than a promissory note of a sort.

Furthermore, Aquinas's position on theology, presented throughout the second to the seventh article, outlines a conception of a hierarchy of the sciences in which theology is the first and most fundamental. Aquinas begins with the argument that theology is a science, and that it is moreover a single, unified science about God primarily, and secondarily about all things in relation to God as their "principle and end" (*principium vel finem*), since all things are creatures. Theology is also a theoretical science, but inasmuch as humans may find perfect bliss in God, it includes practical science. Theology is higher, or "nobler" (*dignior*), than all other sciences because human reason can err in other sciences, but theology comes from divine revelation, and it also concerns the highest good toward which the goods of all other practical sciences are ordered. It is "wisdom" (*sapientia*) because its principles derive from divine knowledge, and thus it orders all other sciences—as an architect orders all other workers to build an edifice—and judges their principles.

Therefore, what Aquinas does in the first question is to define theology as a first science, continuous with all other sciences, which are in his time Aristotelian in their modes of inquiry. In this "science," it is revealed that God is the "origin," or the highest cause, rather than "nature." Furthermore, he defines theology as a science partly by responding to objections from the Aristotelian tradition. For example, Aristotle is cited against his position that theology is a unified science and that it is identified with "wisdom," to which he responds that theology, properly understood, fits Aristotle's criteria as quoted in the objections. Although not explicitly stated, some of the key objections against Aquinas's position that theology is a science, and a science "nobler" than others, are due to the Aristotelian conception of intellectual inquiry. The objection states that science proceeds from self-evident first principles, whereas theology does not; likewise, the principles of a nobler science are more certain, but theology does not proceed from self-evident, certain first principles, but those accepted in faith. To this, Aquinas responds that the principles from which theology proceeds to its other truths are more certain than those from human sciences, precisely because they are from God himself. The significant point here is that Aquinas does not argue against Aristotelian tradition for his position on theology, but rather argues how theology, in some sense, *is* an Aristotelian science, and indeed, more an Aristotelian science than all other sciences. He does so while upholding the core of the Augustinian position that all other sciences are to be ordered by this science of divine revelation.

Rogers argues for an even stronger interpretation of the relation between theology and Aristotelian science for Aquinas: "In the equation 'sacred doctrine is *scientia*' [*ST* I.1.2], Thomas has structured or set up sacred doctrine so that (1) *the more Aristotelian it is, the more scriptural it is.* That relation requires as a presupposition that (2) *the more Aristotelian it is, the more christoform it is.*"[9] Rogers describes how the "science" of the "sacred doctrine," that is, theology, is set up in the ideal structure of an Aristotelian science, which proceeds from its first principles. Furthermore, he notes, in an Aristotelian conception of science, the "propositional" or "noetic" first principles are, or at least are inseparable from, the real or ontological first principles to which they refer. Likewise, the first principles of theology, for Aquinas, are not the propositions of the scriptures per se, but the divine revelation upon which the scripture is founded,

which is the actual person of Jesus Christ, who reveals an otherwise unknowable God.

However, Rogers argues further that the *Summa* as a work of Christian theology does not simply relate faith to reason, or theology to philosophy, but "represents an essay to *co-opt* Aristotelian *scientia* for the
interests and purposes of the sacred doctrine."[10] In the *Summa*, Aristotelian philosophy becomes "tools," constrained so that it can lead only to
Christ, and thus to God. There are differences between Aquinas and
Aristotle. For example, although an Aristotelian science and theology
begins from the "first principles," Rogers writes: "[For] Thomas, unlike
Aristotle, the structural first principles of the world—its set-up—lie
radically outside the world, in the mind of an unreachable God. And for
Thomas the intellectual first principles of understanding—that which
the human creature demands and desires—lie radically beyond our capacity."[11] However, when such disagreements arise, Rogers notes, Aquinas will "co-opt him by using one part of Aristotle against another" to
reach the God of the Christian revelation. For example, he "[uses] the
Metaphysics to move from teleology to christology," and then "uses *De
anima* to move from 'that which is' to the effects of God, from the effects
of God to the unknown essence of God . . . to faith, and from faith, to
'the One who is believed.'"[12]

Aside from the question whether there is a consensus on Rogers's
argument among Thomistic scholars,[13] what he would agree on with a
number of other writers, especially with MacIntyre, is that for Aquinas
Christian theology from divine revelation is an Aristotelian science.
What seems problematical in Rogers's account, however, is that it seems
to imply—rather like Russell's accusation—that to some degree, Aquinas
only pretends to be an Aristotelian, precisely because he uses the findings
of Aristotelian philosophy elsewhere against Aristotle himself to reach a
conclusion that is consistent with Christian revelation. However, as I
have argued in chapter 5, the concept of "dialectics," which is crucial for
an Aristotelian conception of intellectual inquiry, invites the participants of its intellectual tradition to do precisely what Aquinas does, so
that its inquiry can progress further.

I would rather say that Aquinas genuinely believes, and indeed argues from an Aristotelian tradition, that the Christian revelation is the
final end of Aristotelian philosophy. This understanding of the relation

between Christianity and Aristotelian philosophy, rather than "co-opting," seems to be the "essay of the *Summa*," as Rogers would call it. Thus, if it seems at times that Aquinas is "co-opting" Aristotle so that the latter's philosophy "can lead only to Christ," this is because the *Summa* is the result of a highly successful project of synthesizing the two traditions. Furthermore, his supposedly "different" position on the "first principles" from Aristotle, which Rogers mentions, is precisely that which enables this synthesis.

Aquinas's Account of Truth and the Mind of God

Aquinas's position that the first principles are found "radically outside the world," in the "mind of God," is closely related to his position on truth. Aquinas presents a double concept of truth. The first concept derives from Aristotle and is about the nature of things, whereas the second is a concept of truth in relation to God.

For Augustine, truth is "that which is" (*id quod est*), which denotes his understanding of truth as ontological substance; however, for a number of medieval writers, this did not sufficiently "express that by which 'truth' *qua* concept (*ratio*) differs from 'being.'"[14] That is, "what is," or "being," differs conceptually from "truth." The difference is that truth is to be understood in relation to the intellect, an Aristotelian point that Aquinas follows. Aertsen summarizes this position:

> In summary, Thomas follows the Aristotelian approach to truth: the place of truth is not in things, but in the mind. . . . Thomas regards as Aristotle's "definition" of truth a statement in the fourth book of the *Metaphysics*: "To say of what is that it is, and of what is not that it is not, is true." This "definition" indicates a perspective on truth quite different from that of Augustine. The true is not "that which is," but is *to say* of that-which-is that it is.[15]

Thus, Aquinas's definition of truth is the "adequation of thing and intellect." However, as we have seen, this position on truth seems at first to imply a conception of intellectual inquiry in which God plays no part.

That is, for the Augustinian tradition, God *is* Truth, that which *is*, but if truth becomes adequation of the human intellect to the thing, God no longer plays a part in knowing the truth. This is significant especially since philosophy is, according to Aristotle in the second book of the *Metaphysics*, "the science of truth." Thus, since truth is "to say of what is that it is," and in the Aristotelian conception of inquiry, what a thing is is its nature, philosophy as an intellectual inquiry of truth seems to no longer require God. This problem appears in the *Summa* when Aquinas describes one of the objections to his position that the existence of God is not self-evident. The objection, which we examined in the previous chapter, argues that it is self-evident that truth exists, and God is truth, to which Aquinas responds that it is self-evident that truth exists, but not that First Truth exists. What Aquinas is arguing is that it is "truth," as an "adequation of the thing and intellect," which is self-evident to us, and this is not God.

However, Aquinas does argue, following not only Augustine but the scriptures, that God is "Truth." How so? For Aquinas, truth is the adequacy of thing and intellect, and for human beings, this is to say it is the adequacy of the human intellect to what the thing is. However, for God, this is reversed; for God, truth is the adequacy of the thing to the mind of God, the Creator.[16] In this sense, God is the First Truth. Furthermore, Aquinas concludes from Aristotle's position on the relation between truth and being in *Metaphysics* that truth is consequent on being. That is, again, truth is being, insofar as it is the relation of the intellect to being, or to what is said of being. Thus, only that which is "being itself" is also "truth itself," and thus just as only God alone *is* Being (*ipsum esse*) whereas all things *have* being (*ens*), God *is* Truth (*Veritas*), whereas all *things* are *true* (*verum*).[17]

However, how does Aquinas justify what seems to be an additional and unneeded postulation of "Truth" and "God" over and above the Aristotelian position on truth? This is not to say that what Aquinas says is incompatible with the Aristotelian position; indeed, Aquinas argues from and within the terms of Aristotelian philosophy. The problem is whether his "postulation" of God as Truth is necessary. To give a similar objection in the setting of our contemporary debate, a Christian theist may successfully argue that the existence of God is compatible with the findings of modern science. However, this alone will not convince the atheist. Of course, if the theist belief in God is incompatible with modern science, most atheists will simply dismiss the theist position.

However, even if the theist shows that belief in God is compatible, an atheist may nevertheless ask why we would need to postulate the existence of an additional being, namely, God. Again, for a theistic worldview, God is not an additional postulation, but for an atheist worldview, God is. Likewise, if Aquinas is bringing together the Christian and Aristotelian worldviews, he needs to answer an objection similar to this. How does he do so?

To present a preliminary answer to this question, I will turn to Richard Lee Jr.'s *Science, the Singular, and the Question of Theology*, which presents an account of science and theology in the Middle Ages somewhat different from Aertsen's. This is not to say that he presents a rival position to Aertsen's distinction between "nature" and "creature." Rather, Lee describes another important aspect of the difference between the Greek and the Christian conceptions of intellectual inquiry.

Lee argues that Greek philosophy seeks what he calls the "rational ground," which explains why things exist and why they are the way they are. However, the distinctive feature of this kind of explanation is that it conceives the answer as that which "appeals to reason (epistemological) and holds that one way or another, the reason is the cause of a thing (ontological)."[18] This position, Lee comments, is found in Plato, but it is Aristotle who presents the "shortest expression of the rational ground" in the *Posterior Analytics*, where he writes that "'we think we know each [thing] . . . when we think that we know the cause through which the thing exists . . .' (71b10)."[19] Simply put, the concept of "rational ground," central to Greek philosophy—and Aristotle—is that the cause of existing things, including their "nature," may be understood in rational terms, or more precisely, that the cause of things is rational.

That the causes of things are rational is not denied by the Christian worldview. What distinguishes the Greek position regarding the "rational ground" from the Christian worldview is its position on the "existing singular," that is, what exists. What is the distinction? If the question "why" is always to be answered in terms of the "rational ground," it implies that what is rational is "prior" to what exists.[20] This, in turn, leads to the notion that to reach this "rational ground" is to ultimately reach a point of complete understanding in which one knows the rational reason why absolutely all things that exist do exist and are the way they are. In the Christian position, however, the "existing singular" has no ultimate rational explanation why it exists, because the cause of existence lies in the inscrutable will of God. That is, reason cannot go beyond creation to the mind of the Creator.

Aquinas, in Lee's account, holds something of a middle position between these extremes. Science, for Aristotle, begins from self-evident principles, whereas for theology, its first principles—namely, God and his essence—are unknown to human reason. Aquinas nevertheless argues in the *Summa* that theology is an Aristotelian science. He does so by defining theology as a "subalternate science."[21] He observes that music and optics do not begin from self-evident principles, but from principles proven by a different, superior science—namely, mathematics. Thus, music or optics is a "subalternate science" dependent on the superior science of mathematics. Likewise, theology takes its principles from the authority of revelation. To be accurate, it is not revelation per se that is the superior science to theology; rather, this science is the "science that God and the blessed have," which is given in divine revelation.[22] Theology is a science because it is subalternate to the first principles in the mind of God, in which there is a perfect and absolute understanding of absolutely everything that exists and also of God. The difference is that whereas God—and the blessed—know the rational *why* of everything that exists and of God, those on this side of heaven do not.

Thus Aquinas preserves the notion of "the rational ground," which is central—arguably even more central than the notion of "nature"—to Greek philosophy in general and to the Aristotelian tradition in particular, by placing this point of complete rational understanding in the mind of God. Yet why would this preserve the notion of such universal "rational ground"? For this, we will turn once again to MacIntyre.

THE FIRST PRINCIPLES AND FINAL ENDS OF
INTELLECTUAL INQUIRY AND GOD

Plato's Conception of Truth and Rational Inquiry

We examined in chapter 3 how, for MacIntyre, the rationality of an intellectual tradition is found in the historical narrative of its intellectual inquiry, a narrative regarding how the inquiry has progressed so far toward its telos, its end or goal. It is this telos which gives direction to such a narrative. MacIntyre's account of this tradition-constitutive, and tradition-constituted, rationality begins from early Greek writers. For our purpose, however, I will begin with his account of Plato.

I begin with MacIntyre's account of Plato for two reasons. First, it is Plato's philosophical positions and his conception of intellectual inquiry that are influential for the Augustinian tradition. Second, according to MacIntyre, Aristotle's position is largely formed from, and extends and completes, Plato's. Thus, the conception of truth and rational inquiry for the two rival intellectual traditions in the time of Aquinas cannot be understood apart from how it was conceived by Plato. Plato begins from his particular historical condition too: "From Socrates, [Plato] inherited both a negative use of deductive argument as deployed in his method of refutation (*elenchos*) and a standard of truth. Like Socrates he believed that the first step toward truth had to be the use of *elenchos* to exhibit the unreliability of our pre-existing beliefs."[23] Yet why does he inherit this method of refutation, and what is this standard of truth he inherits? Plato's position is to be contrasted against the notion of *techne*, or rhetoric, which was influential in the Athenian politics and social life of his time. It is the notion that to convince others, what one needs is simply rhetoric, which merely has to appeal to the audience and win their approval, and thus does not preclude nonrational manipulation. Hence, "truth" in such a society is understood almost entirely as what people agree, or are persuaded by rhetoric, to believe. However, what Socrates—and Plato as his inheritor—and his dialectic through *elenchos* demonstrated was that not everything that people believed on a given subject could be true and that "they had no resources for deciding which parts . . . they believed were false and which, if any, were true."[24] Then, how are we to proceed, and know what is true? MacIntyre writes:

> The Socratic answer is: by starting out from anyone's thesis, our own or anyone else's indifferently, provided that it is rich enough in content and formulated in such a way as to invite serious attempts at refutation. Every attempt at refutation from any point of view should be carried through as far and as systematically as the participants in the enquiry are able. That thesis which most successfully withstands all attempts to refute it—characteristically of course, such a thesis

will have had to be modified and reformulated in the course of its encounters with a variety of objections—is that which claims our rational allegiance.[25]

Thus, Socrates advanced the conception of "true" as opposed to "false," and further argued that something that is true is true of all times and places, regardless of who believes it.[26]

However, to advance theses and evaluate each of them as more or less "rational" or "adequate" is to presuppose a direction to the inquiry. Here Plato expands upon Socrates' conception of rational inquiry and introduces the concept of the telos, the end or the goal of the intellectual inquiry.[27] As we examined in chapter 4, this conception of the telos and the direction of intellectual inquiry defines rational progress of such inquiry as the following. First, the later stage of the inquiry proceeds from the former; second, the later stage is able to account for the errors and difficulties of the former; third, the later stages progress further toward the goal of the inquiry and thus have more adequate conceptions of it. However, the fourth feature of progress is the most significant for our purpose.

According to MacIntyre, the conception of the telos of inquiry, as it becomes more adequate in successive stages, will also be the conception of "what it would be to have a completed enquiry."[28] MacIntyre writes regarding this concept:

One and the same conception [of the completed enquiry] is to provide both the enquiry with its *telos* and the subject matter with its explanation. So that to arrive at it would involve being able to provide a single, unified explanation of the subject matter and of the course of the enquiry into that subject matter. Let us call the conception which provides this explanation the *arche*: adequately specified as it can only be at the point at which enquiry is substantially complete, it will be possible to deduce from it every relevant truth concerning the subject matter of the enquiry; and to explain the lower-order truths will precisely be to specify the deductive, causal, and explanatory relationships which link them to the *arche* and which show that, given the nature of the *arche*, they would not be other than they are.[29]

In this sense, the telos of the inquiry is its end, in that it defines the in-quiry's final, completed state, and also its *arche*, its first principles; that is, the goal of an intellectual inquiry is to reach a point in which it has an adequate conception of its *arche*, the principles of its subject matter, from which, or in terms of which, the inquiry may explain why things are, and why they are the way they are. Thus, to use Lee's terms, the completed inquiry arrives at the "rational ground."

Why is this important for our account of Plato? Because this *arche* that MacIntyre describes is what Plato means by the "Forms" or "Ideas." MacIntyre notes, however, that *The Republic* makes it clear that Plato has not achieved this state of completed knowledge. Plato does not know the Forms:

> [Socrates in *The Republic* disclaims that he] speaks from the stand-point of achieved *episteme*. He remains one who appeals to images and diagrams, and therefore who has not yet apprehended the forms.
>
> *The Republic* is therefore to be understood as presenting, not a completed theory of forms, but rather a program for constructing such a theory.[30]

This means that what is understood as the metaphysics of Plato regard-ing the "universals" existing independently from the "particulars" is in fact derived from, or even identical to, his conception of rational inquiry, and specifically his conception of the various teloses of a given inquiry. However, this leaves Plato's theory "radically incomplete."[31] How so? Plato's account proposes a completed point of inquiry, in which the in-quiry reaches its telos, and thus its *arche*, but it does not propose the means to arrive at such point.[32] Plato was aware of this incompleteness already in *The Republic*. However, what Plato proposed was that this conception of the final ends of the inquiry, which proceeds toward the knowledge of its first principles, is necessary to preserve the rationality of intellectual inquiry as such.

Both this relation between the metaphysics and the theory of in-quiry and the acknowledged incompleteness of this theory are frequently missed by modern detractors of Plato. Bertrand Russell once again is a classic example, when he misunderstands Plato's dilemma simply as the defect of his metaphysical "Theory of Ideas" regarding universals and particulars: "[Plato] fails altogether to realize how great is the gap between universals and particulars. . . . At a later date, he began to see this difficulty [regarding the 'Theory of Ideas'] as appears in the *Parmenides*, which contains one of the most remarkable cases in history of self-criticism by a philosopher."[33] Because Russell did not, as MacIntyre does, connect Plato's Theory of Forms to his conception of intellectual inquiry and its telos, he does not understand that Plato has acknowledged the gap already in *The Republic*. He does not realize that this "gap" is derived from the gap between the end to which a particular inquiry aims and the current status and practice of this inquiry. Nor is he able to understand why, despite the self-critiques Plato levels at his theory in *Parmenides*, the theory is not abandoned, though Russell himself unknowingly writes the reason: "Nevertheless, the theory of ideas is not wholly abandoned. Without ideas, Socrates says, there will be nothing on which the mind can rest, and therefore reasoning will be destroyed."[34] The theory is not abandoned because intellectual inquiry is intelligible only if it has its telos, the goal to which it is progressing. This is why this seemingly problematical metaphysical theory, if abandoned, "destroys reasoning" as such.

Aristotle's Conception of Intellectual Inquiry—To Grasp the First Principles

Because Plato's project was incomplete, Aristotle's theory and conception of rational inquiry was not independent of Plato. Rather, MacIntyre writes, "The questions which Aristotle answers are Platonic questions."[35] In other words, Aristotle answers the question left by Plato's incomplete account: how do we grasp or get at the *arche*? Or to put it another way, if the particulars or the concrete are all we sense and experience, how do we conceive the inquiry to go from here to its telos, or the *arche*?

Aristotle answers it through a method that moves from particulars to universals, which he called *epagoge*. In the terms of inquiry, *epagoge* moves the inquirer from lower, particular truths, or concrete instances, to general truths of the matter. It is in this sense "induction," but MacIntyre warns it is subtly different from the modern philosophical use of the term. MacIntyre himself explains by using an example from modern natural science: "*Epagoge* involves inference, but more than inference; it is rather that scientific method through which the particular varyingly impure or distorted exemplifications of a single form can be understood in terms of that form—as particular varyingly impure examples of carbon can all be understood by chemists to exemplify the single atomic structure which makes them each an example of *carbon*."[36] However, is this form of reasoning enough? Aristotle argues that through further dialectical arguments, with which a thesis or a theory, or conception—presumably arrived at by *epagoge*—is made to withstand "the most cogent objections from different point of view," the *nous*, or the mind, may form its conclusion on the *arche* of a given inquiry.[37]

However, MacIntyre notes, there has been a misunderstanding of Aristotle regarding how he conceived rational inquiry. That is, many modern readers have believed that for Aristotle, knowledge in scientific inquiry is a matter of deductive demonstration. Yet if this were true, MacIntyre argues, there would be a radical discrepancy between how Aristotle characterized science and how he carried out his own scientific inquiries in his *Physics* and biological treatises.[38] This seeming discrepancy can be explained by understanding the former conception of rational inquiry, as found in *Posterior Analytics*, as a conception of perfected science—the completed inquiry—a concept that Aristotle inherits from Plato: "A perfected science enables us to understand the phenomena of which it treats as necessarily being what they are, will be, and have been, because of the variety of agencies which have brought it about that form of specific kinds has informed the relevant matter in such a way as to achieve some specific end state."[39] That is, in a completed inquiry, all the truths in the subject matter are deductively known from their first principle, in a unified, grand explanation of every particular or concrete truth of that subject matter. Again, we have parallels of this notion of inquiry in contemporary modern science; physics, after all, searches for the Theory of Everything, which would explain every physical phenomenon from fundamental laws.

However, such deductive science must be constructed through the *epagoge* and dialectics. This then is what Aristotle is doing, for example, in his *Physics*. In these forms of rational inquiries, the first principles are not known. That is, the first principles, which would provide deductive knowledge *if* the inquiry were to become complete, are at this ongoing stage the unknown and projected end, or telos, of the inquiry. As the inquiry progresses through its successive stages, its characterization of its projected telos—conception of what the first principles would be, if the inquiry were completed—are formulated and reformulated through various dialectical arguments and through the process of *epagoge*.[40] Thus, in any rational inquiry that is still being constructed, its particular understanding of its projected first principles is being constantly revised. Indeed, as our understanding may always change through further inquiry, no conception of the first principle will ever be certain. Thus, MacIntyre quotes Aristotle saying, "'It is difficult to discern whether one knows or not' (*Posterior Analytics* I, 9, 76a26)."[41] Yet even when the final, perfected understanding of the first principle is not reached, or never reached, the narrative of the successive development and progress of a particular inquiry presupposes the direction, thus the *existence*, so to speak, of its final ends and first principles.

First Principles, Transcendentals, and God in Aquinas

Now, it is understandable why the Aristotelian form of intellectual inquiry came to dominate the natural sciences and, more generally, the Faculty of Arts in the time of Aquinas. According to MacIntyre, Aristotle extends the project that Plato began, and thus his conception of rational inquiry is superior to Plato's in that it overcomes and transcends the limitations of Plato's conception. Aristotle is "Plato's heir," or a successor to Plato's intellectual tradition. This is also why it is primarily the Christian, theological core of the Platonic-Augustinian tradition that remained resistant to the challenges, and incommensurable to the claims, of the Aristotelian tradition.

This is why Aquinas follows Aristotle in criticizing the Platonic theory of Forms. In an inquiry into a thing, Platonic inquiry moves away from the thing to something separate and abstract in the intellect rather than inquiring into the intrinsic nature of the thing. Aertsen, in a passage I quoted from in the previous chapter, summarizes the critique succinctly. Here I quote him in greater detail:

> [Aquinas] describes the Platonists as wanting to reduce every composite thing to simple, abstract principles. That is why they posit the existence of separate, ideal Forms of things. They apply this approach not only to the species of natural things, but also to that

which is most common, namely, good, one, and being. . . . Aquinas rejects the first application of the Platonic method, subscribing to Aristotle's criticism that the Platonists project our abstract mode of knowing onto the mode of being of things.[42]

In the terms of MacIntyre's account, we may describe the critique as follows. An intellectual inquiry regarding "species of natural things," as it is practiced in an incomplete stage of such inquiry, learns through the process of *epagoge* and dialectics what a thing is by its intrinsic nature. The "abstract, simple principles" of the Platonists are merely the conception of the telos and *arche* of the inquiry in our current "mode of knowing" in a still ongoing and thus incomplete stage of such an inquiry. However, "it is difficult to discern whether one knows or not," that is, whether we have or will ever reach a completed stage. It is a problem, then, to project such an incomplete conception of the telos, and posit the objects of this conception as separate entities apart from the composite things actually being studied.

However, Aertsen continues on to describe how Aquinas defended the Platonic approach as legitimate in regard to the "first principle" as such, at a level of that which is "most common," namely, "being, one, and good," which are called the "transcendentals" because they transcend Aristotelian categories.[43] To be more precise, Aquinas argues that the Platonic theory of "Participation" is appropriate for understanding the relation between transcendentals and particular things. This is, first, because "being," "one," "truth," and "good" are convertible, that is, "one," "truth," and "good" are ontologically identical to "being" but are conceptually different aspects of "being"; for example, "truth" is "being" in relation to the intellect.[44] Second, "being as such," or "being in general" (*esse commune*) is that which is "most common" (*maxime communia*), and thus the transcendentals are common to all things. However, in *De ente et essentia*, Aquinas establishes that no existing being is such that its essence is its existence. That is, Aristotelian inquiry into the intrinsic nature of things gives us the "rational ground" of why a thing is what it is, but it does not give us the "rational ground" of that which is common to everything that it studies—"being" as such. If "being" is not the intrinsic nature of existing beings, then it is appropriate to use the Platonic language of "participation" in regard to the "being" of things. That is, existing things "participate" in being, or *have* "being," which is separate from their nature.

Thus, for Aquinas, only God *is* Being, One, Truth, and Good. This is not to say that God is "being in general," or "goodness in general." The relation between God and the transcendentals is a causal relation.[45] That is, "being," which all other existing things "have" in participation, is from God, whose nature is to be. This is likewise for the "truth," or "goodness," which are convertible to "being" and thus caused by God, who *is* Truth and the Good. This conception is at the basis of Aquinas's fourth way in the *Summa*. In *Metaphysics*, Aristotle proposes a general position that if A causes B to have a property C, whereas C can be predicated of both A and B, then A is said to predicate C *maximally*; Aristotle then applies this to the notion of truth. Whether this is valid may be questionable—Aquinas also tries to reformulate the argument in his commentary on *Metaphysics*—but since transcendentals are convertible, Aquinas argues from Aristotle, in the fourth way, that God is the "maximum" of the perfections, such as truth and goodness.[46]

At this point, I emphasize that although the doctrine of the transcendentals is a medieval development, it proceeds from and extends the position of Aristotle. That is, it takes as its starting point the discussion of Aristotle regarding "being," "oneness," "truth," and the "good." It is Aristotle who states that philosophy is the science of truth and that the "first science," which is metaphysics, is the study of being as such, or being-as-being, and thus includes "divine science" (*scientia divina*). Indeed, how Aristotle conceives this "first science" of being and its relation to "theology" is still a controversial question; contemporary writers still argue about whether for Aristotle, being-as-being is "a divine substance, to which all other beings are related."[47] It is Aquinas who argues that being-as-being is not God, but a transcendental, which comes from God. Thus, the theory of the transcendentals and its relation to God, which Aquinas develops from a Platonic position, is nevertheless an appropriate, though innovative, extension of Aristotle.

First Principles, Final Ends of Intellectual Inquiry, and the Existence of God

Aquinas's turn to the Platonic approach in regard to the transcendentals and to God is significant precisely because of how the conception of inquiry for Plato and Aristotle are related. That is, Aristotle presents the means, or the actual practice, of science, with which an intellectual inquiry may progress toward what Plato argues is necessary for such inquiry to be intelligible: its telos and *arche*. Thus, for an Aristotelian conception of inquiry, as an heir to Plato's, there is a perfected understanding of a subject matter, which the inquiry has not yet reached, and may never reach in actual practice, yet toward which it is progressing. That is, an inquiry qua Aristotelian inquiry must progress toward a final, unified, comprehensive explanation of all things in that inquiry. This is why Aquinas confidently denies in the Five Ways that there can be an infinite series of causes, even though elsewhere he argues that it is rational to hold that the universe may not have had any beginning in time. Simply put, an explanatory chain in an Aristotelian inquiry cannot continue without an end, that is, without a point of perfected understanding in which everything is explained through the first principles—even if in actual practice, such a point is never be reached—without rendering the very practice of intellectual inquiry pointless.

There are, however, many different philosophical disciplines, different sciences, from mathematics to physics to biology to ethics to politics. These sciences are to be hierarchically organized, so that the first principles of one inquiry are based upon the conclusions of another, and so forth, until there is a "first science," the telos of which is the *arche*— the absolute First Principle—of all that exists. MacIntyre describes this Aristotelian schema:

> It follows from this account that in each distinctive form of achieved understanding, each science, there are a set of first principles, *archai/ principia*, which provide premises for demonstrative arguments and which specify the ultimate causal agencies, material, formal, efficient and final for that science. It follows also that, insofar as the perfected sciences are themselves hierarchically organized, the most fundamental of sciences will specify that in terms of which everything that can be understood is to be understood. And this, as Aquinas remarks in a number of places, we call God.[48]

Thus the Aristotelian intellectual inquiry, characterized by the concept of "nature," and thus previously incommensurable to Christian theology, nevertheless requires a conception of what Aquinas calls God. Or, as

MacIntyre comments, "there is then an ineliminable theological dimension . . . to [Aristotelian] enquiry."[49]

However, in the present stage of inquiry, we do not have such an understanding of such a first principle. That is, human beings have no perfected understanding of all that is, and of that which is Being. Such an understanding would require every science to be perfected, including the first science of being-as-being, a point which in actual practice may never be reached. This is why Aquinas argues that it is not self-evident that God exists because we do not—and indeed, on this side of heaven, cannot—know the nature of God. Nevertheless, the Aristotelian conception of inquiry requires there to be such a point, even if never reached; this is why Aquinas then argues in the next article, which is prior to the Five Ways, that although we cannot know *what* God is, we can nevertheless know *that* God is.

This is because such perfected understanding is in God—not that the mind of God is adequate *to* the nature of all things, but that the being, goodness, and the truth of all things is *in* God. Or, more simplistically, to know such perfected science of all is to know God. Thus, in arguing that it is demonstrable that God exists, Aquinas argues that there are two kinds of demonstrations. First is a demonstration of *why* from causes, and the second is the demonstration *that* there is a cause from effects. We can demonstrate that God is by moving from effects to the cause. Again, using MacIntyre's account, what Aquinas is arguing is that we are not at a point of perfect understanding, in which we know why all things exist, and more to the point, why the very nature of God is to *be*. Nevertheless, the Aristotelian conception of intellectual inquiry is such that there must be such a point.

Now, we may finally answer the question of what the Five Ways do. However, first we need to examine a few other points regarding the Five Ways.

THE FIVE WAYS AT THE CROSSROADS OF WORLDVIEWS

The "Unoriginality" of the Five Ways

What is striking about the Five Ways, and similar arguments Aquinas presents elsewhere, is that it is "unoriginal." Many scholars have argued that what Aquinas presents in the Five Ways is found in older arguments of philosophers before him. Kerr argues regarding this, quoting Edward Silem, "the arguments are quite unoriginal, *and that is Thomas's point*" because he is instructing theologians, so that they have a better understanding of the reasoning of pagan thinkers, as well as the mystery of God.[50] Summarizing an account by Leo Elders, Kerr even briefly outlines the "genealogy" of the Five Ways. The first way, for example, is found in Plato (*Phaedrus* 245c–e) and reformulated by Aristotle (*Physics* 8.10.266a10–267b25; *Metaphysics* 12.6–8.1071b1–1074b15). The second way is found in Plato's *Timaeus*, although also in Christian scriptures in Acts 17:28 and Isaiah 26:12. The third way is prefigured in Plato and Aristotle and formulated by Philo of Alexandria, Proclus, Augustine, and Ibn Sina. The fourth way is found partly in Aristotle, but also in Augustine. The fifth way is found "wherever religion flourishes."[51]

However, this is to be expected from MacIntyre's account of tradition. What Aquinas is doing is to bring into conversation the different writers of the past that belong to the Aristotelian and Augustinian traditions, and this would be the same with the Five Ways. Furthermore, most philosophical arguments about the existence of God in our time are developed from older theistic and atheistic arguments as well; we are still presenting reformulations of ontological, cosmological, and teleological arguments, as well as the argument from evil, and even, according to Flew—a position I have argued is quite wrong—arguments for the "presumption of atheism" from the time of Aquinas. Thus, for Aquinas to present arguments very similar to those of pagan, Christian, or Muslim philosophers before him is to be expected.

What is more interesting, however, is the account of Aquinas's argument that God exists in the *Summa Contra Gentiles*. According to Hibbs, the structure of the first book in *Contra Gentiles* is dialectical, refuting errors of pagan philosophers, such as circumscribing God "by limits of human imagination and conceptualization," "conflating the world with God," and "denying God's intimate causal contact with, and providence over, singular and lowly things," namely his creatures.[52] This is again to be expected, as these positions are implied in some readings of Aristotle, and it is part of the task of Aquinas to argue why Aristotelian philosophy, insofar as it pertains to natural reason, ought to be consistent with Christian doctrine. However, such dialectic is absent in the argument for the existence of God: "Thomas begins the chapter on the existence of God by noting that he is simply restating familiar arguments. The chapter is devoid of dialectical disputation. . . . Thomas typically ends a dialectical discussion by mentioning proponents of the error he has just refuted. No such list accompanies the arguments for the existence of God."[53] What is remarkable about the arguments about the existence of God Aquinas presents is not that Aquinas uses or reformulates older arguments, but that these are *uncontroversial.*

From the context of two traditions in conflict, what Aquinas seems to be doing is to begin simply from the presuppositions of the rival tradition—in this case, largely Aristotelian—and construct a synthesis. This presupposition was what we now read as the argument for the existence of God. What Aquinas seems to do in his arguments to the first cause in *Contra Gentiles* and in *Summa Theologiae*, insofar as these are understood as part of the synthesis of two traditions, is to identify that which in the Aristotelian worldview a protagonist from a Christian worldview may recognize as similar to his or her concept of God. This may be the reason for the refrain in each of the Five Ways—this "everyone understands as God," "names as God," "speaks of as God," "calls God." Aquinas is identifying and naming that which was not "God" for the original writer, such as Aristotle, as the Christian God.

This project is described in greater detail by McInerny's account of how Aquinas reads Aristotle's *Metaphysics*. McInerny writes that the precise ordering of the twelve books of *Metaphysics*—though now questioned by a number of modern commentators—is crucially important for Aquinas, because it gives direction to Aristotle's philosophical inquiry in which he progresses toward God. Through his reading of *Metaphysics*, Aquinas understands Aristotle to define wisdom, and indeed philosophy, as a search to explain all things through the knowledge of their first causes and principles. Then, each book of the *Metaphysics* moves toward the first causes through the discourse on properties of being, substance, and ultimate cause for each of the four kinds of causes: material, efficient, formal, and final. Eventually, the subject of metaphysics is defined as being-as-being. In the twelfth book, Aquinas sees the culmination of Aristotle's metaphysics, as its search for the first cause of being moves from perishable to immaterial substance, to the ultimate cause of being, which Aristotle describes as "Pure Act, Thinking Itself, Goodness,

Delight."[54] Aquinas identifies this passage as the *praeambula fidei*, the culmination of pagan philosophy, the limit to which human reason may know of God without the aid of revelation.[55]

Thus, a significant part of Aquinas's argument that God exists consists precisely in finding and identifying concepts or positions in the rival tradition or worldview that seem to reach closest to the Christian concept of God.

The Five Ways and the Conflict of Traditions

MacIntyre, however, presents yet another aspect of what the Five Ways do. His account, again, begins from the conflict of traditions. When two comprehensive and incommensurable philosophical positions, that is, intellectual traditions, are in conflict, the problem of truth arises. Within a worldview or a tradition that has no notion of a rival, comprehensive, and incommensurable position, it would be "immensely plausible" to "identify truth with warranted assertibility" as a number of philosophers in our time have done.[56] This is because the mode of reasoning and standard of justification of such a tradition would be considered absolute, and thus a concept of "truth" beyond what is warranted in its mode of inquiry, as well as the conjecture that its conceptual framework as a whole may be in error, would make no sense. That is, without the notion that there are rival, incommensurable, and comprehensive positions alternatives to our own, it would make no sense to say that even if our belief is perfectly warranted, it may still be untrue precisely because what gives it its warrant may be wrong.

However, when the incommensurability of rival positions is recognized, then warranted assertibility no longer defines what is true. MacIntyre describes the problem that results:

> Yet if one is compelled to enquire where the truth lies between alternative, rival, and incommensurable overall points of view, one cannot but entertain the possibility that either or both of these points of view is systematically false, false as a whole in its overall claims (that does not of course mean that *every* particular judgment made from within it is thereby false), just because and insofar as one

cannot but recognize that any such overall scheme of concepts and judgments may fall into a state of epistemological crisis.[57]

Thus, what arises is the concept of "truth," or "reality," which is beyond any particular, comprehensive position and its standard of justification, and which may be impossible to understand or speak of coherently from within one particular standpoint, yet perhaps not so from within its rival. Thus, MacIntyre continues:

> Hence in judging of truth and falsity, there is always some inelim-
> inable reference beyond the scheme within which those judgments
> are made and beyond the criteria which provide the warrants for as-
> sertibility within that scheme. Truth cannot be identified with, or
> collapsed into warranted assertibility. And a conception of *what is*
> which is more and other than a conception of *what appears to be the*
> *case in the light of the most fundamental criteria governing assertibility*
> *within any particular scheme* is correspondingly required, that is, a
> metaphysics of being, of *esse*, over and above whatever can be said
> about particular *entia* in the light of particular concepts.[58]

This is what Aquinas presents in one of his earliest works, *De ente et essentia*, and later, in the early questions of *De veritate*.

Now, according to Aertsen, the Aristotelian inquiry is led beyond the "nature" of things to the first cause of all things by (1) the concept of the transcendentals and (2) the position that no particular being is such that its intrinsic nature is its being; MacIntyre's account suggests that this process signifies an important turning point for conflicts between intellectual traditions. What such metaphysical concepts of being and truth provide—recall that for both Plato and Aristotle, metaphysics is inseparable from their conception of intellectual inquiry—is precisely the notion of the perfected understanding of the first principle of all things, which intellectual inquiry as such, organized into hierarchical sciences, progresses toward, but has not yet reached and may never reach. Thus, for Aquinas, what *is* and what *is truth* at the ultimate level is beyond any particular, comprehensive intellectual position at any particular time. It can thus be the crossroad of the Aristotelian and the Christian worldviews.

What MacIntyre is arguing, therefore, is not only that for an Aristotelian conception of intellectual inquiry to be intelligible, it requires a point of perfected understanding beyond itself, which Aquinas calls "God," but that such a conception is also required in the context of a conflict between two rival traditions, because without such a conception, both would fall into an epistemological crisis:

> It is these [notions of truth and being] which are analyzed and disclosed in the *Quinque Viae* [the Five Ways] of the *Summa Theologiae* ([I.2.3]), each of which relies on a principle or principles without which the objects of enquiry, theoretical or practical, cannot be rendered intelligible. To reject the *Quinque Viae* would be to reject the conception of enquiry shared by both Aristotelians and Augustinians. It was into the common framework furnished by this conception, thus spelled out analogically, causally, and practically that Aquinas integrated both rival schemes of concepts and beliefs.[59]

Thus, what seemed to be "unoriginal" arguments turn out to be an act of identifying and disclosing that which both rival, incommensurable forms of intellectual inquiry hold, and that without which the intellectual inquiry of both would be rendered unintelligible and impossible to practice.

At this point, I must clarify one key point about Aristotle's conception of inquiry. MacIntyre notes how today's usage of the term "principle"—or more widely put, "truth"—is different from Aristotle's. That is, we usually consider a principle, or understanding, or explanation, or truth about an object, as "mind's apprehension through language of what it is."[60] This, however, is to divide what in Aristotle—and Aquinas—unites. To explain an object as so and so is to move toward the telos of the inquiry regarding that object. This is to say, a perfect understanding of an object is what the object is in itself *and* our mind's adequacy to it.[61] This is important because, if it is true, what Aquinas presents is not a "transcendental argument," which argues that God exists by appealing, so to speak, to the structures of our mind, or how we think. For both the Aristotelian and the subsequent Thomistic tradition, the first principle without which an intellectual inquiry is unintelligible is not merely a mental concept, but that which *is*.

The Existence of God and the Construction of a Worldview

Again, the Five Ways constitute only a small portion of the *Summa*. This is because the "God" that is demonstrated in the Five Ways is not yet God. What Aquinas has demonstrated is a concept that is indispensable for the Aristotelian tradition qua intellectual inquiry, a concept that Christians would call God. We briefly examined in chapter 5 how both Kretzmann and Hibbs argue that *Contra Gentiles* is a project of constructing a comprehensive position of which the argument that God exists is only a starting point. Furthermore, especially according to Hibbs, the previous sections are to be reread and understood in the light of later conclusions.

We may make a similar observation for the Five Ways in the *Summa Theologiae*. Without the later sections in the *Summa*, the Five Ways do not actually demonstrate the existence of "God" in any recognizable sense of the word. Indeed, it is only through further arguments, mostly by arguing from what God is not—or more precisely, that God is unlike any other existing being—that even the most general traits of God are established. It is after presenting his Five Ways, in question 3, that Aquinas argues that God is simple and that the *esse* of God is identical to his essence. It is again in question 3 that Aquinas argues that God is One, and only in questions 4 through 6 that perfection, goodness, and infinity are ascribed to God. Moreover, from the Five Ways alone it may be argued that it is still the Aristotelian tradition which is superior to the Christian, Augustinian tradition. It is only through the *Summa* as a whole, through its dialectics on not only the existence of God but also ontology, ethics, politics, and so forth, that Aquinas establishes the truth of the Christian worldview as a whole, albeit integrated with the Aristotelian conception of rationality and science.

Furthermore, such a worldview is to be understood as historically extended. The Christian worldview, of course, presents a narrative of itself that continues from the biblical times. However, Aquinas also presents a narrative of philosophical inquiry from the pagan standpoint, from the pre-Socratics to Plato to Aristotle and so forth, where each stage philosophical progress is characterized by a more adequate conception of the ultimate first principle and final end of intellectual inquiry as such, and in turn, becomes closer to the concept of what Christians would call "God."[62] This narrative also remains open; that is, the comprehensive intellectual position he presents is nevertheless "essentially incomplete," as MacIntyre describes it, in that it is simply the "best answer so far."[63] As the narrative continues into the next generations, the Christian worldview as Aquinas presents it is open to more adequate answers, deeper understanding of God and the world, and so forth. However, such new answers will compose a continuous narrative of the Christian worldview tradition's journey toward its ultimate destination, in which its past steps are joined to the present and will extend to the future.

THE FIVE WAYS AND THE CONTEMPORARY DEBATE

Again, the account of the Five Ways that I have presented is not intended to be a contribution to Thomistic scholarship; it is a response to the general position in the contemporary debate about God. This position understands arguments for the existence of God as "proofs," or at least, as presentation of rational evidence in a "neutral" standpoint, which tends to be identified with the "presumption of atheism." Flew, who proposed this position, in turn, understands the Five Ways of Aquinas precisely in the terms above. I have argued, however, that the presumption of atheism is not a neutral standpoint—there is no such thing—but one that is specific to a particular worldview in the debate. What is required of a rational case for—or against—the existence of God is not proofs or refutations of such proofs per se, but a larger project in which each position seeks to bridge and engage the other position as a comprehensive framework of concepts and beliefs. Indeed, a successful argument in such a project would require that the party constructing the argument have an extensive and profound understanding of what is central to the other's standpoint, and begin—though it is not where the project will end—from such core presuppositions or concepts of the other position. The arguments of the last two chapters were intended to present a case that, generally speaking, this is what Aquinas does in his *Summa Theologiae* as a whole and through the Five Ways in particular.

In my account, the Five Ways are neither proofs nor even a "hypothesis," as Kretzmann called it. Rather, we may call it a kind of "meta-hypothesis," which frames the form of life that proposes, confirms, or rejects hypotheses to proceed further in understanding the world. That is, it is the conception of the ultimate level of reality, by which an entire worldview is guided in forming, evaluating, revising, and abandoning its beliefs, toward which its intellectual, rational inquiry progresses, and through which it functions. This is what Aquinas found in the rival, Aristotelian worldview and identified as "God." Furthermore, this is only one stage—a significant starting point to be sure, but no more—of Aquinas's overall project. In this sense, it is akin to our explorers in the parable, realizing that both of their positions assume some kind of ruler—or at least, some kind of governance—to govern over societies; this becomes for them the starting ground for a cooperative task of drawing from their knowledge of both sociopolitical systems to understand what exactly governs the native society. I have argued that this is a more adequate understanding of Aquinas's position than that of Flew.

What then misleads Flew in his account of Aquinas? There is a tendency for the worldview to be invisible to those who inhabit it, and this is also the case for the nontheist position, which purports itself to be the point in the debate where contemporary arguments for the existence of God begin. Thus, when Flew describes the Five Ways of Aquinas as "an attempt to defeat this presumption of (an Aristotelian) atheist naturalism," he does not adequately grasp that this naturalism is itself a particular framework, a worldview in itself, despite even naming the particular tradition in question.[64] Flew may even be misdescribing the Aristotelian position when he understands it as an "atheist naturalism," precisely because he understands the term "nature" solely from within his worldview. As we have examined, "nature" for Aristotle is simply that which defines what a thing intrinsically is; it is not quite the same concept as "nature" as a singular, closed system, as we usually understand it today. However, this raises an interesting question; how did such an assumption emerge, and how did it become so invisible to us? Or, more to the point, is the kind of atheism Flew proposes, in which one "simply does not affirm" that God exists, actually how modern atheism developed in history? That is, did modern atheism historically emerge simply from a series of negations of theistic beliefs?

SEVEN

The Fork

The Emergence of Modern Atheism as a Worldview

I have argued that a rational case for or against the existence of God is situated in the context of the encounter between rival, comprehensive, and historically contingent frameworks of beliefs and concepts, exemplified in the concept of worldviews. In doing so, I have called into question the view that what theistic arguments do, or ought to do, is to simply present proofs or evidence for positing the existence of an entity—namely, God—in addition to the "universe," or "nature." Examining the Five Ways as an exemplar, I suggested that what theistic arguments do at the crossroads of worldviews is to present a starting point for constructing a comprehensive position in which two rival worldviews, often with incommensurable beliefs, concepts, standards of rationality, and forms of intellectual inquiry, may be dialectically brought together. For Aquinas, this involved identifying and disclosing that without which the intellectual inquiry qua inquiry for both the Augustinian and Aristotelian worldviews ceases to be intelligible. All this undermines the view that atheism, insofar as it "simply does not affirm" that God exists, is a neutral position in the debate—by default, as it were; I have argued in response that such a position is itself a particular worldview and that

there is no "default" standpoint in the debate, metaphysical or procedural. However, the question remains as to how this view, which I shall
call "default atheism"—that is, "atheism-by-default"—was formed historically. Here, I will argue that this kind of atheism, as with any other
worldview, was formed through a series of historical developments.[1]

There are three reasons why such a historical account of the development of "default atheism"—namely, how such a view emerged from a
predominantly theist intellectual milieu of the Christian West—is relevant for our purpose. First, I have argued so far, from MacIntyre's account of tradition, that the intellectual position of a particular worldview
is inseparable from its historical narrative of how it came to its present
standpoint. My account of this atheist position in the debate as a particular worldview would therefore be incomplete without some kind of
narrative—at least, in very general outlines—about how it has historically developed *as* a worldview. Second, the historical narrative of a particular worldview regarding itself and its rival will differ from its rival's
narrative of that worldview. For example, my account of Aquinas differed
from Flew's; likewise, my position implies a narrative regarding how the
"default atheist" position developed, a narrative that differs from any that
would be told by those who hold this position. Third, to answer the
question whether what Aquinas accomplished through the *Summa*, and
the Five Ways specifically, is doable in the contemporary debate, it is
important to retrace the paths through which two rival worldviews in our
contemporary debate have reached their respective positions. This is because this may reveal or at least suggest a point, in the course of such
paths, at which two rival worldviews may yet again be bridged. I will
therefore begin to present a preliminary outline.

However, the historical emergence of atheism as an intellectual position and a worldview constitutes a vast, complicated narrative. The
most significant recent work is *A Secular Age*, by Charles Taylor. In it, he
argues against the "subtraction" narrative of secularism, which understands the emergence of secularism as that of the simple "loss of belief."
Taylor argues that this is far too simplistic and inadequate an understanding of what happened; rather, secularism was made possible by a
construction of a number of concepts, including that of the disengaged
"buffered self," which created a distance from the self to God.[1] The narrative I will present has a similar position, but it follows just one portion

of a particular strand of this far larger narrative; the atheist worldview, and specifically its denial that God exists, developed through particular *theistic* moves in its intellectual history.[2]

Again, I emphasize here that this is one particular strand from a complex weave of numerous historical and intellectual developments, which constitute the narrative of the Enlightenment and the modern age. I seek here only to raise one simple point. That is, the atheist position emerged not by simply rejecting—let alone by "simply not affirming"—belief in the existence of God, but as a result of a number of intellectual formulations and justifications of particular theological or philosophical positions, primarily in a theist—and more specifically, Christian—worldview after Aquinas. More precisely, that there were such particular steps in the complex tapestry of events that form the narrative of the Enlightenment makes untenable any simplistic account of atheism as a position which "simply does not affirm" the postulation of an unwarranted entity. Thus, at this point I acknowledge that the historical account I will present in this chapter will be far from adequate, even regarding the particular strand of the development that I will follow. However, my primary purpose here will be accomplished unless a rival account can somehow refute that such concrete and historically contingent steps—some of which I will identify in this chapter—were present in the historical development of modern atheism.

THE CONSTRUCTION OF THE DENIAL THAT GOD EXISTS

The Emergence of "Neutral" Rationality

The Enlightenment and its epistemological project remains an important influence for the development of the modern atheist position. This is the claim, as we have seen, that there is a neutral viewpoint completely independent of any sociocultural, historical, or philosophical background or assumptions, from and with which to rationally evaluate every knowledge claim, for any position, for all time. Such a viewpoint claims to perform such evaluations by ensuring that each knowledge claim is supported adequately by the "foundation" of knowledge, which will be composed only of what is indubitable, namely what is incorrigible, self-evident, or evident to the senses. Since belief that God exists is not "indubitable" in this way, the existence of God must be demonstrated from or supported by this foundation of knowledge, as with any other belief that is not a part of the foundation. Thus, a "default" intellectual position, which is initially composed only of such foundational, indubitable claims, is atheist insofar as the foundation does not include belief in God. It is to this position that theists must present their proofs or evidence. Of course, those who hold this classical foundationalist epistemology regarding the existence of God are not necessarily atheists; historically, most were not. A theist may believe that though the existence of God is not a part of the indubitable "foundation," it may nevertheless be proved by an argument from such foundation.

However, the terms in which such a theist will understand what it is to argue that God exists will differ significantly from the terms Aquinas used. At first glance, the terms used by the two may seem similar, since Aquinas argued that the existence of God is not "self-evident" and proceeded to demonstrate that God exists. But, as I have repeatedly argued, he presents his argument from the standpoint of a particular, historically extended intellectual tradition, or more specifically from a crossroad of two such rival traditions, rather than from some neutral, timeless standpoint. For Aquinas, the existence of God that his argument demonstrates is not supported by some "indubitable" beliefs from a universal, timeless foundation of knowledge, but is rather intertwined inseparably with the conception of intellectual inquiry qua inquiry that those particular, rival worldviews at the crossroad—in this case, the Augustinian and the Aristotelian traditions—both hold. Thus, if his argument fails, it will not be a failure to prove that God exists, but rather a failure of his project to bring together the two rival worldviews. What will then result is not atheism—not even the kind that "simply" does not affirm the existence of God from the lack of evidence. Rather, it is two worldviews with incommensurable differences, each unable to even begin engaging its rival in any fruitful debate regarding the existence of God. Indeed, this was precisely what characterized the intellectual background in which Aquinas began his project of synthesizing the Augustinian and the Aristotelian traditions. It may be what will increasingly characterize our debate today.

What then happened to this project, within which his argument for the existence of God was inseparably situated? MacIntyre argues that the project was abandoned after Aquinas not simply because of the condemnation of his position in 1277, or even because of the rejection of his key theses by the "most influential writers of the next generation." Instead, he writes:

> What defeated Aquinas was the power of the institutionalized curriculum. Neither theology nor the subordinate *artes liberales* could in the middle or late thirteenth century find room for the Aristotelian system, in the form in which the Islamic commentators had transmitted it, *as a whole*, either in its Averroist version or in Aquinas's. What then made an impact were particular Aristotelian theses, arguments, and portions of theory detached from the whole of which they were parts, and this systematically unsystematic reception and response to this or that in Aristotle or Averroes or Avicenna resulted in a series of equally *ad hoc* revisions of Augustinian positions in theology and of the received positions in other disciplines.[3]

That is, the piecemeal way in which Aristotelian philosophy was understood and taught in the theological faculty precluded a holistic understanding of that philosophy's position. This would in turn preclude an adequate understanding of Aquinas and his overall position, including what he was doing in his argument for the existence of God, even by those who "followed" Aquinas but were taught by such a curriculum.

MacIntyre is concerned here with how the intellectual debate proceeded in the universities after Aquinas and distorted his position. MacIntyre continues:

> So I have argued, that the thirteenth-century university confrontation between Averroist Aristotelianism and Augustiniansim [*sic*] had two distinct and contrasting outcomes: Aquinas's own constructive correction, reinterpretation, and integration of the contending traditions into a new dialectical synthesis which had the capacity for directing enquiry still further beyond itself, on the one hand, and on the other the ensuing development of both the university curriculum

and of the dominant tendencies in intellectual and moral debate, a development which excluded for the most part engagement with Aquinas's thought understood systematically and not just as a set of discrete theses.[4]

That is, by understanding Aquinas's position as "a set of discrete theses," those who came after him failed to understand it as a comprehensive, holistic system in which two rival traditions are integrated together, thereby presenting a viable starting point to extend the inquiry further from the increasingly sterile debate between otherwise incommensurable intellectual positions. There are, of course, different assessments of the philosophical and theological development subsequent to Aquinas; this is to be expected, since, as MacIntyre himself points out, historical narratives such as these are inevitably partisan.[5] However, these accounts do not concern us here significantly, since I aim to outline a problem that is different from, though closely related to, what MacIntyre is describing.

Another important problem in the situation that MacIntyre describes is that in such a setting, the differences between the Aristotelian and the Augustinian positions would not be understood as incommensurable. Recall how I observed in chapter 2 that incommensurable differences in the contemporary debate regarding the existence of God, such as between the Reformed epistemologists and the evidentialists, may be mistakenly seen as mere disagreements when their positions regarding a particular issue—for example, on classical foundationalism—are understood in isolation from their philosophical or theological positions as a whole. Likewise, if the Augustinians were to understand the rival Aristotelian philosophy as a "set of discrete theses," the incommensurability between their position and their rivals' would be obscured. Such seems to have been the case after Aquinas, as increasingly, theologians like Duns Scotus made what MacIntyre calls *"ad hoc"* revisions of Augustinian positions in response to Aristotelian philosophy, rather than engaging it as a whole system.

The point I am raising is that in a mere generation or so after Aquinas, the particular kind of intellectual project in which Aquinas was engaged, and in which his argument for the existence of God was situated, was not only abandoned, but abandoned in such a way that its significance—that is, the significance of what he was doing, rather than his particular intellectual position or arguments—was not truly understood by those that followed. That is, they failed to understand that Aquinas was not addressing the problem of merely incompatible differences between the Augustinian and the Aristotelian traditions, but incommensurable ones. However, if the possibility of alternative, incommensurable, comprehensive intellectual positions is systematically excluded in this way, it opens a way—a logical space, so to speak—for proposing a "neutral" rationality.

Emergence of Skepticism regarding Religious Belief

I have suggested that the first part of the Enlightenment epistemological project, which is a significant basis for "default atheism," was the exclusion of the possibility of alternative, incommensurable positions. This has made possible the notion of a universal—thus neutral—kind of rationality. The second part is to consider the existence of God as something to be proved or else disbelieved in such a "neutral" position, which purportedly led to the general skepticism toward religious belief. This is understood, by those who would hold the position of "default atheism," as a process in which Western society became more skeptical toward religious belief as it became "more rational," until it simply stopped believing—what Taylor would call a variant of the "subtraction story" of atheism.[6]

However, is this the case? In *The History of Scepticism*, Richard Popkin outlines the influence of modern skepticism in the West, from its revival beginning in the late-fifteenth-century Renaissance, through the subsequent religious turmoil and the intellectual crisis during the Reformation, to the threshold of the Enlightenment. He narrates how skepticism and the responses to it have formed the crucial component of the development of modern worldviews, including the rise of secular, atheist positions.[7] Whereas in popular usage, "skepticism" is contrasted with "faith," Popkin argues that the two are, and were historically, compatible for fideistic thinkers. If we do not know whether a belief system is true or false, we may either become an unbeliever or accept it with faith. "Skepticism" instead finds its opposite in "dogmatism," which is the claim that we do know, and know for certain.[8] Popkin also distinguishes between the "Academic" and the "Pyrrhonian" skepticisms. The first is the claim that we cannot know, whereas the latter is the claims that we do not know whether we can know. In practice, the former often leads to a denial of some beliefs, but the latter to a "suspension of judgment." Popkin thus characterizes academic skepticism as a "negative dogmatism."[9]

It is the Pyrrhonian kind which plays a pivotal role in introducing skepticism to the modern West. During the Middle Ages, Pyrrhonian positions were known through the classical works of Sextus Empiricus, Cicero, and Diogenes Laertius. However, it was in the Renaissance that these writings became widely known. Then, with the Reformation came the intellectual crisis regarding how to interpret scripture and make judgments on what it says. This questioning of the criteria divided the Protestants, who argued for a kind of "inner light," against the Catholics, who in turn argued for the adjudication by church traditions. Each side sought to dismantle the other's position by employing skeptical arguments, often drawn from the writings of Sextus Empiricus, as in the case of the followers of Savonarola. The Catholic Reformation that followed further employed skeptical arguments, which questioned certainty in matters of doctrines, but concluded that one ought therefore to simply remain in the traditional rulings set by the church.

However, in the late sixteenth century, skepticism quickly spread beyond religious truths to sciences, ethics, and philosophy as the new Pyrrhonists, such as Michel de Montaigne and Pierre Charron, now directed the arguments of Sextus Empiricus to all natural knowledge. They were largely fideistic, exhorting their readers to suspend all judgment and remain open to direct revelation from God, which is now the only possibility for knowing truth. The subsequent intellectual history of the West thus became the project of either refuting this skepticism or living with it. After the simple denouncements of skepticism or reiterations of Aristotelian philosophy over skeptical claims, some, such as Pierre Gassendi, Marin Mersenne, and Francis Bacon, argued for a "constructive" skepticism in which certainty of beliefs regarding reality is given up in favor of the pragmatic or empirical goals of science. This, Popkin notes, became the root of modern science, but it did not become widely accepted until a new dogmatic system, that of Descartes and his heirs, failed conclusively to solve this skeptical crisis.[10]

Descartes is significant in this history because he sought to find certainty in knowledge through skepticism. Using a radical skepticism, which Popkin calls a "super-pyrrhonism," he sought to clear away all beliefs until he discovered a foundation which could not possibly be doubted.[11] This led to his *cogito*, from there to his clear and distinct ideas, then to an idea of the perfect God, who would guarantee our knowledge about reality. This system withered under skeptical criticisms, as Descartes did not find a way to conclusively prove that his clear and distinct ideas—including that of God—were not merely "subjective" and susceptible to Pyrrhonist doubt. As this system failed, some, such as Blaise Pascal, again advocated a form of religious fideism in the revealed Christian doctrines, while others, like John Wilkins and Robert Boyle, formed a way for science to make progress and solve problems without making metaphysical claims susceptible to skeptical challenges.

Popkin then describes how skeptical arguments then turned, from writings of Isaac de la Peyrère and Samuel Fisher, to question the authenticity of scripture. Specifically, they argued that the Bible used now must be different from the "original," and that purported authors, such as Moses, could not have written the parts they were said to have written. All this questioned the divine authorship of the scriptures, and thus the very foundation of revealed knowledge. Popkin argues that from this, later thinkers, like Baruch Spinoza, would take a skeptical position— academic rather than Pyrrhonian—to undermine and explicitly deny any religious belief, while remaining dogmatic about the certainty of natural, philosophical or scientific knowledge. Popkin summarizes:

> The scepticism with regard to religion coupled with dogmatic antiscepticism about knowledge became a model for many English deists and French Enlightenment thinkers who pursued the many sceptical points raised by La Peyrère and Spinoza until they had reached a point where they thought they had abolished traditional religion, and they tried to do so during the Reign of Terror. D'Holbach could, for instance, argue dogmatically for a naturalistic metaphysics at the same time the work *The Treatise of the Three Impostors, Moses, Jesus and Mohammed or the Spirit of M. Spinoza* was circulating, first in manuscript and then in printed copies, one done by D'Holbach himself.[12]

That is, it is not only out of skepticism toward specifically religious claims, but out of the particular combination of this skepticism and the "antiskepticism" about the particular, Enlightenment view of rational inquiry and knowledge, that modern disbelief emerged.

What is significant about Popkin's historical account is that the narrative of how modern atheism developed from skepticism is not a narrative of Western society simply becoming more skeptical toward religious belief due to the lack of proof or sufficient evidence. Indeed, the narrative does not begin from a skepticism toward the existence of God; rather, the early skeptics in the Renaissance were skeptical toward natural knowledge, and consequently called for a fideistic theism. Even the skepticism toward religion much later on is at first directed not at the belief in the existence of God per se, but at the status of a particular religious text, from which religious life is practiced. Furthermore, from the skeptical challenges of the early Pyrrhonists develops what is at first a pragmatic, but eventually dogmatic affirmation of the findings of the natural sciences, and from the same challenges develops what is at first Pyrrhonic, but eventually dogmatic—that is, "academic"—skepticism regarding religious belief.

That is, it is through a number of highly specific intellectual moves regarding where and how to apply one's skepticism that religious belief—including specifically the "existence of God"—came to be doubted. Consider, for example, how from early modern philosophy onward until recently—perhaps ending only with contemporary revival of theist positions through figures like Swinburne and Plantinga—the rational justification for the belief in the existence of God was expected to fulfill the rigorous standard of Enlightenment foundationalist epistemology, while considerably less rigorous and even pragmatic standards were applied to scientific findings, as well as most everyday beliefs such as the belief in other minds, the external world, memories, and so forth. Thus, the Enlightenment epistemological project alone is insufficient for skepticism regarding religious belief to emerge. This also required a view on what is to be rigorously submitted to its standards. I am not arguing at this point, as Plantinga does, that the existence of God ought to have been treated as a kind of "basic belief" like the above examples. Rather, I am asking what changed from the early Renaissance such that the skepticism that once led to fideism now leads to atheism. Part of the answer, I suggest, lies in Popkin's account itself.

The Emergence of "Default Atheism" as the "Fall-Back" Position

A significant yet underemphasized feature of Popkin's narrative is that a skeptical argument does not, and cannot, stand by itself; it is followed by what I would call a "fall-back" position. That is, when everything is questioned, there is a kind of a "default" position one adopts nevertheless as a worldview. This is in some sense inevitable, as I have argued for the inescapability of our worldview in our thinking. What is striking—though not surprising, if we remember Wolterstorff's argument in chapter 2— is that often this happens to be what one already lives by. That is why, despite questioning all knowledge, early Pyrrhonians appealed to faith, the grace of God, and direct divine revelation. It seems rather simplistic to dismiss this as an attempt to avoid religious persecution, especially because such skeptical arguments were already being used against religious positions during the highly charged religious conflict that characterized the period during the Reformation. A more likely explanation is that the Christian way of life was the only existing practicable way of life. Thus, where there is only one comprehensive belief-system, or way of life, skeptics remain merely "Pyrrhonic," suspending any absolute judgments while living and believing what they have always believed. Their arguments remain a mere cautionary against dogmatism.

However, what if there were more than one comprehensive belief-system to "fall back" to? Only then would the skeptical arguments gain a truly disruptive force, which explains their frequent uses during the Reformation. A true "atheist" skeptic—so radically different from the fideistic early Pyrrhonists—would have therefore required just such a "fall-back" position, which provided an alternative to Christian theism. That is, such a skeptic required a *construction* of a comprehensive, alternative intellectual belief-system—a *worldview*—from which skeptical arguments could be leveled against theist positions. This fall-back position would in turn be exempt from the kind of skepticism the atheist skeptic would level against the rival. It is here that Popkin's discussion of Descartes and Spinoza is invaluable. Descartes and the epistemological project he began unwittingly provided the foundation and the means to construct such an alternative, which Spinoza did to a great degree.

However, what would prompt such a massive undertaking? Or to put it in the context of the history of Christian faith, what kind of crisis would necessitate such an enterprise? It cannot merely be the skeptical challenge. What it would require is that the existing "fall-back" position has become sufficiently unbearable, and its way of living, unlivable. This is precisely what Stephen Toulmin suggests in his account of the development of the Enlightenment epistemology in *Cosmopolis*:

> The 17th-century philosophers' "Quest for Certainty" was no mere proposal to construct abstract and timeless intellectual schemas, dreamed up as objects of pure, detached intellectual study. Instead, it was a timely response to a specific historical challenge—the political, social, and theological chaos embodied in the Thirty Years' War. Read in this way, the projects of Descartes and his successors are no longer arbitrary creations of lonely individuals in separate ivory towers, as the orthodox texts in the history of philosophy suggest. The standard picture of Descartes' philosophical development as the unfolding of a pure *ésprit* untouched by the historical events of his time, so graphically presented in the *Grande Encyclopédie*, gives way to what is surely a more lifelike and flattening alternative: that of a young intellectual whose reflections opened up for people in his generation a real hope of *reasoning* their way out of political and theological chaos, at a time when no one else saw anything to do but continue fighting an interminable war.[13]

That is, the violence of the religious wars in the seventeenth century prompted the quest for a method by which the very questions and issues that had caused these conflicts could be answered rationally, and with certainty. What happened instead was the realization that such a method cannot answer the questions it was designed to answer. This, in turn, combined with a construction of an alternative "fall-back" position, would develop into atheism, which would understand itself as emerging from a "rational disbelief" regarding religion.

John Clayton also suggests another strand to this narrative regarding how the atheist position came to be. He points out how in sixteenth-century Europe, atheism as an intellectual position was "unthinkable."

However, with the recovery of classical learning came the widespread awareness of ancient pagan atheists and their philosophy. From the missionaries in faraway places, such as the Americas and China, came stories of societies that were seemingly atheist. Clayton writes: "Discussion generated [from the account of these atheist societies] forced into European consciousness the thinkability of the denial of God. It was not only the Fool who could entertain the possibility that there is no God. Both the ancient wise and the remote worthy, each of whom was regularly idealized, could clearly think the unthinkable."[14] From this possibility of atheism came the need to somehow defend the belief in God through philosophy. However, this hypothetical atheist, Clayton remarks, "is a far greater threat than any real Other, since the one responsible for writing his brief was an insider who knew all the weaknesses of the case for Christianity."[15] The theologians of different philosophical schools, especially in France, began to debate against each other, assuming the position of the hypothetical atheist, and arguing all too well that the position of their rivals entailed atheism. However, what the debate seemed to indicate, for the educated elite who followed it, was that (a) proof for the existence of God is foundational for religious belief, and (b) the existence of God cannot be proven. Clayton remarks: "One eighteenth-century freethinker quipped that it would never have occurred to anyone to doubt God's existence if theologians had not tried so hard to prove it. This gibe . . . may contain in it rather more substance than one might have imagined."[16]

However, Clayton's narrative is significant for our purpose for reasons other than the caveat on founding religious belief on rational, indubitable proofs. It is that the emergence of atheism in this case required two particular steps. First was the availability of a worldview alternative to theism, whether actual or imagined. Second was the failure of the philosophical justifications by which this particular kind of Christian worldview consciously sought to measure itself against this rival position. That is, this theist position at least implicitly spelled out what it would mean for it to fail, in an intellectual setting where such failure would lead to an adoption of a rival worldview. Again, this account reveals a narrative where the emergence of atheism was contingent upon a number of very particular intellectual developments and movements, often from within the theist worldview.

I have so far outlined how what seems at first to be an act of "simply not affirming" the existence of God turns out to depend upon a number of historical developments, the most significant of which is the availability, or construction, of a worldview alternative to theism. However, with the notion of "neutral" rationality, and the contrasting lack of any notion of the possible incommensurability of alternative intellectual positions, it will have seemed to those who came to inhabit this different worldview that they have done so by "simply not believing" a particular religious belief. All this, however, is a narrative concerning those who moved away from the existing theist—specifically, Judeo-Christian—worldview to its alternative. What is even more remarkable is the other side of this narrative, where a significant portion of this newly emerging worldview was constructed from and by theists, for religious reasons. I will now examine two writers who sketch how the development of modern atheism as a worldview was to a significant extent contingent on particular intellectual formulations of, and historical movements in, historical Christian theism.

THE DEVELOPMENT OF ATHEISM FROM THEISM

Turner's Account of How Atheism Emerged from Theism

Without God, Without Creed by James Turner is a narrative that describes how "it became possible not to believe in God" in the West, and especially in the United States.[17] He argues that, surprisingly, it is neither the modern scientific discoveries nor socioeconomic changes that discredited religion or caused unbelief. There were enormous changes both in the conceptions of the cosmos, rationality, and human nature, and in the forms of society, economy, and moral practice, during the seventeenth to the nineteenth century. However, these changes did not cause unbelief. Turner sums up his surprising conclusion this way: "On the contrary, religion caused unbelief. In trying to adapt their religious beliefs to socioeconomic change, to new moral challenges, to novel problems of knowledge, to the tightening standards of science, the defenders of God slowly strangled Him. If anyone is to be arraigned for deicide, it is not Charles Darwin, but his adversary Bishop Samuel Wilberforce, not the godless Robert Ingersoll, but the godly Beecher family."[18] That is, it was how the theists adapted their religious belief to these changes that caused unbelief. Specifically, it was the effort to change the conception of God so that it conforms to an overly human set of terms—and I add, particularly to that of the European seventeenth to the nineteenth century—so that God is ultimately defined, measured, confirmed, and even falsified and morally condemned by those very same particular, historically and culturally contingent standards. That is, subjecting God absolutely to such standards made it possible to displace God and reject religious belief by these very same standards.

This development began in the mid-seventeenth century, as the scientific revolution, the invention of the printing press, the emergence of the new intellectual elite, and the overall decline in the ecclesiastical authority undermined the earlier medieval Christian worldview and its way of life. This drove the church to seek a new support for its beliefs. One solution was to revise Christian beliefs to "fit the new intellectual style."[19] Specifically, this style was the new rationalistic method, which emphasized precise definitions, measurable data, and observable effects. Such a method fit the new conception of the universe, a universe that "constituted a kind of cosmic mechanism, cranking along according to regular natural rules that were expressed mathematically."[20] By reconceptualizing God to fit closer to this development, Christian thinkers greatly deemphasized the incomprehensibility and mystery of God in traditional theology. Instead, they asserted that the existence and the nature of God could be known clearly, rationally, and indeed, scientifically. This trend even affected religious living, and observable moral life, always a significant concern for Christian living, now became almost its sole concern, displacing all other aspects.

During the Enlightenment of the eighteenth century, these tendencies were pushed further. As science revealed more seemingly impersonal laws of nature that "governed" every aspect of the "machinery" of the universe, certitude concerning the existence of God—albeit only as its Designer—became well established. This was, in fact, a scientific conclusion, as Turner notes: "Natural philosophers . . . did not regard God as external to their work but rather incorporated Him into their systems and hypotheses. God was not, from a scientific point of view, an extrascientific issue on which scientific evidence happened to bear; He was in the fullest sense a strictly scientific cause, essential to explanations of nature."[21] God was essential because some key features of the universe—generally speaking the orderly "laws" of nature, and specifically the origin of life and species—required a hypothesis of an intelligent Designer/Creator. Yet this same scientific certitude, eagerly embraced by numerous church leaders, also dispensed any need for the divine action *in* nature. That is, science seemingly affirmed the existence of God as the hypothetical "first" cause, as the Engineer or Lawgiver of the universe, yet denied his involvement and presence beyond this role: "[In] day-to-day scientific work . . . scientists had no need to continually invoke the hand of God. Astronomy in particular showed by the late eighteenth century a practical tendency . . . to treat God as a passive First Cause now retired from the scene—a posture that chemistry and geology began to emulate."[22] Thus, belief in God became a part of existing scientific theories about Nature, a part that was in actual scientific practice rarely if ever needed. The overall result was a conception of God that became increasingly distant and impersonal.

Such a conception of God posed problems. First was its radical divergence from the traditional personal God of the Christian faith, whom people still worshiped. Second, this rationalistic concept of God was becoming more and more difficult to differentiate from Nature itself. Turner describes the effect this way: "The outcome was a schizophrenic conception of God. Intellectual assurance came from the Divine Engineer; a personal religious experience assumed the Heavenly Father. . . . In strict logic the two were compatible, but psychologically, they now stood light-years apart. The personal God retreated into an impalpable spiritual world. The everyday world was left to the Designer God, drifting ever closer to identity with the anonymous forces of nature."[23] These problems continued during the rise of evangelicalism in the nineteenth century. While rebelling against this rationalized form of Christianity, most evangelicals nevertheless adopted its key assumptions. Its innovations were its emphasis on the individual, emotional response to faith and its introduction of "intuition" as another path to knowledge.[24] Yet such innovations remained largely indistinct from human art, poetry, and culture, and this Christianity's concept of the "intuitive" knowledge of God remained woefully underdeveloped. The intellectual foundation for the evangelical faith remained dependent on the scientific design arguments, especially that of William Paley.[25]

Other, related strands of this development need a brief mention. During the eighteenth century, the concept of Divine Providence, which referred to God's active care of his creation, was redefined as the immutable laws of nature, designed by God, which would guide humanity to scientific and moral progress. Morality, divorced from its traditional context as a part of humanity's journey to God, changed to a concern to be defined solely in terms of human welfare or suffering. Or, as Turner aptly quotes an Anglican divine in 1776, "Cruelty is ATHEISM."[26] The rise of evangelicalism continued this trend, as it emphasized moral excellence and social progress and even identified these, at times, with the personal response to faith in Christ. The result, however, was the implication that the moral authority of God depended on God's conformity to a humanitarian moral standard.

It was precisely in this setting that Darwin's theory of evolution had its lasting impact. The history of subsequent scientific breakthroughs, culminating in Darwin, "proved that the big problems could be explained without God, and they had thus shown God to be unnecessary in [science]."[27] Simply put, there was now nothing in science itself that necessitated a belief in God: "Where science had once pointed beyond nature to God, it now pointed only to nature, behind which lay, if anything, the Unknowable. One might choose to call nature or force or the Unknowable by the name of God. But science offered no justification."[28] That is, the first cause beyond nature no longer resembled the Designer God; indeed, the first cause now became unknowable by science, beyond its inquiry and no longer its concern. This may still seem an open-ended assessment as to whether God exists, but for this: "Religious leaders had, since Newton, insisted on linking science and God. In the half century before Darwin, the certainty of knowledge of God through science had been drummed into Christians more insistently than ever before."[29] Thus, the previous theistic demand for and assumption of scientific certitude regarding the existence of God, met previously by the design argument, backfired into an explicit denial of belief. Furthermore, Darwin's theory posed a further intellectual crisis for the conception of God now made subject to a humanitarian moral standard regarding pain and suffering. For if nature, understood in terms of the new theory of evolution, "were design, its sloppiness and inefficiency suggested gross incompetence; and if this were benevolence, the designer exercised it with a paradoxical delight in suffering."[30] This, along with the history of human suffering, in wars, famines, poverty, and disease, led to the conclusion that God had failed his moral obligation; indeed, it demanded that the believers must abandon their belief in God for moral reasons.

What went wrong? Turner points to a particular development in Christian theism during this period, a development that implicitly demanded that God must measure up to human standards of comprehensibility, knowledge, and morality. Previously, influential figures like John Calvin and Jonathan Edwards were interested in science and extolled the God of nature, yet warned against limiting God to human scientific and moral standards. These warnings, as well as the long Christian tradition that emphasized the ultimate mystery and incomprehensibility of God, largely went unheeded, with disastrous result. Turner concludes: "Put slightly differently, unbelief emerged because church leaders too often forgot the transcendence essential to any worthwhile God. They committed religion *functionally* to making the world better in human terms and *intellectually* to modes of knowing God fitted only for understanding the world. . . . [But] if belief is to remain plausible over the long haul, they cannot regard God as human, sharing human interests and purposes, accessible to human comprehension."[31] It is difficult to say, however, what the Christian leaders should have done instead. Emphasis on transcendence, mystery, and incomprehensibility could have well led to irrelevance of the Christian faith in the increasingly secular, industrialized society. Simply making God incomprehensible may make faith in God incomprehensible.

Turner's final conclusion, however, hints at a deeper problem. "And both believers and unbelievers ought to keep in mind that no one way of knowing reality is the last, best form of human knowledge—more: no one form of knowing can possibly navigate the labyrinth of reality. . . . The universe is not tailored to our measurements. Forgetting that, many believers lost their God."[32] The words I would emphasize in his claim above are "last" and "best"; that is, unbelief had to emerge because the theist conception of God became inextricably wedded to a particular formulation of understanding reality and morality specific to a historical period, which would inevitably be superseded. In allowing this to happen, the theists in question ensured that their belief would rise and fall with the scientific theories and the judgments in moral standards that were fashionable in their time. This is not to say that there is some kind of ahistorical knowledge of God. On the contrary, MacIntyre's account regarding the historically extended forms of rational inquiry that characterize intellectual traditions implies that no understanding of a core set of beliefs in a given worldview can, or does, remain absolutely fixed in its particular formulation and configuration, throughout the long journey through its history. To remain so would be to fail to recognize that human standards of knowing, or living, at any time, are insufficient. It was this that seemed to have been overlooked in the particular intellectual moves made by the Christian theists in Turner's account, spellbound by the promise of certitude and precision offered by what seemed to be an unshakable foundation in the existing sciences and the standards for rational judgment of their day.

Perhaps a question may be raised at this point: did Aquinas not do the same in his formulation of the Christian worldview in his *Summa* when he integrated the theological Augustinian tradition with the predominant sciences and philosophies—namely, Aristotelian intellectual tradition—of his day? A simple answer was already given in chapter 6: Aquinas considered his project essentially incomplete—what he presents is the "best answer so far." However, our emphasis in examining what the Five Ways do, rather than what they argue, should hint at a more proper, and hopefully profound, answer. Before we explore this question, though, we need to further understand the intellectual significance of the particular theistic moves that formed the foundations of modern atheism.

Buckley's Account of the Problematic Development of Theism

In his work *At the Origins of Modern Atheism*, Michael J. Buckley places the root of atheism in the moment the religious apologetics of early modernity declared Newtonian science and mechanics as the "first foundations of religion."[33] The implicit premise of such a strategy was that what is uniquely religious, in experiential, traditional, institutional, liturgical, and social dimensions, was cognitively empty—a premise that contradicted religion and would eventually be actualized in the negation of theism, namely, in the emergence of atheism. He defends this claim further in *Denying and Disclosing God*, by responding to a criticism that his argument is "dialectical and over neat," arguing that what he is presenting is not some Hegelian Idealist theory but an actual, confirmed—indeed, confirmed in other places—pattern in the history of ideas.[34] However, his most significant claim, for our purpose, is summed up in the following:

> Inference cannot simply substitute for experience. One will not long affirm a personal God, who is fundamentally inferred as a conclusion, rather than disclosed as a presence. . . . The most compelling witness to a personal God must itself be personal. To attempt something else as foundation or as substitute, as has been done so often in an effort to secure by inference the reality of God, is to move into a dialectical process generated by internal contradictions of which the ultimate resolution must be atheism.[35]

That is, for Buckley, the problem is in relying upon an inference of God as the foundation for belief, and replacing personal experience with such an inference. Such reliance is precisely the implicit, contradictory premise that what is uniquely religious cannot support a belief in God.

Buckley begins by arguing that examining early, influential figures in science belies the popular belief that modern science and Christianity were antagonistic. Galileo was firm in his conviction that science and religion, as "separate languages," would never truly contradict each other. However, Johannes Kepler went even further, believing that the features of the universe, ascertained from mathematics and observation, may be deduced from Christian theology.[36] Newton followed with the position that "universal mechanics," with which science understands the physical world, could establish a "fundamental religion," "prior to all revelation."[37] That is, science reveals a kind of general religion, prior to any particular religions like Christianity, upon which faith in God is rationally grounded. From the seventeenth century onward, Christian theology increasingly adopted this Newtonian position. Thus, the central claims of the Christian worldview increasingly relied on philosophy, and especially "natural philosophy," as science came to be called, to establish the foundation of that worldview in the form of "fundamental religion."

Buckley outlines the histories of this strategy, which would eventually generate atheism. Descartes, who assumed that the question of the existence of God was to be answered mainly by philosophers rather than theologians, proposed two separate domains, matter and the mind. "Mechanics" was the operating principle only of the former, and the clear and distinct ideas in the latter demonstrated the existence of God. Likewise, Newton asserted that matter was inert and that God was the sole, non-mechanical, first cause that imparts motion to all matter, as the Designer of the mechanical universe. However, Diderot and d'Holbach rejected Descartes's assertion that the mind is a separate sphere. They then argued against Newton that matter itself is inherently dynamic and in motion, and did not need nonmechanical force—namely, God. Similar inversion occurred in biology as a Designer God was thought to be necessary to explain the complexity of living organism until Darwin revealed that biology, just like physics, did not require God. Buckley summarizes the problems that were inherent in this strategy: "[Atheism] arose from the contradiction immanent within the orthodox tradition itself and its apologetic strategies. As dialectical, these . . . embodied an initial contradiction both in content and in form: the impersonal was made the fundamental warrant for the personal; inferential reasoning substituted for disclosure, communication, and real assent. As dialectical, the fatal contradiction was not mounted from the outside; it was immanent within the total career of the argument."[38] The issue at hand is more than that these particular philosophical or scientific positions could not support the belief in God. Rather, placing these as the intellectual foundation for belief was itself a *contradiction*. That is, impersonal, universal, ahistorical features of nature or reason were taken as the only valid kind of support for a personal God, revealed to particular individuals and communities, in particular moments in history, modes of living, and experiences. These strategies, moreover, sought to infer God from the various features of the world or the human subject, as if God is somehow never experienced as a living presence.

Buckley describes a similar pattern during another period in the history of theistic strategy, in the eighteenth century. During this period, starting largely from Locke's *An Essay concerning Human Understanding*, the inquiry into the thinking subject—the human knower—became yet another "foundational" discipline.[39] This alternative "foundation" provided another strategy for intellectually grounding belief in God, though this time, in human nature. Thus, Kant sought to infer God as the necessary postulate for humanity's ethical enterprise, and Schleiermacher sought to place God in the human experience of absolute dependence. "In both," Buckley notes, "God emerged as a necessity to deal with human life and experience. God was an entailment, not of design in nature, but of the human."[40] However, Ludwig Feuerbach, Karl Marx, Nietzsche, and Sigmund Freud turned this project on its head by arguing that it is the human that is necessary for God. That is, God is merely the projection of humanity, its noble or base qualities, its hopes and fears. As such, God is antihuman—a product, or even the cause, of humanity's radical misunderstanding of itself and its conditions, thereby alienating humanity from itself and its destiny.

Buckley identifies the contradiction implicit in this strategy:

> The conclusions reached in each of these systems and habits of religious thought overtly and emphatically affirmed the absolute centrality of God, with the human being finite and created. But the drift of the philosophical arguments by which this conclusion was sustained depended increasingly, though covertly, upon the absolute centrality of the human being, conferring on God a useful function or allotting value from the manner in which he touched human life. . . . God and the human being had in this way been placed initially in an unrecognized struggle for primacy. In this unspoken polar opposition, one must perish that the other may live as absolute and central.[41]

That is, affirmation of God inferred through the human subject already implied the primacy of the human and left both in a destructive competition for supremacy.

The main theme of Buckley's account in *Denying and Disclosing God* is similar to Turner's in that the particular intellectual moves by theists during the seventeenth to nineteenth centuries generated atheism. However, Buckley identifies what may be called a coherence, or logical, problem. That is, whereas for Turner, the moves introduced a vulnerability to the Christian conception of God, for Buckley, the moves introduced a contradiction. For Turner, unbelief emerged from theistic development that led to a limited and restricted conception of God, unnecessarily vulnerable to new discoveries and social changes. For Buckley, the theists misunderstood the *kind* of evidence appropriate to the *kind* of God it sought to prove. The belief in a unique, personal God requires a particular, religious mode of thinking, and indeed, a way of life—a life of saints that manifests God concretely. In this way, Buckley anticipates Moser's argument briefly mentioned in chapter 2; we can even understand Moser's account of the kind of evidence and reasons needed for the belief in God as a corrective response to precisely the kind of contradiction Buckley identified in the development of modern Christian theism.[42] This is not to say that Buckley believes "critical reasoning, institutions, science, and philosophy" have no place, but rather that they are inseparable, intellectually, from the personal, religious, and experiential dimensions of faith.[43]

THE SUBORDINATION OF GOD IN THE NEW, MODERN WORLDVIEW

A significant point that both Turner and Buckley raise, but that neither examines thoroughly, is that the intellectual moves made by Christian theists constituted a significant change to their worldview as a whole, directly affecting their concept of God and consequently their concepts of nature, humanity, and others. Consider, for example, Turner's contention that God was made subject to human standards: this does not simply make the belief in God vulnerable; it radically changes the concept of God, its content and its function in that worldview. That is, this move changes the concept of God from that of transcendent, and largely unknowable God—who is, for Aquinas, "Being," "Truth," "Goodness" itself, and who is thus the standard by which humanity is measured and the ultimate telos to which every inquiry proceeds—to that of a particular piece in that worldview, now subject to a higher standard. Simply put, in Turner's account, "God" is no longer God; he is dethroned. There is now something higher—human standards of morality, scientific knowledge, and so forth, to which "God" submits. God is shorn of his divine qualities, which are given to another.

A similar point may be made regarding Buckley's account. For God to be known only through inference, his presence must be removed; it must be removed from what we come to know through our sciences, our history, our moral endeavors, and so forth, before it becomes necessary to infer his existence back from them. However, this is not possible in the Thomistic standpoint, where God is already present through his creative act in all that exists, as "Being," "Truth," and "Goodness" itself. Again, it nearly seems banal—but is nonetheless significant—that divine qualities of God were somehow stripped away in the modern Christian worldview and given to something else, thereby distorting the core Christian concept of God and his relation to the creation.

A remarkably similar assessment is made recently by Hanby, who presents perhaps the most thorough account of such distortions to Christian theology from which the modern atheist position emerged.[44] He argues that tacit metaphysical, theological assumptions and judgments underlie modern science, and thus scientific atheism, insofar as these assumptions and judgments denote the *kind* of "God" atheism disbelieves. Yet these assumptions, which became metaphysical foundations of Newtonian physics and consequently of the mechanistic understanding of nature, came about by a redefining of key concepts such as cause, matter, and motion, and reducing or even abandoning a substantive understanding of being, truth, essence, and indeed, "universe" itself as "unity of being."[45] However, these were precisely the concepts that had continued to develop from Greek philosophy and through Christian thought, and with which one may properly understand notions of "creation" and "God." Thus, subsequent understandings of God and creation were altered so that "nature" became "artifice," "creation" became "manufacture," and "God" became an "artisan" in the same order of being as the rest of creation.[46] It is this "God" that Darwinism understands itself to have successfully displaced.

Consequently, in the contemporary debate about God that involves natural science, such as the creation-versus-evolution debate, both sides of the debate expect the doctrine of creation to answer questions it was never meant to answer. The question that concerns the participants of such a debate is *how* or even *why* the universe came to be, whereas the primary question that the doctrine answers is *what* the universe *is*.[47]

Thus, from the very start, the debate about science and God, and likewise the debate about the existence of God that stands upon it, is tainted with a distorted theology of God and creation, developed from a series of particular missteps in the Christian theological worldview and incorporated into modern atheism during the construction of its worldviews in the last three centuries. All of this was what modernity now understands as coming to "merely disbelieve" the existence of God.

Let us narrow our attention, however, specifically to the concept most relevant to the Five Ways. How has the concept of God, as the "first cause" in the intellectual inquiry of rival worldviews or traditions, changed through this period? An example of a conventional account of this change is given in Diogenes Allen's *Philosophy for Understanding Theology.* Allen begins his account of the beginning of modern philosophy by remarking how it was from the work of Galileo and Descartes that "Aristotle received his fatal wounds," because both of them, "for different reasons, considered only the *mathematical* properties of bodies as essential and objectively present in bodies."[48] This view implied that bodies consist of nothing more than extension, geometrical shape, and capability of physical motion or rest, and if the view was accepted, most of the metaphysical properties, through which Aristotelian intellectual inquiry formed its conceptions of reality—that is, the very means through which such inquiry was possible—would become obsolete. The theory of impetus, proposed by Galileo, which advocated a radical change in the conception of motion, exacerbated this problem. Allen notes that "for Aristotle a moving thing has a mover acting on it *while* it is moving. Motion requires the *continuous* action of a mover."[49] The theory of impetus, however, provided a better explanation of how a projectile moves despite being no longer in contact with its original mover.[50] This particular defeat led to the abandonment of the entire Aristotelian intellectual system.

The conception of God as the first cause, so closely bound to Aristotelian conceptions, also became obsolete. The Aristotelian theory of motion that "whatever moves has a mover continuous with the motion (or has something always in the state of act)" implied that all motion, at all times, requires God as the First Mover.[51] That is, each cause of the motion in the chain of causes must continuously be in act to cause the motion, and such chain goes on until it reaches God, who must also always be in the act of causing that motion to the rest of the chain. The theory of impetus and inertia denied this Aristotelian notion of God. However, Allen writes: "Deity was not wholly excluded by the new mechanistic science. God's continuous presence was not needed, but nonetheless a deity was required. Although nature was able to keep moving once set in motion, it had to get its *first* push from somewhere, and indeed its very existence."[52] This then led eventually to the further conception that this "first cause" must be intelligent because of the orderliness and design in nature.

Herein lies the development of the "first cause" in the modern sense—a significant divergence from what Aquinas had accomplished through the Five Ways. What I am concerned about here is not the abandonment of Aristotelian physics or its metaphysics, and with it Aquinas's synthesis, which had profound theological consequences as Hanby has argued. Here, I am arguing that the new conception of God as the "first cause" simply *did not accomplish* what Aquinas's conception did. In the new development, God becomes a hypothesis, albeit for that time a crucially important one. Whereas Aquinas identified as God that without which intellectual inquiry as such in the Aristotelian worldview becomes impossible and to which all inquiry ultimately aims, God in the Newtonian system and onward becomes a particular hypothesis without which a particular stage in its intellectual inquiry is incomplete. To put it differently, whereas for Aquinas, God of the Five Ways was disclosed as that through which theory making as such—or simply, science itself—proceeds, in the modern conception, God is that which a particular scientific theory at a given point in time renders necessary or probable. Thus, God becomes merely one of the components in the new worldview, subordinate to a higher standard that directs its intellectual inquiry; the concept of God is now a piece of the worldview, used as a tool for that which modern science seeks—the "Truth" of "Nature." "God" is no longer "Truth" itself. "God" is no longer God.

Let us recall at this point the caveat noted in chapter 5 regarding how the word "existence" is used by Aquinas. I suggest that herein lies one of the reasons for the key difference we noted in what Aquinas means by the "existence" (*esse*) of God, and how the word "existence" is generally defined. Particular, individual components of our worldview "exist" in the way we generally define "exist." That is, they are particular beings whose existence our intellectual inquiry may theorize or encounter, confirm, or disconfirm. However, that which is in the very thinking of the intellectual inquiry of our worldview does not "exist" in that sense. This is how God is transcendent in the Christian worldview; God is not a member inhabiting the domain of its reality.

Yet on the other hand, precisely because God is transcendent in this way, God is also immanent in all that exists. That which Aquinas identifies as God in both the Christian and Aristotelian worldviews through the Five Ways is such that every rational inquiry, indeed every experience as rationally understood, holds the presence of God; that is, God is the principle of being of each and every existence for all time. Thus, in this, Allen's account quoted above is misleading; for the Thomistic standpoint, the conception of the active presence of God in nature does not primarily depend on Aristotle's position on the spatial motion of bodies. However, in the modern conception, God becomes, in Buckley's words, an "inference"; indeed, whereas for Aquinas, God as the "first cause" implies the presence of God in all things, for the modern, mechanistic worldview, God as the "first cause" came to imply the absence of God in all other things. That is, this conception of God as a component in a theory—metaphysical or scientific—by which I mean a part of a world-picture rather than its very basis, limited God to a corner of that picture and excised his presence from the rest.

It is only in this context that divine action is necessarily understood, in popular terms and by a number of scientists, as an unnatural "intervention" in Nature. Such a view assumes that aside from the first act of setting the universe into motion to evolve according to the preset laws of nature, any natural event is by definition precluded from being specifically an act of God.[53] Yet such an exclusive disjunction would be unintelligible for the Thomistic understanding of God. Likewise, it is only in such context that the immanence of God becomes an incoherent concept apart from a significantly pantheistic concept of God, in which Nature becomes increasingly equated with God. This modern conception of God as the first cause thereby marks the beginning of the contemporary meaning of the word "Nature," with a capital "N." Simply put, those who affirm the existence of "God" in such a changed worldview no longer affirm the "God" that the Five Ways are pointing to.[54]

The problem I have outlined so far in the intellectual moves by theists to adapt their conception of God as the first cause in the modern scientific age resulted at the very least in their failure to accomplish in the new, modern forms of intellectual inquiry what Aquinas accomplished for the Aristotelian forms. Yet such failure may have been inevitable. This is because we are only now, through the works of those like Kuhn, Lakatos, and MacIntyre, understanding how the form of intellectual inquiry which we call modern science is really carried out. It may have been impossible to accurately identify, as Aquinas did with Aristotelian conceptions of inquiry, what features if any in science enable it to be a rational inquiry as such—let alone ask how the conception of God as the first cause relates to these features. However, in failing to identify those features, theists impoverished or even distorted the concept of God, and combined with the particular historical moves and developments narrated above, this provided the conceptual foundation from which modern atheism as a worldview could be constructed and then understood in terms of simple negation.

EIGHT

To Set Out

Arguing from the Crossroads to God

A metaphor, or a picture, can hold captive our philosophical understanding, especially when it is not recognized as a metaphor.[1] For the debate about the existence of God, an example of such a metaphor is the view that Nature is a "machine," and God is its no-longer-present "Designer," the existence of whom we must *posit* in addition to the universe by inference from its mechanical structures. Another important example is Flew's parable of the two explorers, searching for an invisible, and again absent, "gardener." Such metaphors and pictures pervade our discourse and shape the terms and the language with which the debate proceeds, and in turn are reinforced. What I have presented through yet another parable of the two explorers is also a metaphor, which suggests a different understanding of what it is to argue about the existence of God. To be precise, it is a subversion of the metaphor; what seemed to be a straightforward debate is revealed—through the introduction of the larger context, namely the background of the explorers themselves—to be in fact sterile, with incommensurable differences between rival positions. However, from our standpoint, there is a different way to proceed in the debate, a different way for them to understand and address the question. This is what I have proposed for the debate about the existence of God.

For this argument, I have first presented a growing case against yet another set of philosophical metaphors—that is, the Enlightenment picture of rationality as a timeless, neutral "mirror of nature," in which we find the indubitable beliefs that constitute a single, universal "foundation" upon which every form of intellectual inquiry must "build" its body of knowledge. In contrast, I have argued from the contemporary conceptions of rationality, especially from MacIntyre, for a different metaphor—that of intellectual inquiry as a "quest," or a "journey." The debate regarding the existence of God between theists, atheists, and so forth represents a crossroad of such journeys—a crossroad of worldviews. The dominant "pictures" that held us captive in regard to how we ought to answer the question of whether God exists are in significant ways defective—they have led to an "odd" way of arguing about the existence of God—and there is a more promising, fruitful picture. In this way, what is being proposed is quite literally a Gestalt-switch from one picture to the other.

These different metaphors lead to a different understanding of what it is to argue that God exists. For those who are "held captive" by the metaphors rooted in the epistemological ideals of the Enlightenment, the belief that God exists is argued from, and supported by, the "foundation" of knowledge. In this understanding, the existence of God as the first cause is a *postulation*, which is "proved" by rational argumentation. For those who follow the metaphor of the no-longer-present "Designer" God of a "machine" universe, God is posited as an explanatory hypothesis for a particular scientific world-picture at a particular stage in its inquiry. In such a case, the "God" of such a hypothesis is discarded whenever such world-picture is revised or changed in significant ways—as was the case when the new theory of evolution explained the seeming design of living creatures, and will be the case if, say, the "multiverse" hypothesis is ever confirmed, thus explaining the "fine-tuning" of the universe. However, from the metaphor of the crossroads of worldviews, I suggest a different understanding of what it is to say that God exists. I have argued that for Aquinas, the existence of God is that which renders intelligible and possible the rational inquiry with which each rival worldview at the crossroad forms, revises, or abandons its intellectual positions. That is, God is that which is present in, and inseparable from, the *journey itself* to its ultimate destination, and in that sense is present in the very road that leads to the destination, including the road already traveled and the road yet to be traveled. Here, God is not a "hypothesis" that may be discarded when a worldview is revised or changed, but that *through* which, and *about* which, such changes can take place.

One significant question I have left unanswered is how we are to argue about the existence of God in the contemporary debate if this is the case. A complete answer to this, however, cannot be given in the context of this work precisely because such an answer would require the kind of extensive project exemplified by the entire *Summa Theologiae* of Aquinas. That is, a complete answer, which constitutes an actual case for or against the existence of God, is inseparable from such a large-scale project. However, I will suggest the beginning of such a project, from the standpoint of a theist.

THE ARGUMENT SO FAR AS A STARTING POINT

The Argument So Far as an Example of MacIntyrean Rational Argument

Consider the argumentation of this book so far. The particular form of its argumentation and its standards of justification have in fact followed what I have proposed as the most promising conception of rationality and justification so far—that of MacIntyre—which responds adequately to the difficulty that inevitably arises in the debate between rival worldviews in contemporary philosophy.

For example, what I have presented regarding the shift in our conception of rationality and intellectual inquiry consisted primarily in a narrative of a particular development in philosophy. It first described what was once the predominant philosophical position on rationality, namely the Enlightenment epistemology and its contemporary classical foundationalist variants, and proceeded to outline the difficulties and failures that the proponents of this position recognized, or ought to have recognized, as failures in its own terms. The narrative then sketched out how the conceptions of rationality and knowledge consequently shifted and developed through the writings of figures like Quine, Kuhn, and Rorty. Through this, I argued how MacIntyre especially presents the best understanding of rationality and intellectual inquiry so far, insofar as this understanding explains why the Enlightenment position regarding these conceptions encountered insoluble difficulties, and inevitably so, in ways that the proponents of this position could not understand from their standpoint. Furthermore, in doing so, I observed how these new conceptions present a more accurate account of the actual, historical practices of rational inquiry, such as those followed in the natural sciences. Thus, the narrative I presented, though necessarily selective, is consciously structured to describe comparatively in what ways the "best" position so far develops from, and transcends the limitations of, the prior positions. That is, the form of argumentation I present follows that which MacIntyre describes in his account.

The argument of this book regarding the debate about the existence of God also presents such a narrative. I have described how our understanding of what it is to argue about the existence of God has led to a number of seemingly insoluble problems, interminable arguments and counterarguments, proliferating variations and configurations of opposing positions, and the incommensurable differences between them. Then, I proposed a particular understanding of the debate with which we may explain how these difficulties arise, and often inevitably so, thereby presenting a viable way to resolve these difficulties and surpass the limitations of our present positions. I described how this understanding derives from the most promising philosophical position so far regarding rationality and intellectual inquiry—a position argued as rationally superior, precisely by resolving the problems and transcending the limitations of the other positions. Finally, I have specified how the particular understanding I propose presents a more accurate account of an actual, historical exemplar of theistic arguments, namely, the Five Ways of Aquinas.

That is, the main argument of this book itself consciously follows the standard of what it has proposed as the most promising account so far regarding rational argumentation for or against large-scale, comprehensive intellectual positions, such as worldviews. How is this relevant to the question of whether God exists in the contemporary setting? Just as how I have argued throughout this book follows the general form of what I have presented as the best form of argumentation for the kind of questions I raised, the argument about the existence of God implicit in my position has followed what I have argued is the best form of argumentation from and to rival worldviews so far—namely, how Aquinas argued by bringing together rival intellectual traditions, as described by MacIntyre. That is, my argument so far is itself also an argumentation at a crossroad of worldviews, or more precisely, the beginning of such an argument.

The Argument So Far as a Beginning of the Argument at the Crossroads

Again, consider the argument so far. It begins by describing the position which both theists and atheists seemingly share—a particular understanding of what it is to rationally argue about the existence of God—and then specifies the difficulties and limitations of such a position. What I have proposed as a more promising understanding is in fact constructed from the significant concepts and positions from the intellectual history of both worldviews. The term "worldview" is itself an important concept with a long philosophical history in both intellectual positions, to the extent that to say theist and atheist positions are "worldviews" would have been a banal statement were it not for the contemporary philosophical shift in our understanding of rationality and intellectual inquiry relevant to the concept. This shift, which includes the writings of Quine, Kuhn, Rorty, and others, is in turn a contemporary development in the history of secular, and nontheistic, philosophy. However, in developing my position from their works, I am certainly not arguing from some neutral standpoint—nor is a "neutral" position necessarily secular, as I have argued precisely against this very possibility. Neither am I arguing simply from a nontheist position; MacIntyre—at least in his later writings—belongs to a theist, Thomist intellectual tradition, and the primary historical exemplar I examine is Aquinas.

Therefore, I am arguing from a crossroad of particular worldviews, a place where their narratives intersect. That is, my argument begins from the current standpoint of both the atheist and the theist intellectual positions regarding the conceptions of rationality, intellectual inquiry, and worldviews that are relevant to the question of the existence of God. Simply, it begins from what would be considered the best answers on these related issues so far, for both positions.

Furthermore, as I have consciously and repeatedly remarked, what I have argued, insofar as it argues from the positions of those like Kuhn, Rorty, and others, does not depend on the more controversial aspects of their works such as the implication of relativism or irrationality of science, or the rejection of any substantive notion of truth. This is not simply because I seek to avoid controversy; it is because those who actually participate in a "rational" debate about the existence of God tend to hold a particular set of assumptions regarding the rationality of science, notion of truth, and so forth that are contrary to those controversial perspectives. Thus, I am arguing from a particular crossroad of two particular kinds of rival worldviews, more specifically, the crossroad of a Christian, Thomistic intellectual tradition on the one hand and scientific naturalism and its variants on the other. What I would have argued throughout this book, and the writings I would have examined, would have differed greatly if the crossroad had been between, for example, a Christian and a Nietzschean worldview, not only because the topic of the book would differ, but more importantly, because the *crossing point* of the two positions—assuming such exists in this case—would have differed.

This then is the beginning of an answer to a possible set of objections from a key movement in philosophy of religion, Continental postmodern philosophy, discussions of which were conspicuously absent in this book. The proponents of this movement would apply the works of Continental philosophers like Heidegger, and especially Derrida—far too briefly mentioned in chapter 3—to question any claims of coherence, wholeness, and totality, which are features I will seem to have presented as characterizing worldviews. The reason why participants in such a key movement are not covered in this book is that, as far as I can tell, they are not among the primary participants of the contemporary "rational" debate about the existence of God; their position would preclude them from participating. That is, the movement is not among the intellectual positions that will be present at the particular crossroad in which the existence of God is debated through what is purported to be rational argumentation. This is certainly not to say that the objections they would raise against the debate itself, or some of the features inherent in the very concept of worldviews, are not significant for my argument so far—but the kind of questions I have raised so far in this book leads us to a different crossing point of intellectual positions than the one we would have arrived at had we engaged their position.[2] That is, to participate in the rational debate about the existence of God implies a particular kind of crossing, involving a particular kind of worldviews.

All of this is why in chapter 4 I argued specifically against the notion of a worldview-by-default, composed only of scientific statements, which is what scientism claims itself to be; it is a particularly widespread view of one of the worldviews at this kind of crossroad, and more importantly it is a view that precludes its proponents from even perceiving the crossroad. Scientism, as examined in chapter 4, itself holds a particular position in metaphysics and epistemology—and, as it turns out, a self-referentially incoherent one at that. However, I considered this to be an insufficient (though significant) critique of scientism. This is because from the standpoint of those who hold such a worldview, it would seem that they are "merely" starting with, or "simply" affirming, only the scientific knowledge, without necessarily claiming a metaphysical position that states that the only things that exist in the world are those known scientifically. Thus, I began from this standpoint, to eventually conclude that even the "scientific" worldview characterized in this way cannot avoid—and in fact, has already answered—the nonscientific, metaphysical questions regarding the laws of nature, scientific concepts, the relation and organization of different scientific disciplines, and so forth that inevitably arise from the solely "scientific" body of knowledge it claims to affirm; without answers to these questions, it becomes incoherent and unintelligible to itself.[3] Again, this type of argument was required because to argue from the crossroad of worldviews, a participant must pose such a critique from within, and in the terms and frame of, the particular, rival worldview at the crossroad.

To sum, if I have argued convincingly for a new way of understanding what it is to argue about the existence of God, it will be because I have presented a plausible case from the standpoints of both the particular atheist and theist positions in the debate and solved the problems, difficulties, and limitations that are recognized—or ought to be recognized—as such in the terms of those who hold these positions.[4] Moreover, in this new understanding, some of the significant terms and assumptions from which the debate about the existence of God has proceeded so far will need to be abandoned. There is no neutral rationality, nor a "by-default" or "purely scientific" worldview. The debate does not begin from the "presumption of atheism." The holistic conception of belief systems and worldviews implies that there is no "properly basic belief," which serves simply as a completely independent "foundation" of epistemological justification; rather, each worldview has a set of core beliefs that are partially revisable. More importantly, it is not the case that the theist "posits" or "postulates" the existence of God *in addition to* the "universe," in a neutral framework of inquiry.

Such a shift in our understanding of what it is to argue about the existence of God redefines what it would be to have argued successfully, for both the theist and the atheist positions. Thus, I have first shown how the conventional arguments about the existence of God in the contemporary debate are generally faced with significant difficulties, and necessarily so, from the standpoint of the most significant contemporary conception of rationality and intellectual inquiry, summed up in the concept of worldview. Then, I have proposed through the example of the Five Ways of Aquinas a different way to argue for the existence of God, even though the theist and the atheist positions in the debate are comprehensive and incommensurable worldviews. What is significant here is that what my arguments *do*, so far, parallels what the two articles in the *Summa*, prior to the Five Ways, also *do*. In the first article, Aquinas argues that the existence of God is not self-evident, by explaining how the major arguments for the existence of God, such as arguing from the concept of God to his existence, are simply untenable. In the second article, he argues that the existence of God is nevertheless rationally demonstrable, and defines what kind of argumentation does in fact demonstrate God's existence. Thus, just as Aquinas presents the arguments of the first two articles, which lead to the Five Ways, what I have argued is a necessary preliminary to the new "Five Ways."

However, what would be the "Five Ways" of our day?

FINDING GOD AT THE CROSSROAD OF WORLDVIEWS

Identifying That Which Is in the Thinking of Both Worldviews

Again, a complete answer to this is beyond the scope of this work. However, from the argument of this book so far, through our examination of MacIntyre's account of rationality and intellectual inquiry and what the Five Ways of Aquinas accomplished, we can outline what such an argument at the crossroad will be in our contemporary debate.

First, a theist will need to identify and disclose that which is already in some significant way present in the rival worldview, which the theist—or more specifically a Christian—would "call" God. Conversely, a theistic argument that posits an additional entity, namely God, which is central to the theist worldview but foreign and unnecessary to its rival, will tend to fail. However, the problem then is whether it is possible to identify anything in the rival worldview as something which the theist would "understand as God," as Aquinas puts it, and if so, how.

However, there are some further guidelines. Phillips argued, as we saw in chapter 2, that the existence of God is a "basic" belief for practicing theists, in the sense that it is that which is in the very reasoning and thinking of what we would call a worldview and is that which stands or falls together with the entire worldview itself. Furthermore, as we have seen in MacIntyre's account of intellectual traditions, a worldview is historically extended. That is, a worldview changes and revises its beliefs through time, and it is precisely the historical narrative of how it has rationally formed, changed, revised, or developed its intellectual position in response to its past problems, difficulties, and limitations that constitutes its rationality.

Therefore, what is truly "basic" to a worldview, in the way Phillips defines it, is that which is *in* this very narrative—*in* the journey itself, so to speak. Such a belief then remains constant through the changes in the worldview, because it is inseparable from the thinking and reasoning of that worldview, through which the worldview changes and develops. To abandon such a "basic" belief, therefore, is to not only abandon a particular intellectual position of the worldview at a particular time, but to abandon the entire worldview as a historically extended tradition—that is, to abandon the journey itself. For a theist worldview, the belief in the existence of God is "basic" in this way. However, the very reason why Phillips has argued that the existence of God is not a matter of rational argument is precisely what makes such arguments possible, in the kind of debate about God I am proposing. That is, a part of the task for a new kind of argument for the existence of God is to identify a belief which is in the thinking of, and is thus "basic" to, the rival worldview, as "God" is in the theist worldview.

However, what is identified and, in Aquinas's words, "understood as God" in the rival worldview is not the belief itself, but the object of such a belief. Thus, to identify what is "basic" in the rival worldview, in our contemporary debate, is primarily an ontological or a metaphysical question. What do I mean? Recall that in the Platonic and Aristotelian philosophy, metaphysics is inseparable from the philosophers' conception of rational inquiry; for example, the Platonic theory of Forms is a theory both of what truly exists in reality—namely, the Forms—and the "program" for constructing an intellectual inquiry through which to know them. Therefore, what a theist is to identify and "understand as God" in the rival worldview is that which is (a) believed to be real, or to exist, and (b) "basic" in that it is in the very thinking and reasoning of the worldview, throughout its entire historical development. In this sense, whatever is to be "called God" would be a necessary being in terms of that particular worldview; that is, it is believed to exist regardless of how the particular set of beliefs in that worldview changes.

Thus, in my position, "God" may be defined as that which exists in every possible world, a statement that interestingly parallels part of Plantinga's modal ontological argument, but with a very different meaning and purpose. First, what is understood as "God" would exist in every possible variation of the intellectual positions in the history of a *particular worldview*, as its "basic" belief. Second, what a theist would identify as "God" would exist in every possible variation of the rival worldview as the object of its "basic" belief. However, this understanding of "God" is not an argument that God actually exists; after all, it is always possible that a theist is unable to identify such a "basic" belief—or to be precise, object of that belief—in a particular rival worldview. Rather, it is a proposal of how a theist may construct a position, a crossroad, from which to begin the project of bringing together rival, incommensurable worldviews.

What I have stated so far underscores the point that there is no "neutral" argument, which works for all—or perhaps even most—worldviews at all times. That is, to begin an argument by "identifying" or "disclosing" that which a theist may call "God" in the rival worldview requires an investigation of a particular worldview, understanding its beliefs from within its standpoint and in its own terms. What is identified as "God" in such a case will be particular to that worldview. Thus, the example of the beginning of an argument I will propose below is an argument from the crossroad of specifically Christian theism and scientific naturalism.

Identifying That Which We Call "God" as the First Principle of the Sciences

How are we then to argue from a crossroad specifically between Christian theism and scientific naturalism? That is, how would a theist find what he or she may identify as "God" in a rival worldview that denies that God exists? Again, our account of Aquinas in chapter 6 offers further directions.

In chapter 6, we examined how Aquinas identified "God" with the absolute "first principle" of the "first science." For both of the rival traditions, the Augustinian and the Aristotelian, there is a notion of a perfected science, or a completed inquiry, in which everything in the subject matter is understood in a unified, grand explanation, because in such a perfected science, every concrete, or particular, truth in it is known deductively from its first principle. Furthermore, sciences are hierarchically organized, so that the first principles of one science are based upon the conclusion of another, and so forth, all the way to the first principles of the "first science." Thus, in this hierarchy, the first principles of every science ultimately derive from the absolute "first principle," which Aquinas identifies as God. This knowledge of the "first principle" is the knowledge of God himself, regarding himself and all of creation, and thus is divine omniscience. Thus, human beings cannot reach this state of understanding in this life, but unless there is such an understanding, the intellectual inquiry as such of both the Augustinian and Aristotelian traditions will be rendered unintelligible.

However, this particular conception of God, as described in chapter 6, would enable a theist to identify what may be called "God" only in worldviews that have similar conceptions of intellectual inquiry. That is, to use this particular strategy to identify "God" in a rival worldview would require that the particular worldview holds similar conceptions of first principles, a hierarchically organized set of sciences, and a notion of a perfected, or completed, inquiry in a given subject matter. This is precisely what a worldview such as scientific naturalism does hold.

I briefly mentioned in chapter 4 that there are a number of positions regarding how sciences are to be organized hierarchically and how some even include ethics, metaphysics, or theology in the hierarchy. Murphy, for example, argues that sciences may be organized as a hierarchy in terms of either "increasing complexity of systems studied," or "more encompassing wholes."[5] According to the former criterion, the "more complex system" of "higher" sciences would be based on the more fundamental "lower sciences"; thus the order from lower to higher science would go from physics, to chemistry, to biology, eventually to psychology, and finally to the social sciences. According to the latter criterion, the highest science would be cosmology, which encompasses everything. The details of how sciences are to be organized do not concern us here, but simply that there is such a hierarchy.[6]

What is of interest is the reference at this point to Arthur Peacocke's proposal that "theology should be seen as the science at the top of the hierarchy, since it is the study of the most encompassing system possible—God in relation to everything else that is."[7] This, of course, is not the case for scientific naturalism. However, although "theology" is not the highest science for such a worldview, I have argued that the scientific naturalist position inevitably raises what we may term "metaphysical" questions regarding the laws of nature, scientific concepts, and so forth. That is, the "highest science" for scientific naturalism seems to be—instead of "theology"—its implicit and usually unrecognized intellectual position regarding these metaphysical questions. If a theist is to find what he or she may call "God" in scientific naturalism, it will be at this level of its worldview. What will it be? Here I will suggest one candidate that seems to fit what I have described so far.

"God" and the "Laws of Nature"

In modern science, the concept of the laws of nature is that which is closest to the Aristotelian conception of first principles. To know the laws of nature is to know how the world is; a perfected science is precisely the complete knowledge of all the laws that govern the behaviors of things in that subject matter. Such sciences are hierarchically—and often reductively—organized so that the laws of "higher" sciences that study more complex systems, such as biology, may be reduced to, or at least will be based on, the "lower," or more fundamental science, such as physics. In such a hierarchy, there would be a set of "ultimate laws" in the most fundamental science, which explains—at least in principle, insofar as the "laws" of other sciences are based upon these laws—the existence and behavior of everything. Stephen Hawking, in *A Brief History of Time*, speaks of the quest of physics for such "ultimate laws," and describes its significance: "However, if we do discover a complete theory . . . [if we find the answer to] why it is that we and the universe exist, . . . it would be the ultimate triumph of human reason—for then we would know the mind of God."[8] Hawking invokes the term "mind of God," and indeed "God," as a metaphor. Although he does not explicitly state his atheistic position regarding the existence of God in this book—which he does elsewhere—*A Brief History of Time* has become influential at the popular level as a classic work—almost a Bible!—of scientific naturalism.

This is precisely because, I suggest, the phrase "laws of nature" function like the word God in scientific naturalism, and thus it is inevitable that the narrative of the quest for such laws, written by a foremost scientist of the age involved in such a quest, becomes so significant in this worldview. In this case, it is even more significant that for Hawking, knowing the ultimate laws of physics is equated, however metaphorically, to "[knowing] the mind of God." This almost divine status of the laws becomes even more evident in Hawking's most recent book, where he writes: "Because there is a law like gravity, the universe can and will create itself from nothing. . . . Spontaneous creation is the reason there is something rather than nothing, why the universe exists, why we exist. It is not necessary to invoke God to light the blue touch paper and set the universe going."[9] That is, if the laws of nature explain how the universe began, then there is no need for God, because the universe "[creates] itself from nothing," because of the laws.[10]

The precise content of the ultimate laws of nature is debated in science, but that the laws *are* is affirmed by Hawking emphatically. Consider Hawking's words again: "As I shall describe, the prospects for finding such a theory [of ultimate laws of nature] seem to be much better now because we know so much more about the universe. But we must beware of overconfidence—we have had false dawns before! . . . Having said this, I still believe there are grounds for cautious optimism that we may now be near the end of the search for the ultimate laws of nature."[11] It may seem odd to assume that there are such "ultimate laws," let alone to hold a "cautious optimism" that we are close to discovering what they are. After all, such a claim, by Hawking's own admission, turned out repeatedly to be "false dawns." However, I note the parallel here with Aquinas's position that we cannot know what God is, but *that* he *is*. That is, rather like the concept of God as the first cause in Aquinas, the concept of the laws of nature at the ultimate level is a concept without which scientific inquiry as such would cease to be intelligible.

It may be argued that a scientific naturalist is not required to hold such a belief in the "ultimate laws." To this I reply first that nevertheless, the concept of the laws of nature in general—though perhaps not the "ultimate laws"—is indispensable to science as an intellectual inquiry. Second, a number of influential proponents of this worldview, such as Hawking, do hold such a belief in "ultimate laws," and a theist argument at the crossroad, in this case, would differ depending on this particular variation in the scientific naturalist worldview. Moreover, it seems to me that most scientific naturalists would see no reason to reject the notion of such laws, because of the past successes of science. Therefore, the concept of the laws of nature seems to possess characteristics similar to those of the concept of "God" as the first cause, understood in the context of its place in the Augustinian and Aristotelian conception of intellectual inquiry. That is, it is what a theist may "call God," in a scientific naturalist worldview.

A further case for this is found when Alister McGrath presents what he describes as a "general consensus on the nature and scope of the 'laws of nature,' within the scientific community, set out by Paul Davies":[12]

In general terms, the "laws of nature" can be considered to have the following features.

1. They are *universal.* The laws of physics are to be assumed to be valid at every place and every time. They are held "to apply unfailingly everywhere in the universe and at all epochs of cosmic history."
2. They are *absolute*—that is to say, they do not depend on the nature of the observer. . . . The state of a system may change over time, and be related to a series of contingent and circumstantial considerations; the laws, which provide correlation between those states at various moments, do not change with time.

3. They are *eternal*, in that they are held to be grounded in the mathematical structures which are used to represent the physical world. . . .

4. They are *omnipotent*, in that nothing can be held to be outside their scope.

It will be clear that these attributes show remarkable affinities with those which are traditionally applied to God.[13]

In the last observation McGrath is echoing Paul Davies, who writes: "Curiously, the laws have been invested with many of the qualities that were formally attributed to the God from which they were once supposed to have come."[14] What is "remarkable," or "curious," may be explained—as we have examined in chapter 7—when we consider how modern atheism emerged in significant ways through a number of theological moves in Christianity that divested God of key qualities. However, what is important for our purpose here is that if a theist seeks to identify what he or she would "call God" in a scientific naturalist worldview, in the way that Aquinas does in the Five Ways, the laws of nature increasingly seem to be the best candidate with which to begin.[15]

ARGUMENT FOR THE EXISTENCE OF GOD

The Issues That "Dissolve" in the New Debate on the Existence of God

What follows is a suggestion, a possible way a theist may begin an argument for the existence of God at a crossroad between Christian theism and scientific naturalism. The purpose of this suggestion is to outline how the debate about the existence of God will proceed differently if we hold the kind of understanding I have proposed regarding what it is to argue about the existence of God.

The observation that there is a parallel between "the laws of nature" and "God" is, at first glance, not a significant nor a novel claim. However, I have argued that a rational argument for the existence of God at the crossroad begins—and here I must emphasize that it is only a beginning of such an argument—precisely from identification of such a parallel. Standard contemporary theist arguments put forth the laws of nature, and thus the order of the cosmos, as evidence for the existence of God. The scientific naturalist therefore asks why we must posit the existence of God in addition to the universe governed by such "laws of nature." The debate then becomes whether the laws of nature are sufficient to explain the universe, or whether we need to postulate something else, namely, God. Or in the case of Swinburne, whether all the "brute facts" described by these different laws are "simpler" than the hypothesis of God that brought these laws into being. However, what I have proposed as an argument does not posit an additional entity; it simply identifies what the scientific naturalist already believes, a belief which is "basic," and thus necessary, to its worldview, as what a theist would call "God."

If the argument begins from this point, a number of significant arguments that scientific naturalism presents for its position and against theism will simply be dissolved. By this, I do not mean that such arguments will be refuted, but that the implication of such arguments regarding the question about the existence of God will no longer be considered significant or interesting. For example, consider Mackie's position that religious experience and miracles may be explained in natural terms, that is, by the "laws of nature," or Hawking's claim that "ultimate laws" will explain the existence of the universe. Such arguments question the need to posit the existence of God in addition to the laws of nature. However, if at this point "God" is identified in some way with "laws of nature," then such questions simply cease to be significant. That is, even if the laws of nature eventually explain why the universe began, or why people have religious experience, or why a particular "miracle" happened, and so forth, if such concept of the laws of nature is identified with that which Christians would "understand as God," then such an explanation no longer will have any implication for whether "God" exists.

This is because these arguments all belong to a particular kind of argument—that the scientific naturalist worldview can sufficiently explain and understand the world without the theist concept of God. Again, in the contemporary debate, the standard theistic response, as exemplified by Swinburne, regarding this naturalist position is to use probabilistic arguments to claim that a theist worldview, which postulates the existence of God to explain the universe, consciousness, religious

experience, and so forth, is more probable than an atheist, scientific naturalist worldview. As we have seen, this response faces three difficulties.
First, such arguments tend to assume, wrongly, that the only significant
dispute between the theist and the atheist worldviews—at least, the only
one that is relevant for the debate—is that one posits the existence of
God, while the other does not. Second, the standards according to which
to "calculate" the "probability" of the worldviews differ for each worldview. Third, because the debate proceeds in terms of whether or not to
"postulate" an additional being with particular attributes, namely God,
the question inevitably arises regarding the "probability" of a being with
such attributes. Thus, a probabilistic argument will fail to decisively refute the naturalist position that the naturalist worldview can sufficiently
explain the world without "God."

However, if the first step of a theist argument is to simply identify that which the theist may "call God" in this worldview, the theist is
now arguing from within the rival worldview, and has thereby "stepped
over" this particular set of objections. That is, arguing from "within"
may overstep other difficulties and disagreements that arise when one is
arguing from the "outside," namely, from the other worldview. Furthermore, from within such a rival standpoint, there may be further points
from which a theist may further build his or her case—points hitherto
unavailable to a debate "stuck" on the question about positing an additional entity.

I refer here to the discussion in *Time* magazine between Francis
Collins, a Christian and the geneticist who headed the human genome
project, and Richard Dawkins, a biologist and an atheist. In the article,
Dawkins speaks regarding the probabilistic argument for the existence
of God:

> [Dawkins]: I accept that there may be things far grander and more
> incomprehensible than we can possibly imagine. What I can't un-
> derstand is why you invoke improbability and yet will not admit that
> you're shooting yourself in the foot by postulating something just as
> improbable, magicking into existence the word God.[16]

Collins replies that God is that which answers the questions of why
things come into existence, not that which requires explanation. Daw-

kins retorts that such an answer is a "cop-out," which evades the intellectual responsibility to explain. Collins agrees that explanation is important, but points out that Dawkins is the one assuming that "anything that might be outside of nature is ruled out of the conversation."[17] Then the two have this following exchange:

> [Dawkins:] There could be something incredibly grand and incomprehensible and beyond our present understanding.
>
> [Collins:] That's God.
>
> [Dawkins:] Yes, but it could be any of a billion Gods. . . . The chance of its being a particular God, Yahweh, the God of Jesus, is vanishingly small.[18]

What is interesting is that what Dawkins says is typical of the naturalist response to theist arguments, yet he then remarks that "there could be something incredibly grand and incomprehensible and beyond our present understanding." What he seems to imagine is something—a deeper reality—that, if anything, science, rather than "religion," would uncover, perhaps in the far future.

In this exchange, Dawkins is led to acknowledge something, but disagrees that this requires him to postulate the existence of some "improbable" being. Again, identifying the laws of nature as a parallel to the Christian notion of God oversteps this objection about the need to postulate something further. Indeed, when Collins identifies that "something" with God, Dawkins then retorts that this is unlikely to be the God of a particular religion. However, at this point the primary question of the debate shifted, rather subtly and unremarked—from whether to postulate the existence of God to whether the "something" that Dawkins already acknowledges is the God of any existing religion.

The Questions of Contention in the New Debate

The most obvious objection to the kind of theist argument I have described so far is that it does not actually argue that God exists. It merely affirms what the atheist already believes, and seems to state belief in God as a kind of word preference. If this is where the argument ends, this will certainly be true. I have argued, however, that a complete argument for the existence of God will be a task with a scope similar to that of Aquinas's *Summa*. Indeed, the Five Ways as an argument for the existence of God are inseparable from the arguments of the *Summa* as a whole. How then are we to set out from merely identifying the concept of the laws of nature as a parallel to the concept of God to arguing that God, as theists, let alone Christians, would understand him, exists?

Again, how Aquinas proceeded from the Five Ways in the *Summa* gives more direction. First, the Five Ways are followed by the question on whether the essence of God is to be, and then by the questions on whether God is one, good, perfect, infinite, and so forth. Thus, as I noted in chapter 6, it is in the questions that follow the Five Ways that Aquinas argues through negative theology that what is "called" or "understood as" God is self-subsistent, one, good, perfect, and so on. Thus, it is *from* identifying what in the rival worldview theists would "understand as" God that a theist may argue further regarding *how* we are to understand *what* this is. Simply put, in a successful theistic argument—or rather, theistic project—the particular conception of what may be "called God" in the rival, atheist worldview is to be changed, through further inquiry, into that which resembles the Christian understanding of God.

This is precisely why I have on several occasions raised the questions about how we are to understand the notion of the laws of nature, such as whether the laws really do exist, or are merely projections from our minds. This is because this is a question that is raised from within the framework of the scientific naturalist worldview. However, it is also the question that has the potential to be used as a theist argument. What such an argument may be can be partly glimpsed in Keith Ward's *God, Chance & Necessity*, in which he analyzes and refutes the claim that scientific explanation, from cosmology, biology, and sociobiology, undermines belief in the existence of God.[19] His arguments—at least, his refutations of the naturalist argument against theism—are good examples of arguing from the scientific naturalist position in defense of a Christian, theist worldview. However, what is of interest here is his following remark on the laws of nature:

> We can say that there does exist a Platonic universe of mathematical entities, including quantum laws and all sorts of other laws too. But

they do not exist in some half-real realm, neither fully actual nor merely possible. These entities exist in a cosmic mind. They are the thoughts of a cosmic mind, thoughts that exist by necessity, just as they are. That cosmic mind causes one set of those laws—a supremely elegant, well-ordered set—to apply to a physical reality.[20]

What he suggests is a particular understanding of the laws of nature—as "thoughts" of God. He argues further: "The existence of laws of physics does not render God superfluous. On the contrary, it strongly implies that there is a God who formulates such laws and ensures that the physical realm conforms to them."[21]

Ward's choice of words here unfortunately suggests that the theist is again positing God; however, I would argue that a more significant question he should have pursued more thoroughly is whether the laws do resemble, analogously, "thoughts." To argue that they do would be to identify the laws of nature with the biblical concept of the Logos of God, and possibly even to raise theological questions regarding the role of the Logos in divine revelation and in the incarnation in Jesus Christ, again from a question that is raised from within the secular, naturalist worldview. Also, note that this is where the identification with the "laws of nature" with what Christians may call "God" is further refined. The "laws" are what Christians understand not simply as "God," but as the *Logos of* God—who, according the first verse of the Gospel of John, is with God, and is God.

Likewise, there are other important issues regarding how we are to understand what the laws of nature are, which would include, for example, the question whether the laws of a "higher" science may be entirely reducible to the laws of a "lower" science. If the laws of nature are such that human social behavior is reduced entirely to deterministic chemical processes in the brain, then those laws will be incompatible with the theist notion of free will. Furthermore, in a holistic, interconnected web of beliefs that characterizes the worldview, this conclusion, in turn, will affect the theist conception of God. Thus, if human behavior is entirely determined by seemingly impersonal laws of nature in the "lower" science, it will be theists who need to revise their conception of God until it increasingly resembles the impersonal laws of nature of the scientific naturalists.[22]

The theistic project may also proceed to raise other questions, such as the coherence or adequacy of the particular configuration of meta-physical concepts or premises that are inseparably related to the scientific naturalist understanding of reality—that is, of what may be "called God" in that worldview. This move alone, in the context of the debate between incommensurable worldviews, would be inadequate, as we have seen, without also asking whether the conceptual resources of Christian theism can resolve the problems or difficulties such a position has encountered in its own terms. That is, the theistic project would follow MacIntyre's account of how incommensurable intellectual traditions resolve their debate. In this case, it would involve an extensive historical account of the formation, development, and encountered problems of the tacit metaphysical position of scientific naturalism, as well as detailed analysis and critique of the definitions, structures, and interrelations of its concepts and premises. All of this may well resemble, for example, Hanby's argument throughout *No God, No Science?*, where he presents an account that begins from Greek philosophy, which raised the question of the unity of being—thus, the very concept of the "*uni*verse"—then proceeds to explain the answer eventually given by the Christian doctrines of creation and incarnation, and then identifies the subsequent theological distortions in Renaissance Christianity and in modernity that even now tacitly underlie the supposed naturalist assumptions of modern science, compromising and even crippling science's conception of nature despite its stunning successes.

Thus, in the debate I have proposed so far, a whole array of questions may be raised, unfolding from the kind of theistic argument that I have suggested—the kind of questions that are rarely, or only marginally, asked in the contemporary philosophical debate about the existence of God proper. Likewise, such questions go beyond whether to posit the existence of God, to what our conception of reality—what we may otherwise "call God"—ought to be.

Significance of Particular Historicity of the Worldview in the New Debate

Another significant question of contention would be that of "miracles" and "religious experiences." Hawking states, for example, that the crucial question about the existence of God is whether there are "miracles," which he defines as "exception to the laws." Without such miracles, he notes, God is simply an "embodiment of the laws of nature."[23] In the argument for the existence of God that I am proposing, whether there are "exceptions to the laws of nature" ceases to be a significant question, at least until we have a complete knowledge of every law of nature. This is because if what the scientific naturalist calls the laws of nature is actually the Logos of God, then the claim that there is an exception to this—that is, an exception to the all-encompassing thoughts of God upon which the intelligibility of the universe is founded—will simply be incoherent to the theist. Rather, the distinction for the theist simply will be between the aspect of the Logos of God that sciences have discovered and defined and that which they have not. Thus, Hawking's contention that without "miracles" God is simply "an embodiment of the laws of nature" ceases to be significant or even intelligible, because just what these laws are— that is, whether we ought to understand them as the Logos of God—is precisely what will be contested. On the other hand, "miracles" as such will be defined in terms very different from Hawking's.[24]

What *will* be contested is whether there historically have been particular miracles or religious experiences. The standard theist argument in the debate has been that we are warranted in believing that God exists because of the general fact that there are religious experiences and reports of miracles. This, in turn, raises either the question whether miracles in general are possible, and if so, how, or whether religious experiences may be explained naturally. However, because such a question becomes unintelligible in the kind of debate I have proposed, what remains is the question whether the particular events and experiences deemed significant for a particular religious worldview indeed happened. This is crucial because, as MacIntyre argued, an intellectual position—including that which is composed of religious beliefs—has a particular history. That is, the rationality of such beliefs is inseparable from the particular, historical narrative of how such beliefs were formed, revised, and developed. A theist argument of the kind that I propose will thus present particular, historical—or at least believed-to-be-historical—events of significance for the religious tradition.

To understand why this is important, consider how a particular scientific inquiry will justify its theory. It will not argue for its position from the general fact that there are verifiable, experimental observations, but rather by specifying which particular observation in which particular experimental context leads one to confirm, abandon, or revise which particular scientific hypothesis. As MacIntyre points out, it is just such a narrative that defines the rationality of accepting a scientific theory. A significant question regarding the existence of God—and at this point, specifically the Christian God—will then be how the Christian worldview came to hold, change, or revise its beliefs through its very particular set of past, revelatory experiences.[25]

Thus, specifically Christian beliefs such as the resurrection of Jesus Christ become inseparable from the philosophical question of whether God exists. Similarly important is what Moser would emphasize as the right kind of evidence of God—not a third-person account of religious experience, but a personal encounter and continued relationship with God, which will be considered as continuation and confirmation of the particular experiences and events that have made the Christian worldview what it has become. Likewise, particular kinds of experiences that speak against this Christian understanding of God, namely suffering and evil, will become another key question. However, the existence of suffering and evil will raise many other possibilities than merely that God does not exist—such as that "God" is uncaring, impersonal, evil, and so forth—and the Christian theist answer will need to begin by considering how to interpret these experiences within a Christian worldview.[26]

Lastly, the Christian worldview, constructed from this crossroad, will be understood as a part of its historically extended narrative into the past and to the future. Its position will be, as MacIntyre put it, "essentially incomplete," and therefore open to change. However, the position it has held, and the position it holds now, and the position it will hold will be a part of its continuous narrative, a continuous journey through history. Already within even the biblical narrative, there has been a significant shift in its worldview; for example, through the narrative of the Old Testament, the understanding of God, the conception of the covenant relationship with him, and so on develop and thus change from, say, the period of the Judges to the period after the Babylonian exile. Nevertheless, the particular understanding of the world and God held by the ancient Israelites, though no longer held precisely in the same way by contemporary Christians, is still the root of their contemporary worldview. It is this continuity in the historical dimension of the Christian worldview that makes intelligible to a significant degree its claim that Christians are open to corrections to their beliefs while firmly holding onto the core doctrines of their worldview. In this sense the core of their worldview has remained intact.

THE EXPLORERS AT THE CROSSROAD

We again return to the parable of the explorers at the crossroad. If I have made a case for a different understanding about what it is to argue about the existence of God and for a different way of proceeding in that debate, I have moved us to a new perspective, comparable to that of the readers of the parable, who can understand the predicament of the explorers precisely because their perspective enables them to understand why the arguments of both explorers were unfruitful. This volume leaves a number of this project's questions unresolved. First, how should we then understand the specific arguments for and against the existence of God, such as those we mentioned in chapter 2, if we were to proceed in the debate in the way I have proposed? Second, of course, would be what concrete steps are we to take in the debate after accomplishing what the Five Ways did? Beyond the speculations we have examined above, such questions must remain unanswered at the close of this volume.

However, we can begin by noting that if I have succeeded in my arguments, I will have, in turn, moved the debate into a far broader arena of discussion. That is, just as, from our perspective, the debate between the two explorers ought to have involved far-ranging questions regarding equality, liberty, individualism, and so forth, the kind of debate about the existence of God envisioned by what I have proposed will necessarily involve far-ranging questions and issues. It will involve, of course, the more traditional philosophical questions, although in a different and larger context. That is, existing philosophical arguments about the existence of God will be posed differently, being situated in a debate that begins from the existence of "what Christians would call God"—though of course, "what may be called God" may in the end turn out to be something else. The primary question of this debate will be not whether God exists, but how we are to understand or engage our reality, and whether the way we do so will resemble what the theists see as interaction with God. Such a question will extend into various issues in science and theology, as well as history, revelation, and even personal testimonies and experiences. The kind of debate that I envision emerging as a result will in different aspects reflect the kinds of ideal practice of philosophy of religion that a number of recent writers have outlined—a practice, however, that they have been precluded from realizing by the very way the question of the existence of God has been posed and answered so far.

Consider, for example, Cottingham, and especially Moser, who envisions a debate where the most pertinent evidence on whether God exists is that which arises from direct, personal relationship with God—the kind of evidence we ought to expect from a God who is worthy of worship and with whom we interact. I would suggest that Moser, however, underestimates the extent to which a rival worldview, with conceptual schema, mode of reasoning, and even language, can systematically exclude the possibility of recognizing such as an evidence. For example, if a particular worldview's explanatory schema is such that every instance of what theists would call an encounter with God, personal transformation from divine grace, and so forth is explained in terms of how that schema represents reality—such as by particular laws or principles of the human psyche or moral character and so on—then such seemingly direct evidence will be interpreted in a different way that will once again raise the question why one must "posit" an unwarranted being.[27] In this sense, the situation will be rather like how the process of election or referendum simply was not considered "evidence" for the skeptic in the parable. What I argue the Five Ways do is to establish the crossroad, a place in which proponents of both worldviews are brought to understand their difference as asking "what" or "who" is the reality we are engaged with. Only then does *how* we engage with this reality—or how it engages us— become a substantial question.

Or consider Paul Draper and Ryan Nichols, who claim that there is widespread bias and partisanship in philosophy of religion, and thus recommend that its practitioners eschew apologetics, make a practice of constructing arguments against their own position, and accept genuine risk.[28] Whether there is such bias is questionable, especially in the way Ryan and Nichols have outlined.[29] However, in my account of worldviews that form the context from which these different and allegedly "partisan" positions in philosophy of religion debate each other, what Draper and

Nichols may speak of as "bias"—such as confirmation/disconfirmation bias—is a feature in how rationality works in regard to large-scale intellectual positions. Indeed, if certain philosophers perceive such bias in the proponents of one particular position—which happens to be that of their opponents—in regard to issues of evidence, standards of justification, and the like, yet not in their own, my account would suggest that it is they who may be blind to the assumptions of their own worldviews. However, Draper and Nichols's recommendation to respond to these biases is to a great extent what would be required to construct a successful argument from the position of one worldview to its rival's. If anything, Draper and Nichols vastly underestimate the task at hand. The kind of project I have proposed from the example of Aquinas's *Summa* requires more than just constructing arguments against one's own position; it requires understanding the opposing intellectual position *in its entirety*, including its tacit and implicit premises and extending well beyond what is conventionally understood as "the question about the existence of God," and beginning the task of dialectically integrating the opposing position into its own worldview, along with the risks and changes this will bring to one's previous position.

Or consider the concept of "skeptical religion" that J. L. Schellenberg proposes.[30] Schellenberg's position cannot be categorized as any of the standard positions of theist, atheist, or even the agnostic groups in the contemporary debate. His position of "ultimism," which is skeptical to both the theist and the atheist, scientific naturalist claims, but argues for the possibility of an ultimate level of reality and goodness, seems at first glance similar to what I argue the Five Ways disclose in rival worldviews. However, in my account, what the Five Ways do is not to posit some "ultimate reality" in addition to the kind of reality affirmed by worldviews such as scientific naturalism, but to identify what already functions within such a worldview in a manner similar to how such a reality functions in a theistic worldview; also, such an argument is intelligible only at the crossing of rival worldviews. Furthermore, the kinds of debate that will follow the identifying of what may be "called God" in the opposing worldview and the establishing of a crossroad of worldviews are open to the possibility of developing precisely the variant position regarding reality that does not fall into an either-atheist-or-theist divide. However, beyond the critiques that may be leveled against Schellenberg's particular standard of defining or evaluating evidence, I would caution here that he may be greatly underestimating the extent to which a particular worldview tradition is able to change some of its beliefs yet retain its core beliefs and preserve the continuity of its position. That is, even if one can somehow argue that existing theist or atheist positions are philosophically inadequate, this will be far from establishing that they will continue to be so. Thus, in arguing for his position, Schellenberg may be underestimating the sheer number of possible, different, and hitherto unimagined kinds of paths of understanding, experiencing, and knowing reality that can lead out from any one particular worldview in the debate as a result of crossing paths with another.

The debate I envision, therefore, is one in which a particular worldview tradition, such as Christian theism, continues to enrich its interaction with, and thereby its understanding of, reality as "God," through its journey onward both from its past travels—composed of concrete and revelatory experiences, historical events, and intellectual accomplishments—and from the challenges, insights, and resources of the travels from other worldviews it encounters at the crossroads. At such a crossroad, arguing about the existence of God will in a sense become the telling of a story—a story of a journey of ourselves and our rivals, in which both sides are invited to see what had been so familiar and prevalent in their past travels in a new, transforming light, one that will illuminate their path forward.

NOTES

ONE   To Step Back: Rethinking the Question

1. This position, for example, is presented by Peter Winch, *The Idea of a Social Science* (New York: Humanities Press, 1958), regarding "non-scientific" belief in witchcraft by the Azande tribe.

2. It seems to me that the significance of this—that is, the question of who is crafting the parable—is seldom mentioned in the discussion of the famous article by Antony Flew, the opening of which my parable consciously mimics. Antony Flew, R. M. Hare, and Basil Mitchell, "Theology and Falsification," in *New Essays in Philosophical Theology*, ed. Antony Flew and Alasdair MacIntyre (London: SCM Press, 1955), 96–108.

3. In David Brin, *The Postman* (New York: Bantam, 1985), a number of people in a postapocalyptic United States falsely believe that their central government is restored, because the main character acts as a postman. In George Orwell, *Nineteen Eighty-Four* (London: Secker and Warburg, 1949), the entire society is indoctrinated by its tyrannical, mind-controlling government to follow its leader, the "Big Brother," who, the book reveals, may not even exist.

4. Note how these "evidences" may be phrased to be a kind of causal or design argument, such as the following: "Roads, postal service, schools, military, law enforcement, etc., exist, and are organized in this manner, because there is a nationally elected governing office that set them up," rather like "the universe, order in nature, consciousness, etc., exist because there is an intelligent first cause that created and designed them." Consider also how the difficulties of, or objections to, such arguments would parallel those that typically arise in the debate regarding the cosmological arguments and the various arguments about God from natural science.

5. Note how all of these features were present in some forms in the history of the United States during the nineteenth century. Consider also how such debate would likewise have interesting parallels to the debate regarding arguments from evil or unanswered prayers.

6. It seems an obvious point to observe that historically, non-Western cultures that encountered accounts of democratic political systems of the West did not seriously question whether a "ruler exists" in those societies. They did raise questions, but their primary question was whether the ideas of democracy and equality that those other societies believed in were workable, and if so, how those ideas could be applied to their own society. For examples of the history of democracy in the non-Western world, see Ainslie T. Embree and Carol Gluck, eds., *Asia in Western and World History* (New York: Armonk, 1997), and John Dunn, *Democracy: The Unfinished Journey, 508 BC to AD 1993* (Oxford: Oxford University Press, 1992).

7. This would be a considerably more difficult question to answer for the explorers than one might expect. Imagine, for example, how one would perceive the differences between the lives of average working-class families and the members of Forbes 400 in a modern, democratic society, if the only categories one possessed to understand the differences were those of a feudal society.

8. Of course, it is possible that the natives are living in small tribal societies, or even in a state of anarchy, with no higher "ruler." However, for these two explorers, this would require more than a mere refutation of this or that evidence for their respective positions; it would require a development or even construction of a hitherto utterly unimagined concept, with its own unique set of social features.

9. To be clear, I am not at all comparing the theist position to a democracy, or the atheist position to feudalism, or vice versa. Indeed, I could easily have switched the sociopolitical systems of the explorers to raise the same points I have so far outlined.

10. Alasdair MacIntyre, *God, Philosophy, Universities* (Lanham, MD: Rowman & Littlefield, 2009), 76–77. MacIntyre was giving an account of Thomas Aquinas's position on the existence of God, which I will also give in greater detail in chapters 5 and 6.

11. Thomas S. Kuhn, *The Structure of Scientific Revolutions*, 3rd ed. (Chicago: University of Chicago Press, 1996; first published 1962), 114.

12. MacIntyre, *Whose Justice? Which Rationality?* (Notre Dame, IN: University of Notre Dame Press, 1988), 380.

TWO   Where We Stand: The Contemporary Question

1. "Incommensurability" is a significant and complex concept, first introduced in philosophy of science by Thomas S. Kuhn and Paul Feyerabend independently in 1962. There are many definitions of this term, many of which are controversial. See Kuhn, *Structure of Scientific Revolutions*; also Paul K. Feyerabend, "Explanation, Reduction and Empiricism," in *Minnesota Studies in the Philosophy of Science*, vol. 3, *Scientific Explanation, Space, and Time*, ed. H. Feigl and G. Maxwell (Minneapolis: University of Minnesota Press, 1962), 28–97. For our purpose, I am limiting what I generally mean by "incommensurability" to what I already described in chapter 1, which largely follows MacIntyre's definition.

2. For one of the most recent examples, the disputes at the three levels are discussed in Herman Philipse, *God in the Age of Science? A Critique of Religious Reason* (Oxford: Oxford University Press, 2012). Philipse, who argues emphatically for atheism, contends that to build a rational case for the existence of God, an intellectually responsible theist needs arguments that follow a very particular type of reasoning similar to that of scientific disciplines. Thus, his position leads him to argue—though rather all too briefly—for very particular stances in all three levels of disputes.

3. "The Great Pumpkin" or, more recently, "The Invisible Pink Unicorn" is popularly used to parody theists for believing in something that atheists suggest is at least equally unconfirmed, and unconfirmable, and thus "believable." Likewise the "Flying Spaghetti Monster" parodies the theist position that God created the world—though it targets primarily the proponents of Intelligent Design—which it suggests is no different, cognitively, from proposing that an invisible, undetectable, omnipotent "flying spaghetti monster" created the world.

4. Admittedly, I have organized and phrased the characterizations in a particular way here to reveal at least a sense of the radical nature of their differences. However, examples of these positions, in some form or variation, described, assumed, or argued, can be found throughout the history of the debate up to the present. Perhaps the diversity of positions and stark contrast between them can most readily be glimpsed in anthologies on philosophy of religion such as the following: Charles Taliaferro, Paul Draper, and Philip L. Quinn, eds., *A Companion to Philosophy of Religion*, 2nd ed. (Malden, MA: Wiley-Blackwell, 2010); Michael Peterson, William Hasker, Bruce Reichenbach, and David Basinger, eds., *Philosophy of Religion: Selected Readings*, 4th ed.

(Oxford: Oxford University Press, 2010); Louis P. Pojman and Michael C. Rae, eds., *Philosophy of Religion: An Anthology*, 5th ed. (Belmont, CA: Wadsworth, 2008); Michael L. Peterson and Raymond J. VanArragon, eds., *Contemporary Debates in Philosophy of Religion* (Malden, MA: Blackwell, 2004).

5. Richard Swinburne's theistic argument would be the most notable example of this position, which he presents in *The Existence of God* (Oxford: Clarendon Press, 2004; first published 1979).

6. Kai Nielson, *Naturalism and Religion* (Amherst, NY: Prometheus Books, 2001), 279, especially exemplifies this atheist position.

7. I believe a number of contemporary theists, such as D. Z. Phillips, hold positions similar to that of such a theist. An example of Phillips's work that exemplifies this is *Religion without Explanation* (Oxford: Blackwell, 1976).

8. Richard Gale, *On the Nature and Existence of God* (Cambridge: Cambridge University Press, 1991), is a good example that examines the deductive arguments both against and for the existence of God. Inductive argument for the existence of God is exemplified in Swinburne, *Existence of God*. A more recent example of a likewise comprehensive case against the existence of God, including the critiques of the theist arguments, can be found in Nicholas Everitt, *The Non-Existence of God* (London: Routledge, 2004).

9. Yujin Nagasawa, *The Existence of God: A Philosophical Introduction* (New York: Routledge, 2011), offers a concise, historically nuanced account mainly of these three classes of arguments. Other significant arguments for the existence of God include the argument from consciousness, from morality, from religious experience, and from miracles. There are atheist arguments against the existence of God, the most significant being the argument from evil, in both deductive and inductive forms, and the deductive argument for the incoherence of the concept of God.

10. David Hume, *Dialogues concerning Natural Religion*, ed. Richard H. Popkin (Cambridge: Hackett, 1998; first published 1779).

11. Kant's influential series of critiques against the three classes of theistic arguments, which he calls the ontological, cosmological, and the physico-theological proofs, can be found as a part of his discussion of "the Ideal of Pure Reason" in *Critique of Pure Reason*, trans. N. K. Smith (New York: St. Martin's Press, 1965; first published 1781, 1787), specifically in book 2, chapter 3.

12. Everitt, *Non-Existence of God*, xiii.

13. Graham Oppy, *Arguing about Gods* (New York: Cambridge University Press, 2006), is a recent work that presents a fairly comprehensive list of the contemporary variations of ontological, cosmological, and teleological arguments, along with other arguments such as those from religious experience and morality, and the atheist argument from evil. His list is by no means exhaus-

tive, but even the general descriptions there reveal numerous new forms of arguments.

14. Norman Malcolm, "Anselm's Ontological Arguments," *Philosophical Review* 69 (1960): 41–62; Charles Hartshorne, *Anselm's Discovery: A Re-Examination of the Ontological Proof for God's Existence* (La Salle, IL: Open Court, 1965); Alvin Plantinga, *God, Freedom, and Evil* (Grand Rapids: Eerdmans, 1974); and Plantinga, *The Nature of Necessity* (Oxford: Oxford University Press, 1974).

15. William Lane Craig, *The Kalam Cosmological Argument* (London: Macmillan, 1979).

16. Swinburne, *Existence of God*; William Wainwright, *Mysticism: A Study of Its Nature, Cognitive Value, and Moral Implications* (Madison: University of Wisconsin Press, 1981); William Alston, *Perceiving God: The Epistemology of Religious Experience* (Ithaca, NY: Cornell University Press, 1991).

17. Richard Taylor, *Metaphysics* (Englewood Cliffs, NJ: Prentice-Hall, 1963); Bruce Reichenbach, *The Cosmological Argument* (Springfield, IL: Thomas, 1972); William L. Rowe, *The Cosmological Argument* (Princeton: Princeton University Press, 1975).

18. Rowe, *Cosmological Argument*, 136.

19. Bernard Lonergan's *Insight: A Study of Human Understanding*, vol. 3 of *The Collected Works of Bernard Lonergan* (Toronto: University of Toronto Press, 1997; first published by Longmans, Green, 1957), which is among the most influential works in the twentieth century for contemporary Catholic philosophy and theology—including its discussion about the existence of God—is a case in point; it is a comprehensive examination of cognition and knowing, which includes extensive critiques of the epistemological positions of Hume and, especially, Kant.

20. Oppy, *Arguing about Gods*, 414.

21. Ibid., 425.

22. Philipse, again, is one of the most recent examples, considering Swinburne's arguments as the "toughest case" for philosophers of religion in *God in the Age of Science?*, 91. Most of this book is spent on arguing that Swinburne's cumulative Bayesian case for the existence of God fails to satisfy the standard of scientific reasoning Philipse claims theist rational arguments, such as Swinburne's, ought to be aiming for.

23. Swinburne, *The Coherence of Theism* (Oxford: Clarendon Press, 1977). Mackie specifically mentions Swinburne's arguments in *The Coherence of Theism* on religious language with approval in J. L. Mackie, *The Miracle of Theism* (Oxford: Clarendon Press, 1982), 3.

24. Swinburne, *Coherence of Theism*, 92.

25. Mackie, *Miracle of Theism*, 4.

26. To be more precise, such a cumulative case for the existence of God justifies using what Swinburne calls the "principle of credulity" regarding religious experience, which is to say that religious experience ought to be taken as veridical. The most recent form of his whole argument, along with the account of his probabilistic reasoning, is found in the second edition of *The Existence of God*. In his preface, Swinburne states that the second edition revises and updates some of his arguments in a "minor" way, but the general approach and argument remains the same as the first edition.

27. Swinburne, *Is There a God?*, rev. ed. (Oxford: Oxford University Press, 2010; first published 1996), 120–21. Swinburne published the first edition as a concise and readable summary of the first edition of *The Existence of God*, and likewise, he followed the second edition of *The Existence of God* with this revised edition. Because of this, and because for our purpose we require a general overview of his argument, rather than the precise reasoning based on his probabilistic calculus, I will mostly reference this work for this discussion.

28. See Hume, *An Enquiry concerning Human Understanding*, ed. Antony Flew (La Salle, IL: Open Court, 1988; first published 1748), and *The Natural History of Religion*, ed. H. E. Root (London: A & C Black, 1956; first published 1757).

29. Mackie, *Miracle of Theism*, 130–31.

30. Ibid., 252–53.

31. Some readers may be confused by the use of the word "disembodied" here, since this is not a term employed in any traditional theist, or Judeo-Christian, description of God. "Disembodied mind" and "disembodied person" are terms used primarily in the context of the contemporary debate about the existence of God, arising from the atheist—specifically the materialist—argument that the very notion of spirit, or mind without a body, that is, mind that is *not* embodied, is incoherent. Thus, one of the notable contentions in the debate is precisely whether the notion of "disembodied" being as such is intelligible.

32. Mackie, *Miracle of Theism*, 253.

33. Swinburne, *Is There a God?*, rev. ed., 37–38.

34. Swinburne, *Is There a God?* (1996), 42–43. This passage was removed and simplified in the revised edition, possibly because the meaning of the word "complicated" here is rather unclear. I use this older formulation of his argument here because the wording gives a clearer contrast between Mackie's and Swinburne's positions.

35. Swinburne, *Is There a God?*, rev. ed., 40.

36. Mackie, *Miracle of Theism*, 252.

37. Richard Messer, *Does the Existence of God Need Proof?* (Oxford: Oxford University Press, 1993), 22n53.

38. Swinburne, *Is There a God?*, rev. ed., 1–2.

39. Ibid., 44–45. It is notable that boldface emphasis in the passage above was added in the revised edition in 2010, which seems to indicate Swinburne's growing awareness of the importance of this difference. Note also that by calling God a "simple being," he raises—whether consciously or not—a theological question of the nature of God, which reveals yet another use of the word, "simple."

40. Oppy, *Arguing about Gods*, 10.

41. Ibid., 11.

42. Ibid., 7.

43. Ibid., 8.

44. Ibid., chapter 3.

45. Ibid., 168–69.

46. Ibid., 173.

47. Ibid., 414.

48. This principle is explicitly declared by Michael Scriven, *Primary Philosophy* (New York: McGraw-Hill, 1966), 103. This position is a significant part of what I will argue against in chapters 3 and 4. Furthermore, in chapter 7, I will give a brief account of how this notion that the atheist "merely disbelieves" seems to have developed historically.

49. Antony Flew, "The Presumption of Atheism," in *God, Freedom, and Immortality* (New York: Prometheus Books, 1984), 14. First published in "The Presumption of Atheism," *Canadian Journal of Philosophy* 2 (1972), 29–46.

50. Ibid., 20.

51. Swinburne, *Coherence of Theism*, 6.

52. Alvin Plantinga, "Reason and Belief in God," in *Faith and Rationality: Reason and Belief in God*, ed. Alvin Plantinga and Nicholas Wolterstorff (Notre Dame, IN: University of Notre Dame Press, 1984), 72. Yet despite Plantinga's claim, an evidentialist need not be a foundationalist, and a foundationalist—for example, a neopositivist—need not hold these three theses.

53. Ibid., 59.

54. Ibid., 60.

55. Ibid., 79–81.

56. For the details of this argument, see Plantinga, *God, Freedom, and Evil*, 85–113.

57. Ibid.; see also "Reason and Belief in God," 84.

58. Norman Kretzmann, "Evidence and Religious Belief," in *Philosophy of Religion: A Guide and Anthology*, ed. Brian Davies (New York: Oxford University Press, 2000), 95–107 (esp. 99–100), an edited version of "Evidence against Anti-Evidentialism," which originally appeared in *Our Knowledge of God*, ed. K. J. Clark (Dordrecht: Kluwer Academic, 1992), 17–38.

59. Everitt, *Non-Existence of God*, 26.

60. Ibid., 28–29.

61. Nicholas Wolterstorff, "Can Belief in God Be Rational?," in *Faith and Rationality*, 159.

62. Ibid., 163.

63. Ibid., 155.

64. Plantinga, *Warrant and Proper Function* (Oxford: Oxford University Press, 1993), 46–47 especially.

65. Plantinga, *Warranted Christian Belief* (New York: Oxford University Press, 2000), 243–44.

66. Ibid., 290–404. Some of the defeaters he considers are projective theories in psychology, historical biblical criticism, postmodernism, and pluralism, as well as the issue of suffering and evil.

67. Plantinga, *Where the Conflict Really Lies: Science, Religion, and Naturalism* (New York: Oxford University Press, 2011), ix.

68. Flew, "Theology and Falsification."

69. Charles Taliaferro, *Evidence and Faith: Philosophy and Religion since the Seventeenth Century* (New York: Cambridge University Press, 2005), chapter 8.

70. Ibid., 351. The argument he quotes is in Swinburne, *Coherence of Theism*, 104–5.

71. Fergus Kerr, *Theology after Wittgenstein* (New York: Blackwell, 1986), 154. The original quote is found in Ludwig Wittgenstein, *Culture and Value*, trans. Peter Winch (Chicago: University of Chicago Press, 1980; first published as *Vermischte Bemerkungen* [Frankfurt: Suhrkamp Verlag, 1977]), 82.

72. Kerr, *Theology after Wittgenstein*, 29–30.

73. D. Z. Phillips, *Faith after Foundationalism* (New York: Routledge, 1988), chapter 4.

74. Ibid., 41.

75. Ibid.

76. A concept from W. V. O. Quine and J. S. Ullian, *The Web of Belief*, 2nd ed. (New York: Random House, 1978; first published 1970).

77. Phillips, *Concept of Prayer* (New York: Schocken Books, 1966), 81–82.

78. Messer, *Does the Existence of God Need Proof?*, 45.

79. Ibid., 46.

80. This assessment of the cosmological argument is found in Phillips, "From World to God?" in Phillips, *Faith and Philosophical Enquiry* (London: Routledge & Kegan Paul, 1970).

81. Messer, *Does the Existence of God need Proof?*, chapter 6.

82. Kerr's point mentioned above is one such critique. A recent example is found again in Philipse, *God in the Age of Science?*, 28–29, where he argues this in his very brief mention of Phillips.

83. Philipse's *God in the Age of Science?* explicitly claims to have answered the disputes in all three levels ([1] whether the existence of God is subject to rational arguments, [2] whether evidence is required to rationally believe in God, and [3] whether there is sufficient evidence for belief in God), and to have refuted the theist position that God exists, by specific references to Phillips, Plantinga, and Swinburne. However, although reviewers commended his work for rigorous and systematic arguments, they identified several problems. Among the problems was a failure to defend, or even assuming outright, a number of premises or definitions of concepts (such as causation) that are critical to his arguments and relevant to the debate, yet are intensely disputed among philosophers. Thus, for example, his entire argument against the notion that God is the ultimate cause is undermined. Another problem reviewers identified was the severe limits of the applicability of his critique of—and sometimes even outright misunderstanding of—the different but very significant variations of the theist positions of those he examined: whether the different theist understandings of what constitutes a case for the existence of God, each of which includes revealed theology, or the precise defense of Reformed epistemology. In this way, his work seems to have run afoul of precisely the kind of difficulties I am sketching out at the end of this chapter.

See Jim Slagle, review of *God in the Age of Science? A Critique of Religious Reason*, by Herman Philipse, *Philosophy* 88 (April 2013): 325–29, or Andrew Pinsent, review of *God in the Age of Science? A Critique of Religious Reason*, by Herman Philipse, *Notre Dame Philosophical Reviews*, January 2013, http://ndpr.nd.edu/news/36607-god-in-the-age-of-science-a-critique-of-religious-reason/.

84. C. Stephen Evans, *Natural Signs and Knowledge of God: A New Look at Theistic Arguments* (Oxford: Oxford University Press, 2010), 13–17. Here, Evans proposes what he calls the "wide accessibility principle" (WAP)—human beings are given opportunity to learn that God exists—and the "easy resistibility principle" (ERP): such opportunities can easily be overridden.

85. Details of Moser's position are found in Paul K. Moser, *The Elusive God: Reorienting Religious Epistemology* (Cambridge: Cambridge University

Press, 2008), and *The Evidence for God: Religious Knowledge Reexamined* (Cambridge: Cambridge University Press, 2010). John Cottingham argues for a similar position with frequent references to Moser in his *Philosophy of Religion: Towards a More Humane Approach* (Cambridge: Cambridge University Press, 2014), 17–22 especially. This is not to say Cottingham or Moser entirely eschews discussions in natural theology and arguments drawn from the empirical sciences, although Moser describes them as "at best incidental, even a dispensable sideshow," in *Elusive God*, 25. Cottingham discusses the classical arguments at some length in the chapter entitled "Metaphysics," while Moser devotes the entirety of the first chapter in *The Evidence for God* to refuting the claims that empirical science or epistemology supports naturalism and undermines the rationality of the belief in God.

THREE   The Road: Rationality and Worldviews

1. Although there is a growing voice in the literature on the inadequacy of epistemological foundationalism in contemporary philosophy of religion, this particular observation about evidentialist arguments—and the term "comprehensive philosophy"—is found in Charles Taliaferro, "Philosophy of Religion," in Stanford Encyclopedia of Philosophy Archive, winter 2014 edition, ed. Edward N. Zalta (Stanford, CA: Metaphysics Research Lab, Center for the Study of Language and Information, Stanford University), last substantive revision September 11, 2013, http://plato.stanford.edu/archives/win2014/entries/philosophy-religion/. Likewise, Kai Nielson, *Naturalism without Foundations* (Amherst, NY: Prometheus Books, 1996), offers a nonfoundationalist atheist position.

2. "Modern" philosophy is generally understood to have begun with Descartes in the seventeenth century. It is still debated when the "postmodern" period began, but a concise and general account of its characteristic positions in Anglo-American philosophy may be found in Nancey Murphy, *Anglo-American Postmodernity: Philosophical Perspectives on Science, Religion, and Ethics* (Boulder, CO: Westview Press, 1997).

3. Murphy, *Anglo-American Postmodernity*, 26.

4. Richard Rorty, *Philosophy and the Mirror of Nature* (Princeton: Princeton University Press, 1979), 7.

5. Ibid., 9. Emphasis original in this and all subsequent quotations unless otherwise noted.

6. Ibid., 140.

7. Ibid., 142.

8. Ibid., 152.

9. Ibid., 159.

10. Ibid., 163.

11. Ibid., 8.

12. Ibid., 163.

13. Ibid., 178.

14. Ibid., 170.

15. Ibid., 170–71.

16. Ibid., 8.

17. Ibid., 366.

18. Quine, "Two Dogmas of Empiricism," *Philosophical Review* 40 (1951): 20–43. A revised version also appears in Quine, *From a Logical Point of View*, 2nd ed. (Cambridge, MA: Harvard University Press, 1961), 20–46. Different versions are presented side by side for comparison at http://www .ditext.com/quine/quine.html. All quotations from "Two Dogmas" in this chapter are found in both versions. The term "web of beliefs" is found in Quine and Ullian, *Web of Belief.*

19. Ibid.

20. Ibid.

21. For example, in Newtonian physics, the law of gravitation is more "central," whereas the accepted number of planets in the solar system is more "peripheral." Thus, if the observed orbit of a planet, such as Uranus, conflicts with the prediction of the Newtonian law of gravitation, one may posit an undiscovered planet, which may be affecting its orbit, rather than discarding the concept of gravity. This led to the discovery of Neptune. This raises the question of the role of such ad hoc postulation, or hypothesis, in scientific inquiry. Imre Lakatos, for example, is one of the most significant figures whose work in philosophy of science discusses this issue. See Imre Lakatos, *The Methodology of Scientific Research Programmes: Philosophical Papers*, vol. 1, ed. John Worrall and Gregory Currie (Cambridge: Cambridge University Press, 1978).

22. Quine, "Two Dogmas of Empiricism" (emphasis added).

23. Oppy, *Arguing about Gods*, 8.

24. Gary Gutting, *What Philosophers Know: Case Studies in Recent Analytic Philosophy* (Cambridge: Cambridge University Press, 2009), 13.

25. Ibid., 18–25, 82–83. Gutting notes that Quine's argument has been subject to several significant critiques, H. P. Grice, P. F. Strawson, and Hilary Putnam, among others, and that in the decade or so of discussion that followed his article, some of his critics cited clear cases of the analytic-synthetic

distinction. What this established, however, was that the distinction is "unsustainable" without terms like "necessity" and "self-contradictory." That is, Quine's challenge contributed to a new philosophical understanding that the analytic-synthetic distinction may be formulated in modal terms, but cannot be reduced to nonmodal terms.

26. Ibid., 30.

27. Ibid., 74.

28. Ibid., 74–76. The quotation from Putnam is in Hilary Putnam, "The Analytic and the Synthetic," *Mind, Language, and Reality*, vol. 2 of *Philosophical Papers* (Cambridge: Cambridge University Press, 1975), 35–37.

29. Rorty, *Philosophy and the Mirror of Nature*, 322.

30. Michael Polanyi, *Personal Knowledge: Towards a Post-Critical Philosophy* (Chicago: University of Chicago Press, 1958).

31. Ibid., 53.

32. Kuhn, *Structure of Scientific Revolutions*, 84–91.

33. Ibid., 30–33. An example of this would be Isaac Newton's *Philosophiæ Naturalis Principia Mathematica*, which set the framework of subsequent scientific inquiry in Newtonian physics, defining the terms, relevant data, method of research, and so forth, but was also the concrete historical exemplar of scientific practice and achievement in that field of inquiry.

34. Ibid., 36–39.

35. Ibid., 148–50.

36. Ibid., 150, and also 120.

37. Thomas Kuhn, *The Essential Tension: Selected Studies in Scientific Tradition and Change* (Chicago: University of Chicago Press, 1977), 320–39.

38. Hans Küng, *Theology for the Third Millennium: An Ecumenical View* (New York: Doubleday, 1988); Ian Barbour, *Religion and Science: Historical and Contemporary Issues* (San Francisco: HarperCollins, 1997), especially chapter 5.

39. Gutting, *What Philosophers Know*, 151–52. Gutting quotes John H. Zammito, *A Nice Derangement of Epistemes: Post-positivism in the Study of Science from Quine to Latour* (Chicago: University of Chicago Press, 2004), 53.

40. Gutting, *What Philosophers Know*, 169.

41. Gutting notes this similarity as well, comparing it to Plantinga's position that the existence of God is properly basic and requires no further justification; and Gutting finds the point also comparable to the "ethical and political convictions tied to the practice of our democracy" that underlie John Rawls's theory of justice, which again require no further philosophical foundation to justify them. Ibid., 171.

42. The latter claim would exclude those like D. Z. Phillips, so even this would not be all-inclusive.

43. Consider, for example, how the precise meaning of terms in the core beliefs such as God being "perfectly good," "personal"—which for Christianity is Triune—or "creator" can vary between different theological positions, or even across different periods in the intellectual history of a particular position. For an example of the latter, I have noted briefly in chapter 2 how the precise understanding of God as a "necessary being" has changed, or been refined, from Anselm's understanding that God exists by definition, to contemporary developments of the notion of "necessary existence" and specifically to Plantinga's modal version about a being of "maximal greatness" existing in all possible worlds. Obviously, the differences in the precise meaning are restricted to certain limits or parameters—or else, we would not recognize that different philosophers were using variations of the same term! However, the difference is there, and it can be at the level of terms that compose even a core belief.

44. See Hasok Chang, "Incommensurability: Revisiting the Chemical Revolution," in *Kuhn's "The Structure of Scientific Revolutions" Revisited*, ed. Vasso Kindi and Theodore Arabatzis (New York: Routledge, 2012), 153–76.

45. MacIntyre, "Epistemological Crises, Dramatic Narratives, and the Philosophy of Science," *The Monist*, no. 60 (1977): 453–72; then reprinted in Gary Gutting, ed., *Paradigms and Revolutions: Appraisals and Applications of Thomas Kuhn's Philosophy of Science* (Notre Dame, IN: University of Notre Dame Press, 1980), 59.

46. Ibid.

47. Ibid., 60.

48. Ibid.

49. Ibid., 56.

50. Ibid., 70.

51. An extensive account of the development of MacIntyre's philosophy may be found in Thomas D'Andrea, *Tradition, Rationality and Virtue: The Thought of Alasdair MacIntyre* (Aldershot: Ashgate, 2006). The development from MacIntyre's account of theoretical reason to his more influential work on practical reason is found from 216 onward.

52. MacIntyre, *After Virtue: A Study in Moral Theory*, 2nd ed. (Notre Dame, IN: University of Notre Dame Press, 1984).

53. Ibid., 187.

54. Ibid., 219. Again, I am extracting from the larger context of MacIntyre's ethical theory only the most relevant concepts that concern us. Thus, I am leaving out, for example, his significant discussion on virtues as qualities

that enable a person to achieve internal goods of a practice, or the role of the "quest" in solving the problem of ordering competing goods in human life, among others.

55. Ibid., 222.

56. Ibid.

57. MacIntyre, *Whose Justice? Which Rationality?* (Notre Dame, IN: University of Notre Dame Press, 1988), 7.

58. Alasdair MacIntyre, "An Interview for Cogito," in *The MacIntyre Reader*, ed. Kelvin Knight (Notre Dame, IN: University of Notre Dame Press, 1998), 270. The interview was first published in *Cogito* 5, no. 2 (1991): 67–73.

59. MacIntyre, "An Interview with Giovanna Borradori," appeared originally in Italian in 1991, and in English as "Nietzsche or Aristotle?," in *The American Philosopher: Conversations with Quine, Davidson, Putnam, Nozick, Danto, Rorty, Cavell, MacIntyre, and Kuhn*, ed. Giovanna Borradori (Chicago: University of Chicago Press, 1994); *MacIntyre Reader*, 264.

60. David Naugle, *Worldview: The History of the Concept* (Grand Rapids: Eerdmans, 2002), 259–60.

61. Ibid., 59.

62. Albert Wolters, "On the Idea of Worldview and Its Relation to Philosophy," in *Stained Glass: Worldviews and Social Science*, ed. Paul A. Marshall, Sander Griffioen, and Richard Mouw (Lanham, MD: University Press of America, 1989), 15.

63. Ibid., 16. Wolters also characterizes various Christian positions, such as that of the Anabaptists, Roman Catholics, and Calvinists, as correlating largely to one of his five types; see 24.

64. The Reformed epistemologists—not surprisingly, as Calvinists—also belong to this group.

65. Jacob Klapwijk, "On Worldviews and Philosophy," in Marshall, Griffioen, and Mouw, *Stained Glass*, 49.

66. Wolters, "On the Idea of Worldview," 18.

67. Ibid., 18–19.

68. This is not to say that "philosophy" would simply be indistinguishable from "worldview" without the Enlightenment view of rationality. Rather, the distinction between "philosophy" and "worldview" would not be as clear, nor would there be such a need to expressly define what the relationship between these is, especially in terms of "rationality."

69. Naugle, *Worldview*, 70.

70. Ibid., 104.

71. Ibid., 82.

72. Ibid., 103.

73. Friedrich Nietzsche, *Gay Science, with a Prelude in Rhymes and an Appendix of Songs*, trans. with commentary by Walter Kaufmann (New York: Random House, 1974), 180–83.

74. Naugle, *Worldview*, 117. Naugle is referring especially to Edmund Husserl, *The Crisis of European Sciences and the Transcendental Phenomenology: An Introduction to Phenomenological Philosophy*, trans. David Carr (Evanston, IL: Northwestern University Press, 1970), 389–90.

75. Naugle, *Worldview*, 119. The concept comes from Husserl, *Crisis of European Sciences and the Transcendental Phenomenology*, 121–39.

76. Naugle, *Worldview*, 138.

77. Ibid. Naugle is discussing Heidegger's magnum opus, *Being and Time*. See Martin Heidegger, *Being and Time*, trans. John Macquarrie and Edward Robinson (New York: Harper and Row, 1962).

78. Naugle, *Worldview*, 147. The argument Naugle describes is found in Martin Heidegger, "The Age of the World Picture," in *The Question concerning Technology, and Other Essays*, trans. William Lovitt (New York: Harper and Row, 1977), 115–54.

79. Naugle, *Worldview*, 145–46.

80. Ibid., 145.

81. Ibid., 154.

82. Wittgenstein, *Philosophical Investigations* (Oxford: Blackwell, 1967), section 217.

83. Naugle, *Worldview*, 175.

84. Ibid., 184.

85. Ibid., 187.

86. Ibid., 292. Naugle specifies "philosophically" here, because he writes *from*—the very concept of worldview demands such an approach—a particular worldview, namely, Christianity, and argues that *theological* understanding of the concept is of first importance for Christians.

87. Thus, by "worldview" I will mean, unless otherwise specified, a concept that includes these larger notions, rather than simply a set of beliefs about the world. More specifically, I will be using the term "worldview" interchangeably with MacIntyre's concept of historically extended "tradition."

88. Wolters, "On the Idea of Worldview," 23. There are several writings that exemplify the enterprise of integrating the concept of worldview into the themes of Christian worldview. Again, see, for example, Naugle's *Worldview*, chapter 9. For other worldviews, see Wolters, *Creation Regained: Biblical Basics for a Reformational Worldview* (Grand Rapids: Eerdmans, 1985), or Arthur F. Holmes, *Contours of a World View* (Grand Rapids: Eerdmans, 1983).

89. Naugle, *Worldview*, 295–330.

90. James Olthuis, "On Worldviews," in Marshall, Griffioen, and Mouw, *Stained Glass*, 38.

91. Ibid., 36–38.

92. Holmes, *Contours of a World View*, 44.

FOUR   At the Crossroads of Worldviews

1. This is not to say that presenting a rational case for—or against—the existence of God from and to different worldviews is the sole context and function of such arguments. John Clayton argues in his cross-cultural and historical account of theistic arguments that such arguments have served many different functions in diverse intellectual and social contexts. For example, he argues that many traditional arguments for the existence of God were in fact "intra-traditional," with diverse functions, which included defending the orthodox conception of God to those within the same religious tradition or moving one to worship and praise, rather than arguing to atheists that God exists. For this account, see John Clayton, *Religions, Reasons and Gods: Essays in Cross-Cultural Philosophy of Religion* (Cambridge: Cambridge University Press, 2006). What I am arguing, however, is what Clayton himself would acknowledge—that the contemporary debate about the existence of God does overwhelmingly constitute arguments between worldviews.

2. Phillips would reject the claim that God is an explanatory hypothesis, but this depends on whether a theistic worldview as a whole is a kind of large-scale, comprehensive explanation. Although I believe that a worldview holds an explanatory role, for our purposes it is sufficient to claim that a worldview *can* do so, at least in the case of Swinburne's.

3. Mackie, *Miracle of Theism*, 253.

4. Ibid., 250. For Küng's position, see Hans Küng, *Does God Exist?* (Garden City, NY: Doubleday, 1980).

5. Again, compare Swinburne, *Is There a God?*, 44–45, and Mackie, *Miracle of Theism*, 252–53. Although *Miracle of Theism* was published years before *Is There a God?*, the original argumentation of Swinburne in *The Existence of God* to which Mackie responded is largely the same.

6. There are numerous other examples in the contemporary debate with similar problems, which the concept of worldview may likewise make intelligible. A more contemporary case is *The Non-Existence of God*, by Everitt, especially its critique of the theistic argument from the fine-tuning of the universe (chapter 5), the argument that a vast universe, largely devoid of intelligent

life, counts against the existence of God (chapter 11), and the argument that the concept of God, with such properties as omnipotence and omniscience, is incoherent and logically impossible (chapters 13, 14).

These arguments depend upon prior assumptions and premises, none of which the theist needs to affirm, such as the point that the different possibilities in the universal constants have different probabilistic weight we do not yet know. Likewise some of Everitt's points would seem simply bizarre to many theists, such as that because God has no body and thus cannot, say, scratch his nose (265), he is not omnipotent, or that because God is omnipresent and timeless, he cannot "know" indexical statements such as "what is over there" or "what happens tomorrow" or "Was Kennedy killed forty years ago?," and therefore is not omniscient (293).

However, if conceived as arguing from his particular worldview, Everitt may be understood as presenting an argument that there is no need for those who hold an atheist worldview to abandon it for a theist worldview. Thus, he is arguing that there is no reason to conclude that the anthropic principle constitutes a problem for a naturalist worldview, and that from the standpoint of his worldview, with premises not shared by theists, the concept of God seems incoherent and thus there are reasons to reject it. Like Mackie, he is presenting an adequate intellectual response from an atheist worldview, while simultaneously misunderstanding theist worldviews, especially regarding the concept of God, creation, and so forth, and doing so, it seems, for the same reason as Mackie.

So far, I have limited my examples to Mackie and Everitt because it is still widely assumed that the atheist standpoint is a kind of "default" position, and that its standard of reasoning is universal.

7. Mackie, *Miracle of Theism*, 64–80.

8. Mikael Stenmark, *Scientism: Science, Ethics and Religion* (Aldershot: Ashgate, 2001). Stenmark also identifies and critiques the other claims of scientism that science alone can answer moral or existential questions and thus will displace traditional ethics and religion. The first two claims are more relevant to our purpose and are discussed here.

9. Ibid., 22–23.

10. Michael Hanby, *No God, No Science? Theology, Cosmology, Biology* (Malden, MA: Blackwell, 2013). Hanby would argue, however, that insofar as such a metaphysical position is held tacitly by science and is implicit in its methods, a clear distinction between "science" and "scientism" is unsustainable (2, 11). This is certainly not because scientism is indeed a neutral position that affirms only what is known by "science," but because a significant

portion of the practice of modern science itself is already interwoven with a set of metaphysical and, more importantly, *theological* concepts, definitions, and metaphors—and according to Hanby, deeply flawed ones at that. What I am arguing here is, however, more modest: even if the practice and method of modern science are separable from such a metaphysical and theological framework as Hanby describes, those who participate in the debate about God, even to "merely not affirm" that God exists, are unable to do so by "pure science"—if such exists—alone, but must do so from a particular metaphysical and epistemological standpoint, of which scientific knowledge composes only a part.

11. These are significant debates in philosophy of science, between what is called the regularity and the necessitarian approach and between the realist and the antirealist view regarding the concept of the laws of nature. For example, see Martin Curd and J. A. Clover, eds., *Philosophy of Science: The Central Issues* (New York: W. W. Norton, 1998), chapter 7.

12. Again, this is a classic question in the philosophy of mathematics that divides the mathematical realists and the antirealists, with numerous rival positions within these broadly conceived two views.

13. There are a number of philosophical positions on how the different scientific fields may be organized hierarchically, and on whether each discipline can be reduced to a more "fundamental" discipline. Some even argue that the sciences may be organized to include ethics and metaphysics or theology. For an example of such arguments, as well as a concise discussion of the issues above, see Nancey Murphy and George F. R. Ellis, *On the Moral Nature of the Universe: Theology, Cosmology, and Ethics* (Minneapolis: Fortress Press, 1996), and Arthur R. Peacocke, *Theology for a Scientific Age: Being and Becoming— Natural, Divine and Human*, 2nd enlarged ed. (Minneapolis: Fortress Press, 1993; first published 1990 by Blackwell).

14. Wolterstorff, "Can Belief in God Be Rational?," 159.

15. Naugle, *Worldview*, 260.

16. Ibid., 324.

17. A number of discussions regarding Kuhn's *The Structure of Scientific Revolutions* place this work squarely in the context of the realist-antirealist debate. Likewise, writings on the realist-antirealist debate nearly always mention Kuhn as a significant influence for the contemporary debate. Examples of the discussion regarding this debate can be found in the collection of papers in *Scientific Realism*, ed. Jarrett Leplin (Berkeley: University of California Press, 1984), where Richard N. Boyd in particular describes Kuhn—I think too simplistically—as an antirealist and a constructivist in the chapter entitled "The Current Status of Scientific Realism," 42–81.

18. Rorty, "Pragmatism and Philosophy," in *Contemporary Approaches to Philosophy*, ed. Paul Moser and Dwayne Mulder (New York: Macmillan, 1982), 414.

19. This is, of course, one of Rorty's most controversial positions; the question regarding the notion of truth remains a substantive philosophical issue.

20. Rorty, "Pragmatism and Philosophy," 413.

21. Ibid., 406.

22. Ibid., 422–23.

23. Ibid., 423.

24. Ibid., 424.

25. Charles Taylor, "Overcoming Epistemology," in *Philosophical Arguments* (Cambridge, MA: Harvard University Press, 1995), 2.

26. Ibid.

27. Ibid., 3.

28. Ibid.

29. Ibid.

30. Ibid., 11.

31. Ibid., 12.

32. Ibid.

33. Ibid., 12–13.

34. Ibid., 13.

35. Charles Taylor, "Rorty in the Epistemological Tradition," in *Reading Rorty*, ed. Alan Malachowski (Oxford: Blackwell, 1990), 270.

36. Ibid., 258.

37. Rorty's reply is found in "Taylor on Truth," in *Philosophy in an Age of Pluralism: The Philosophy of Charles Taylor in Question*, ed. James Tully (Cambridge: Cambridge University Press, 1994), 20–33. Taylor replies in the same book in "Charles Taylor Replies" (213–57; he addresses Rorty in 219–22). Gary Gutting presents a summary account and assessment of the debate in *Pragmatic Liberalism and the Critique of Modernity* (Notre Dame, IN: University of Notre Dame Press, 1999), part 1, chapter 4, "The Problem of Truth," 25–32, where he supports Rorty's position against Taylor. I believe, however, that Gutting does so only by missing Taylor's emphasis on how the concept of truth is inseparable from the articulation of our way of living.

38. Naugle, *Worldview*, 186. In 164–70, Naugle argues that Donald Davidson's critique of conceptual schemes is also a critique, ultimately, of the notion that the knower and reality are somehow separated. Davidson's article that he refers to is "On the Very Idea of a Conceptual Scheme," found in

Proceedings and Addresses of the American Philosophical Association 47 (November 1973–74): 5–20, which was originally presented as the presidential address before the seventieth annual meeting of the eastern division of the American Philosophical Association in Atlanta, Georgia, on December 28, 1973. The work appears later in Davidson's book *Inquiries into Truth and Interpretation* (Oxford: Clarendon, 1984), 183–98. Naugle discusses the introduction to *Inquiries into Truth and Interpretation* to provide more context for this article, which argues against the possibility of alternative conceptual schemes. Naugle then lists a number of critical responses against Davidson's argument in *Worldview*, 171–73.

39. Knight, "Guide to Further Reading," in MacIntyre and Knight, *MacIntyre Reader*, 277.

40. MacIntyre, "An Interview for Cogito," in MacIntyre and Knight, *MacIntyre Reader*, 267.

41. Winch, *Idea of a Social Science*, 100.

42. MacIntyre, "Is Understanding Religion Compatible with Believing?," in *Rationality*, ed. Brian R. Wilson (Oxford: Blackwell, 1970), 65. First published in John Hick, ed., *Faith and the Philosophers* (London: Macmillan, 1964), 115–33.

43. Ibid., 71.

44. Although part of the problem in this case is that their belief system is such that it is "practically" unverifiable or unfalsifiable.

45. Ibid., 67–68.

46. Winch, "Understanding a Primitive Society," in Wilson, *Rationality*, 96. First published in *American Philosophical Quarterly* 1, no. 4 (October 1964): 307–24.

47. Ibid., 101.

48. Ibid., 102.

49. Charles Taylor, "Rationality," in *Rationality and Relativism*, ed. Martin Hollis and Steven Lukes (Cambridge, MA: MIT Press, 1982), 98.

50. Holmes, *Contours of a World View*, 50.

51. Ibid., 50–51.

52. Ibid.

53. See Ninian Smart, "The Philosophy of Worldviews, or the Philosophy of Religion Transformed," in *Religious Pluralism and Truth: Essays on Cross-Cultural Philosophy of Religion*, ed. Thomas Dean (Albany: State of University of New York Press, 1995), 17–31. In proposing a philosophy of worldview, Smart criticizes the tendency of philosophy of religion to concern itself mostly with the claims of Western theism, arguing that there are many dif-

ferent religions, and indeed worldviews—among which he includes secular ideologies like Marxism—with vastly different concepts, beliefs, attitudes, and behaviors, all of which are significant topics, yet most of which contemporary philosophy rarely, if ever, addresses. For Smart's work in philosophy of religion that address non-Western religions and secular ideologies, see Smart, *Worldviews: Crosscultural Explorations of Human Beliefs* (New York: Scribners, 1983), or *Dimensions of the Sacred: An Anatomy of the World's Beliefs* (Berkeley: University of California Press, 1996).

54. Ninian Smart, *Religion and the Western Mind* (Albany: State of University of New York Press, 1987), 47.

55. Ibid., 48.

56. The following argument is found in Smart, "Truth, Criteria, and Dialogue," in Dean, *Religious Pluralism and Truth*, 67–71. Smart uses the term "system" interchangeably with "worldview."

57. Taylor, "Rationality," in Hollis and Lukes, *Rationality and Relativism*, 104.

58. Ibid., 100.

59. Wilko van Holten, *Explanation within the Bounds of Religion* (Frankfurt: Peter Lang, 2003). Van Holten emphasizes, however, that this explanatory role is only a part of, and inseparable from, the religious forms of life in which it is situated.

60. Ibid., 125–30. What van Holten argues in his book is what my account regarding arguments about the existence of God more or less takes for granted. Whereas I argue for a shift in our understanding of the rational debate about the existence of God, using the concept of worldviews, van Holten is in a sense describing how theism as a worldview rightly claims to be rational and so participates in such a debate, while largely leaving aside the question whether it is in fact rational.

61. Ibid., 146–47.

62. Ibid., 158–71.

63. Ibid., 169.

64. Ibid., 171.

65. MacIntyre, *Whose Justice? Which Rationality?*, 78–79.

66. Ibid., 79–80.

67. MacIntyre, *First Principles, Final Ends and Contemporary Philosophical Issues* (Milwaukee: Marquette University Press, 1990), 12–13.

68. MacIntyre, *Whose Justice? Which Rationality?*, 166–69.

69. Ibid., 166–67.

70. Ibid., 160–62.

FIVE   The Crossroad We Have Passed: The Project of Thomas Aquinas

1. Flew, "Presumption of Atheism," 27.

2. Fergus Kerr, *After Aquinas: Versions of Thomism* (Cornwall: Blackwell, 2002), 17. MacIntyre argues that this role of Aquinas as a counter to Descartes is a misunderstanding of his position, and that *Aeterni Patris* itself does not imply such a view. He argues in *Three Rival Versions of Moral Enquiry* (Notre Dame, IN: University of Notre Dame Press, 1991), chapter 3, that the very questions of epistemology since Descartes are simply not asked in Aquinas's position. Kerr also notes this in *After Aquinas*, 17–19.

3. Bertrand Russell, *A History of Western Philosophy* (New York: Simon & Schuster, 1972), 463. Originally published as *A History of Western Philosophy, and Its Connection with Political and Social Circumstances from the Earliest Times to the Present Day* (New York: Simon & Schuster, 1945).

4. Anthony Kenny, *The Five Ways: St. Thomas Aquinas's Proofs of God's Existence* (London: Routledge & Kegan Paul, 1969), 2–3.

5. Ibid., 3–4. This assessment is even more remarkable as Kenny is later criticized repeatedly by Gyula Klima for inappropriately using post-Fregean logic and concepts to assess and critique a number of Aquinas's positions, such as his argument that God is *ipsum esse subsistens*—the essence of God is his existence. See Gyula Klima, review of *Aquinas on Mind*, by Anthony Kenny, *Faith and Philosophy* 15 (1998): 113–17, and also "On Kenny on Aquinas on Being: A Critical Review of A. Kenny: *Aquinas on Being*," *International Philosophical Quarterly* 44 (2004): 567–80. What Kenny seems to have done, at least in his later work, namely understanding the position of different intellectual frameworks in terms of his own, thereby misunderstanding it, is precisely what MacIntyre predicts will happen in the earlier stages of the encounter between different intellectual traditions.

6. Kenny, introduction to Thomas Aquinas, *Summa Theologiae*, vol. 1, *The Existence of God, Part One, Questions 1–13*, ed. trans. Thomas Gilby (Garden City, NY: Doubleday Image, 1969), 11–12.

7. Brian Davies, introduction to *Thomas Aquinas: Contemporary Philosophical Perspectives*, ed. Davies (New York: Oxford University Press, 2002), 4–5.

8. In the setting of medieval education, however, such students would be expected to have already trained in philosophical disciplines extensively, and thus be conversant with the arguments and writings Aquinas often only mentions or briefly summarizes in this work.

9. Here on, I will refer to the *Summa Theologiae* simply as the *Summa* and cite it as *ST*, with the section listed in the order of part, question, then article. For example, *Summa Theologiae*, part one, question two, article three will be *ST* I.2.3.

10. B. Davies, introduction to *Aquinas's "Summa Theologiae": Critical Essays*, ed. B. Davies (Toronto: Rowman & Littlefield, 2006), ix.

11. The following observation, of the Latin formula, is largely from Jan. A. Aertsen, "Aquinas's Philosophy in Its Historical Setting," in *The Cambridge Companion to Aquinas*, ed. Norman Kretzmann and Eleanore Stump (Cambridge: Cambridge University Press, 1993), 18–19. Some articles, however, such as the question on whether God exists is self-evident, begins with *videtur quod*, or "it seems," with Aquinas taking the negative response.

12. Kerr begins his discussion of the Five Ways by remarking, "The Five Ways . . . have given rise to so much debate, particularly since the 1920s, that it is almost a shock to return to the text and see how very little space they occupy in the vast expanse of the *Summa Theologiae*." Kerr, *After Aquinas*, 52.

13. I will include original Latin phrases in my discussion when either the concept or the terms seem awkward, unclear, or apt to be misunderstood with only the English translation, or when the precise wording will become important later in this chapter or in the next. Note that Aquinas refers to the verse cited as Psalm 52:1, following the numbering of the Psalms in the Vulgate.

14. The comparison example of "human is an animal," however, is misleading because Aquinas argues in *ST* I.3.5 that God does not belong to a genus in the way "human beings" belongs to the genus of "animals." Thus, not only is it the case that the essence of God cannot be known in this way, but God transcends every category through which we come to understand the essence of things.

15. For our purpose, I describe here only what the Five Ways are arguing for, rather than the details of their argumentation. Several recent works have presented a sympathetic account of Aquinas's theistic arguments using contemporary terms and examples. Of these, a significant work that describes the Five Ways in the context of Aquinas's philosophical and theological position as a whole, but written for a wider, more general audience, is found in Brian Davies, *Aquinas* (New York: Continuum, 2002). C. F. J. Martin, *Thomas Aquinas: God and Explanations* (Edinburgh: Edinburgh University Press, 1997), is another important work from a contemporary philosophical school of analytic Thomism, which presents an account of the Five Ways in the context of the Latin Aristotelian theory of science as "knowledge through explanations."

16. Davies, *Aquinas*, 39.

17. Ibid.

18. Victor White, "Prelude to the Five Ways," in Davies, *Aquinas's Summa Theologiae*, 33–34.

19. Kerr, *After Aquinas*, 52.

20. Plantinga, "Reason and Belief in God," 40–47.

21. Ibid., 47–48.

22. Kretzmann, "Evidence and Religious Belief."

23. Everitt, *Non-Existence of God*, 59–60, 73.

24. Ibid., 66. This again seems to evince Everitt's tendency, noted in chapter 4, to misunderstand and misdescribe the positions of rival worldviews. As we will see, Aquinas rejects the infinite regression not because an infinite chain of causes cannot start, but because the explanation of causes must terminate somewhere in an Aristotelian conception of intellectual inquiry.

25. Flew, "Presumption of Atheism," 27–28.

26. Ibid., 28.

27. The argument is in the second objection in *ST* I.2.3. Again, I include the original Latin here because the wording and concepts will become important in chapter 6 when we examine the function of the Five Ways proper.

28. Flew, "Presumption of Atheism," 29.

29. Ibid.

30. White, "Prelude to the Five Ways," in Davies, *Aquinas's "Summa Theologiae*," 26–27.

31. This may at first seem an inconsequential difference from Flew—it may seem to the proponents of Flew's reading that the difference is between starting from a presumption of atheism as such and starting from such a presumption *because* the larger position in which the Five Ways is set is a Christian theology concerned with responding to those who are atheists. Such differences in motivation would have little relevance to the argument that Aquinas follows a procedural presumption of atheism. However, this seemingly trivial difference will become increasingly important as we go on, to the extent that this "presumption of (an Aristotelian) atheist naturalism" (Flew, "Presumption of Atheism," 28) will be something radically different from the kind of presumption Flew envisioned.

32. White, "Prelude to the Five Ways," 29.

33. Ibid., 31.

34. Ibid., 31–32.

35. Nicholas Wolterstorff, *Reason within the Bounds of Religion* (Grand Rapids: Eerdmans, 1976).

36. Kerr, *After Aquinas*, 57.

37. Ibid., 61. The translation of Romans 1:20 is from Gilby's translation of *Summa Theologiae*, vol. 1, as quoted by Kerr.

38. Ibid., 58.

39. Ibid., 59.

40. Ibid., 58.

41. For an account of this philosophical development in the Middle Ages, and especially Aquinas's place in it, see Jan A. Aertsen, *Medieval Philosophy and the Transcendentals: The Case of Thomas Aquinas* (New York: E. J. Brill, 1996).

42. Kerr, *After Aquinas*, 60.

43. Ibid., 58.

44. A concise, readable discussion of the arguments by negation that follow the Five Ways can be found in B. Davies, "Aquinas on What God Is Not," in Davies, *Aquinas's Summa Theologiae*, 129–44.

45. Eugene Rogers Jr., *Thomas Aquinas and Karl Barth: Sacred Doctrine and the Natural Knowledge of God* (Notre Dame, IN: University of Notre Dame Press, 1995), 136–37. Kerr refers to this work in *After Aquinas*, 63–65.

46. Jean-Pierre Torrell, O.P., *Saint Thomas Aquinas*, vol. 2, *Spiritual Master*, trans. Robert Royal (Washington, DC: Catholic University of America Press, 1993). For his recent biography of Aquinas, see Torrell, *Saint Thomas Aquinas*, vol. 1, *The Person and His Work*, rev. ed., trans. Robert Royal (Washington, DC: Catholic University of America Press, 2005).

47. Torrell, *Saint Thomas Aquinas*, vol. 2, *Spiritual Master*, 27.

48. MacIntyre, *Whose Justice? Which Rationality?*, 172.

49. Kretzmann, *The Metaphysics of Theism: Aquinas's Natural Theology in the "Summa Contra Gentiles"* (New York: Clarendon Press, 1997), 22–23, 27.

50. Ibid., 85.

51. Thomas Hibbs, *Dialectic and Narrative in Aquinas: An Interpretation of the "Summa Contra Gentiles"* (Notre Dame, IN: University of Notre Dame Press, 1995).

52. MacIntyre, *Whose Justice? Which Rationality?*, 172.

53. Hibbs, *Dialectic and Narrative in Aquinas*, 22.

54. MacIntyre, *Whose Justice? Which Rationality?*, 172.

55. Ibid., 166–67.

56. MacIntyre, *Three Rival Versions of Moral Enquiry*, chapter 5.

57. Martin, *Thomas Aquinas*, 25

58. Aertsen, "Aquinas's Philosophy in Its Historical Setting," in Kretzmann and Stump, *Cambridge Companion to Aquinas*, 20.

59. Ibid., 20–21.

60. MacIntyre, *Three Rival Versions of Moral Enquiry*, 107.

61. Ibid., 110.

62. Ibid.

63. Ibid., 110–11.

64. Ibid., 111–12.

65. MacIntyre, *Whose Justice? Which Rationality?*, 168.

66. Aertsen, "Aquinas's Philosophy in Its Historical Setting," in Kretzmann and Stump, *Cambridge Companion to Aquinas*, 21.

67. Ralph McInerny, *Praeambula Fidei: Thomism and the God of the Philosophers*. (Washington, DC: Catholic University of America Press, 2006), 166.

68. Torrell, *Saint Thomas Aquinas*, vol. 1, *The Person and His Work*, 225, 248.

69. Martin, *Thomas Aquinas*, 29.

70. Hibbs, *Dialectic and Narrative in Aquinas*, 14.

71. Aertsen, "Aquinas's Philosophy in Its Historical Setting," 21. Most of his writings on the issues discussed in this article are presented in more extensive accounts found in his two books *Nature and Creature: Thomas Aquinas' Way of Thought* (Leiden: E. J. Brill, 1988) and *Medieval Philosophy and the Transcendentals: The Case of Thomas Aquinas.*

72. Aertsen, "Aquinas's Philosophy in Its Historical Setting," 22–23.

73. Ibid.

74. Ibid., 24.

75. MacIntyre, *Three Rival Versions of Moral Enquiry*, 120.

76. Aertsen, "Aquinas's Philosophy in Its Historical Setting," 25.

77. Ibid., 26.

78. MacIntyre, *Three Rival Versions of Moral Enquiry*, 123–24.

79. Ibid., 122.

80. Ibid., 117.

81. B. Russell, *History of Western Philosophy*, 461–62.

SIX   God at the Crossroads: What the Five Ways Do

1. Again, in a comprehensive, holistic web of beliefs, such as a worldview, all beliefs are interconnected, and this is especially the case for the "existence of God," which is central, or "basic"—in the way D. Z. Phillips uses the term, rather than Plantinga—to the entire worldview. However, some questions are more immediately and directly relevant, and thus I would place these questions as issues near the center of the web, and farther from the "periphery," where beliefs are affected more by particular experiences and susceptible to revision.

2. Aertsen, *Nature and Creature*, 2. MacIntyre, among others, also presents a similar account of this conception of philosophy in *First Principles, Final Ends*, which will be discussed in greater detail later.

3. Ibid., 2–3. For the characterization that the concept of "nature" is central to Greek philosophical thinking, Aertsen cites E. Frank, "Der Wandel in der Beurteilung der Griechischen Philosophie," in *Wissen, Wollen, Glauben: Gesammelte Aufsätze zur Philosophiegeschichte und Existentialphilosophie* (Zurich and Stuttgart, 1955), 44; O. Gigon, *Grundprobleme der antiken Philosophie* (Bern, 1959), 154.

4. Ibid., 3–4.

5. Ibid., 4.

6. Ibid.

7. Ibid., 5.

8. MacIntyre, *Three Rival Versions of Moral Enquiry*, 108–9.

9. Rogers, *Thomas Aquinas and Karl Barth*, 17. The main purpose of the arguments in this work is to narrow the distance between Barth and Aquinas regarding the issue of natural knowledge of God without divine revelation, by examining the similarity of their positions on Romans 1:17–25. With this purpose, Rogers argues that in order to adequately understand Aquinas's position on theology as an Aristotelian science, one must direct careful attention to the role of scripture, and more importantly the significance of the person of Christ, in Aquinas's thought.

10. Ibid., 20.

11. Ibid., 32.

12. Ibid., 33.

13. Kerr, for example, in his survey of the different versions of Thomism, generally agrees with his argument. See Kerr, *After Aquinas*, 61–63.

14. Aertsen, *Medieval Philosophy and the Transcendentals*, 245.

15. Ibid., 250.

16. Ibid., 370.

17. Ibid.

18. Richard A. Lee Jr., *Science, the Singular, and the Question of Theology: The New Middle Ages* (New York: Palgrave, 2002), 1.

19. Ibid.

20. Ibid., 5.

21. Ibid., 36–37.

22. Ibid., 37. The phrase, literally, "the science of God and the blessed" (*scientia Dei et beatorum*), is found in *ST* I.1.2.

23. MacIntyre, *Whose Justice? Which Rationality?*, 71.

24. Ibid. MacIntyre's discussion in this context, and furthermore in this book, largely centers on the issue of "justice," and thus on practical reasoning. However, his account is relevant to theoretical reasoning and metaphysics— especially in these passages—because it describes the conception of "rational enquiry" as such and on the more general issue of "truth." Indeed, the chapter in which he presents his account on Plato is itself titled "Plato and Rational Enquiry."

25. Ibid., 71.

26. Ibid.

27. That is, Plato expands upon what we believe to have been the conception of rational inquiry held by the historical Socrates, as abstracted from Plato's depiction of him. MacIntyre's Plato, as opposed to Socrates, in this case, is depicted by the Socrates of *The Republic*, who is the spokesperson for Plato's position.

28. MacIntyre, *Whose Justice? Which Rationality?*, 80.

29. Ibid.

30. Ibid., 82.

31. Ibid., 83.

32. Ibid.

33. Russell, *History of Western Philosophy*, 127.

34. Ibid., 128.

35. MacIntyre. *Whose Justice? Which Rationality?*, 85.

36. Ibid., 91.

37. Ibid.

38. MacIntyre, *First Principles, Final Ends*, 23.

39. Ibid., 27–28.

40. Ibid., 38.

41. Ibid., 13.

42. Aertsen, "Aquinas's Philosophy in Its Historical Setting," 23. See also Aertsen, *Nature and Creature*, 86–87.

43. Ibid.

44. For an extensive account of Aquinas's position on the transcendentals and their relations to each other, see Aertsen, *Medieval Philosophy and the Transcendentals*, chapter 2.

45. Aertsen, *Medieval Philosophy and the Transcendentals*, 360.

46. Ibid., 381–83.

47. Ibid., 125–26.

48. MacIntyre, *First Principles, Final Ends*, 29.

49. Ibid.

50. Kerr, *After Aquinas*, 70.

51. Ibid., 70–71.

52. Hibbs, *Dialectic and Narrative in Aquinas: An Interpretation of the "Summa Contra Gentiles,"* 36.

53. Ibid., 7. Hibbs then comments, "In the traditions with which Thomas concerns himself in the book, there was no disagreement over the existence of God." This may seem puzzling since in the Five Ways, Aquinas responds to what Flew perhaps hastily termed as "Aristotelian atheist naturalism." I have argued, however, that the "God" of such arguments by itself is not what Christians, including Aquinas, would call God. Aristotelian philosophy was "naturalist" in this sense. What was uncontroversial was the arguments for a kind of ultimate first principle—the first cause—in general. What was not disputed was that there is something like God, and what was disputed in the later arguments against pagan writers was whether that something is "God" in the Christian sense. Or, to put it differently, the dispute was on which position has the best understanding or conception of this ultimate first principle and reality, which Christians understand as "God."

54. McInerny, *Praeambula Fidei*, 219–36.

55. Ibid., 236. The definition of *praeambula fidei* is found in 27–32.

56. MacIntyre, *Three Rival Versions of Moral Enquiry*, 120–21.

57. Ibid., 121.

58. Ibid., 122.

59. Ibid., 123.

60. MacIntyre, *First Principles, Final Ends*, 4.

61. Ibid., 5.

62. Aertsen, "Aquinas's Philosophy in Its Historical Setting," 28–33. Aertsen adds, however, that this final end of inquiry—the ultimate fulfillment of the human desire to know, which is the central notion to Aristotelian philosophy—is not attainable, and thus philosophy is caught in an "anguish." It is, however, given the promise of such blessed knowledge in the Christian revelation. Thus for Aquinas, it is the Christian revelation that shows the Aristotelians the way to encounter the personal reality of what their intellectual tradition was striving toward.

63. MacIntyre, *Three Rival Versions of Moral Enquiry*, 124.

64. Flew, "Presumption of Atheism," 28.

SEVEN   The Fork: The Emergence of Modern Atheism as a Worldview

1. Taylor, *A Secular Age* (Cambridge, MA: Harvard University Press, 2007), 38–41.

2. Such an argument is nothing new; John Milbank's *Theology and Social Theory: Beyond Secular Reason* (Oxford: Blackwell, 1990), which outlined how the secular worldview was constructed largely from the material in Christian theology—or heretical offshoots of it—is one of the most well-known early works of this sort. This book, which led to a major movement in theology called the Radical Orthodoxy, is now more than two decades old. Again, what is relevant here is the implication of such accounts for how we are to conceive of the debate about the existence of God.

3. MacIntyre, *Three Rival Versions of Moral Enquiry*, 151–52.

4. Ibid., 165.

5. Lee, for example, in contrast to MacIntyre, presents a sympathetic account of those who came after Aquinas in *Science, the Singular, and the Question of Theology*, chapter 4 and onward. I argued in the sixth chapter that Aquinas's understanding of theology as a "subalternate science" of the "knowledge of God, and of the blessed" was a crucial part of his position as a whole, including his argument for the existence of God. However, Lee argues that there were a number of difficulties with this conception of theology as a "subalternate science," which Scotus and William of Ockham rightly criticized. This, he asserts, eventually opened the way for modern science.

6. Taylor, *Secular Age*, 22, 23–26. That is, the development of secularism constitutes simply a "loss" of religious belief, a position that Taylor critiques as a simplistic and inadequate understanding of the complex series of developments that made secularism possible.

7. Richard Popkin, *The History of Scepticism from Savonarola to Bayle* (Oxford: Oxford University Press, 2003).

8. Ibid., xxiii.

9. Ibid., xix–xx.

10. Ibid., 127, and discussed throughout chapters 9–11.

11. Ibid., 148.

12. Ibid., 252–53.

13. Stephen Toulmin, *Cosmopolis: The Hidden Agenda of Modernity* (Chicago: University of Chicago Press, 1992), 70–71.

14. Clayton, *Religions, Reasons, and Gods*, 214. It should be noted that such European thinkers who characterized the "far-away" societies like China simply as "atheist" have described these very different worldviews in solely European terms, thereby misdescribing them—as those who encounter intellectual positions incommensurable to their own are apt to do. As further dialogues between the West and other societies progressed, more nuanced comparisons became possible. For an example of such dialogues, among works

too numerous to list, see Hans Küng and Julia Ching's *Christianity and Chinese Religions* (New York: Doubleday, 1989). A key point of this book is that there are many "religious" elements—including what may be characterized as a belief in a personal supreme being—that thread through Chinese intellectual traditions. However, the main point of Clayton's observation stands; what these Europeans saw in these societies—even if it was a result of inadequate understanding—was the *possibility* of a practicable atheist worldview.

15. Ibid.

16. Ibid., 211.

17. James Turner, *Without God, without Creed: The Origins of Unbelief in America* (Baltimore: Johns Hopkins University Press, 1985), xii–xiii.

18. Ibid., xiii.

19. Ibid., 21.

20. Ibid., 16.

21. Ibid., 56.

22. Ibid., 57.

23. Ibid., 59–60.

24. Ibid., 104–5.

25. Ibid., 96.

26. Ibid., 70.

27. Ibid., 180.

28. Ibid., 187.

29. Ibid.

30. Ibid., 183.

31. Ibid., 269.

32. Ibid.

33. Michael J. Buckley, *At the Origins of Modern Atheism* (New Haven: Yale University Press, 1987), 193.

34. Michael J. Buckley, *Denying and Disclosing God* (New Haven: Yale University Press, 2004), xii. He also mentions a seeming misread of his previous work as claiming that this root of atheism begins with Aquinas, a reading he explicitly disclaims.

35. Ibid., xvi.

36. Ibid., 10.

37. Ibid., 21–22.

38. Ibid., 46.

39. John Locke, *An Essay concerning Human Understanding*, ed. Peter Nidditch (Oxford: Oxford University Press, 1975; first published 1690).

40. Buckley, *Denying and Disclosing God*, 79.

41. Ibid., 95–96.

42. Moser in fact references Buckley's work in his discussion in *Elusive God*, 35, 84.

43. Buckley, *Denying and Disclosing God*, 138.

44. Hanby, *No God, No Science?* Hanby's book, briefly mentioned in chapter 4, was published when the completed and revised manuscript of this book, *God at the Crossroads*, had been submitted for review, and this has largely prevented an adequate discussion of his arguments within the confines of this book. Also, his work focuses primarily on metaphysics and theology, whereas my discussion tended to center on issues associated with epistemology—the two are closely related, yet do diverge. However, I would venture to suggest here that the kind of argument he presents in regard to how Christian theology is essential for the metaphysics of science—for science to properly understand itself and its subject of inquiry—may resemble how a theist argument in the debate about the existence of God would eventually proceed under my proposal. It remains to be seen whether or not his arguments are convincing to those inhabiting a scientific atheist worldview.

45. Ibid., chapter 3.

46. This is the precise wording of such theology, which Hanby characterizes as the "traditional Christian theology" that Darwinism both affirms as its foil and denies by its scientific findings. Ibid., 301.

47. Ibid., 5, 324. This, Hanby would argue—and I would concur—is the true question of contention in the debate about God as the first cause. That is, God is not an answer to how or why the universe exists, but *what* reality *is*.

48. Diogenes Allen, *Philosophy for Understanding Theology* (Atlanta: John Knox, 1985), 162.

49. Ibid., 163.

50. Ibid. Hanby would, however, correct a simplistic view that the theory of impetus explained "motion" better than the Aristotelian position, since the theory did so only by redefining and narrowing the meaning of the term, resulting in the loss of a greater kind of knowledge or explanation the term was meant to convey. I will let his words summarize the difference here:

> The operative concept of motion here is obviously very different from Newtonian motion, which is really but measured differences in *stasis* plotted against a motionless backdrop. The moved bodies themselves are internally indifferent to that state, and indeed it makes no difference, from a Newtonian point of view, *what* those bodies are. Aristotelian motion, by contrast, is a function of the priority accorded to form and is therefore an attribute of *things*. It is itself a kind of actuality, in fact, namely, the actuality of a potency *as such*, which we might paraphrase, not inaccurately I

think, as the actuality of chang*ing*. This fundamental meaning of motion applies even in the paradigm instance of local motion, whose medium is not homogeneous space but heterogeneous places more or less conducive to the flourishing of the actual things that find themselves at home and moving in them. This too reflects the ontological priority of form and actual things, for as Joe Sachs puts it, it matters to things where they are (1995: 105). As an attribute of a thing, motion is always dependent on the something that moves, an observation which gives rise to the distinction between "natural motion," which a thing does or undergoes as a matter of *per se* activity, and the indifferent "violent motion," which a thing undergoes *per accidens*. Natural motion, the acorn growing into an oak, for example, reveals the natures of the thing in question, whereas violent motion, an acorn kicked across the sidewalk by my son, does not. That the object happens to be an acorn in this latter example is entirely incidental. (Hanby, *No God, No Science?*, 61–62)

Hanby concedes, however, that Aristotle's metaphysical conception of motion and act was still partly responsible for his error in physics and astronomy, an error that, though secondary to his philosophical position as a whole, was sufficient to bring the entire system into "ill-repute."

51. Allen, *Philosophy for Understanding Theology*, 164.

52. Ibid., 166.

53. Whether an event explainable by laws of nature—that is, a natural event—can be a special act of God, or "miracle," is now one of the first points usually raised and discussed in the contemporary dialogue between religion and science concerning divine action. Alan G. Padgett, for example, begins his article by rejecting this popular disjunction in "God and Miracle in an Age of Science," in *The Blackwell Companion to Science and Christianity*, ed. J. B. Stump and Alan G. Padgett (Malden, MA: Wiley-Blackwell, 2012), 533. Likewise, in Thomas F. Tracy, "Theology of Divine Action," in *The Oxford Handbook of Religion and Science*, ed. Philip Clayton (Oxford: Oxford University Press, 2008), 597–605, the disjunction is brought up by scientific writers as a popular point, and by Rudolph Bultmann as a basis for a systematic theological argument against the idea of particular divine actions. Tracy responds against their arguments by outlining different ways of thinking about divine action, including that of Aquinas.

54. Again, Hanby, in chapter 3 of *No God, No Science?*, especially in 120–29, presents a remarkably similar—though much more thorough—account of the kind of process I have outlined. To do so, however, he closely follows the changing conception of being, cause, motion, matter, space, nature, and other metaphysical concepts that form the theological understanding of God, divine

power, and creation, while I have limited this discussion primarily to the role of the concept of God in intellectual inquiry in a given set of worldviews, and the relation of that concept to argumentation for the existence of God.

EIGHT   To Set Out: Arguing from the Crossroads to God

1. This statement, of course, is a conscious parallel to Wittgenstein's remark: "A *picture* held us captive. And we could not get outside it, for it lay in our language and language seemed to repeat it to us inexorably." *Philosophical Investigations*, section 115.

2. However, I would speculate that any extensive engagement with Continental postmodern philosophy that derives from this work will likely build from MacIntyre's answer to what he calls the genealogy version of moral inquiry, presented in his *Three Rival Versions of Moral Enquiry*. On the other hand, the position presented in my book regarding who is best able to complete a project that brings two incommensurable positions together at a crossroad suggests that a successful project of bringing the Christian perspective and continental postmodern philosophy together at a crossroad would resemble in significant ways the kind of project exemplified in the philosophical and theological works by John Caputo, such as *The Weakness of God: A Theology of the Event* (Bloomington: Indiana University Press, 2006), or *The Insistence of God: A Theology of Perhaps* (Bloomington: Indiana University Press, 2013). Again, however, this remains mere speculation on my part. For a good overview of this philosophical movement, see Caputo, *The Religious: Blackwell Readings in Continental Philosophy* (Oxford: Wiley-Blackwell, 2001).

3. Hanby's *No God, No Science?* again presents a similar but more extensive argument, as we briefly saw in the previous chapter, with a full genealogical account of the construction of the metaphysical and theological position that is implicit in modern science.

4. For example, the contemporary philosophical writings of Quine, Kuhn, Rorty, and others that I have examined constitute significant philosophical developments that have emerged from within a largely scientific naturalist worldview and intellectual tradition, which address questions that were raised by that worldview's particular conception of intellectual inquiry: philosophical and scientific reasoning.

5. Nancey Murphy, *Reconciling Theology and Science: A Radical Reformation Perspective* (Kitchener, ON: Pandora Press, 1997), 16.

6. Again, a significant issue here is whether the "higher" sciences can be reduced to the lower science. That is, whether things in the higher science can

be explained entirely in terms of the lower science, such that behaviors of, say, living beings can be explained entirely in terms of laws of physics. Murphy, for example, takes the position that there are limits to such reductionism, and that there are questions and matters in a higher science which can be answered and understood only at that particular level of analysis. For further discussion, see Murphy, *Anglo-American Postmodernity*, and Nancey Murphy and Warren S. Brown, *Did My Neurons Make Me Do It? Philosophical and Neurobiological Perspectives on Moral Responsibility and Free Will* (Oxford: Oxford University Press, 2007).

7. Murphy, *Reconciling Theology and Science*, 17. Peacocke's position that Murphy presents here is found in its most systematically developed form in *Theology for a Scientific Age*.

8. Stephen Hawking, *A Brief History of Time*, expanded ed. (New York: Bantam Books, 1998; first published 1988), 191.

9. Stephen Hawking and Leonard Mlodinow, *The Grand Design* (New York: Bantam Books, 2010), 180.

10. Here, note the parallel to the doctrine of *creatio ex nihilo*, where "God" is now replaced by "a law like gravity."

11. Hawking, *Brief History of Time*, 172.

12. Alister E. McGrath, *Science and Religion: A New Introduction*, 2nd ed. (Malden, MA: Wiley-Blackwell, 2010; first published as *Science and Religion: An Introduction* [Oxford: Blackwell, 1999]), 91.

13. Ibid.

14. Paul Davies, *The Mind of God: The Scientific Basis for a Rational World* (New York: Simon & Schuster, 1992), 82. It is also notable that McGrath is a Christian, whereas Davies in this work is does not subscribe to any religion, though he is sympathetic to a belief in God (16).

15. The most obvious objection to this point would be that the "laws of nature" are not actually what Christians would "call God." I will address this objection later in the chapter.

16. David Van Biema, "God vs. Science," *Time*, November 5, 2006, 37.

17. Ibid.

18. Ibid.

19. Keith Ward, *God, Chance & Necessity* (Oxford: Oneworld, 1996).

20. Ibid., 52–53.

21. Ibid., 55–56.

22. Again, for a discussion on the philosophical issue of free will and neurobiology, see Murphy and Brown, *Did My Neurons Make Me Do It?* For a series of discussions on the issue of reductionism, especially in regard to neurobiology, see Nancey Murphy, George F. R. Ellis, and Timothy O'Connor,

eds., *Downward Causation and the Neurobiology of Free Will* (Berlin: Springer Verlag, 2009).

23. Hawking and Mlodinow, *Grand Design*, 29.

24. I need not speculate what such alternative definitions will be. For example, in "God and Miracle in an Age of Science," Padgett presents a Christian, biblical definition of miracles as "signs and wonders" that "point to God's work of salvation and redemption" (533–34). Indeed, he finds the notion that miracles "break" the laws of nature theologically "confusing" and imprecise, and philosophically "objectionable" (534–35).

25. There have already been some writings regarding the rationality of theology as a historically extended inquiry that in significant ways also define the terms in which the claims of particular religious experiences throughout the history of a community of faith are confirmed by that community. See for example, Nancey Murphy, *Theology in the Age of Scientific Reasoning* (Ithaca, NY: Cornell University Press, 1990).

26. If I may speculate, such an answer may come to resemble the arguments found in Paul K. Moser, *The Severity of God: Religion and Philosophy Reconceived* (Cambridge: Cambridge University Press, 2013).

27. For the Christian theist perspective, one may perhaps call this "hardening of the heart."

28. For the details of their argument, see Paul Draper and Ryan Nichols, "Diagnosing Bias in Philosophy of Religion," *The Monist* 96, no. 3 (2013): 420–46.

29. A fairly thorough examination and critique of their claims is found in Klaas J. Kraay, "Method and Madness in Contemporary Analytic Philosophy of Religion," *Toronto Journal of Theology* 29 (2013): 245–64. Kraay also discusses and critiques similar criticisms of bias by J. L. Schellenberg, "Philosophy of Religion: A State of the Subject Report," *Toronto Journal of Theology* 25 (2009): 95–110.

30. He presents his position on "skeptical religion" and "ultimism" through a trilogy that consists of J. L. Schellenberg, *Prolegomena to a Philosophy of Religion* (Ithaca, NY: Cornell University Press, 2005), *The Wisdom to Doubt: A Justification of Religious Skepticism* (Ithaca, NY: Cornell University Press, 2007), and *The Will to Imagine: A Justification of Skeptical Religion* (Ithaca, NY: Cornell University Press, 2009).

BIBLIOGRAPHY

Aertsen, Jan A. "Aquinas's Philosophy in Its Historical Setting." In *The Cambridge Companion to Aquinas*, edited by Norman Kretzmann and Eleanore Stump, 12–37. Cambridge: Cambridge University Press, 1993.

———. *Medieval Philosophy and the Transcendentals: The Case of Thomas Aquinas*. New York: E. J. Brill, 1996.

———. *Nature and Creature: Thomas Aquinas' Way of Thought*. Leiden: E. J. Brill, 1988.

Allen, Diogenes. *Philosophy for Understanding Theology*. Atlanta: John Knox, 1985.

Alston, William. *Perceiving God: The Epistemology of Religious Experience*. Ithaca, NY: Cornell University Press, 1991.

Anselm. *Proslogion, with "A Reply on Behalf of the Fool" by Gaunilo, and "The Author's Reply to Gaunilo."* Translated by M. J. Charlesworth. Oxford: Clarendon Press, 1965.

Aquinas, Thomas. *"De ente et essentia": On Being and Essence*. Translated by Armand Maurer. 2nd rev. ed. Toronto: Pontifical Institute of Medieaeval Studies, 1968.

———. *Summa Contra Gentiles*. Book 1, *God*. Translated by Anton C. Pegis. Notre Dame, IN: University of Notre Dame Press, 1975.

———. *Summa Theologiae*. Vol. 1, *The Existence of God, Part One, Questions 1–13*. Edited and Translated by Thomas Gilby et al. Garden City, NY: Doubleday Image, 1969.

———. *The Summa Theologica*. 2nd rev. ed. Translated by Fathers of the English Dominican Province. 22 vols. London: Burns, Oates & Washbourne, 1912–36; reprinted in 5 vols., Westminster, MD: Christian Classics, 1981. E-text at www.newadvent.org/summa, dhspriory.org/thomas/summa/index.html, www.catholicprimer.org/summa/index.html, and www.ccel.org/ccel/aquinas/summa.html.

————. *Summa Theologiae: Latin Text and English Translation, Introductions, Notes, Appendices & Glossaries.* Edited and translated by Thomas Gilby et al. New York: Blackfriars, 1964.

Aristotle. *Metaphysics.* Translated by Hippocrates G. Apostle. Grinnell, IA: Peripatetic Press, 1979.

————. *The Nicomachean Ethics.* Translated by David Ross. Oxford: Oxford University Press, 1980.

————. *Posterior Analytics.* Translated by Jonathan Barnes. 2nd ed. Oxford: Clarendon Press, 1994.

————. *Prior Analytics.* Translated by Robin Smith. Indianapolis: Hackett, 1989.

Augustine. *Confessions.* Translated by Henry Chadwick. Oxford: Oxford University Press, 1991.

————. *On the Holy Trinity.* Translated by Arthur W. Haddan. In vol. 3 of *The Nicene and Post-Nicene Fathers*, Series 1. Edited by Philip Schaff. 1886–89. 14 vols. Reprint, Peabody, MA: Hendrickson, 1994.

Barbour, Ian G. *Religion and Science: Historical and Contemporary Issues.* San Francisco: HarperCollins, 1997.

Brin, David. *The Postman.* New York: Bantam, 1985.

Buckley, Michael J. *At the Origins of Modern Atheism.* New Haven: Yale University Press, 1987.

————. *Denying and Disclosing God.* New Haven: Yale University Press, 2004.

Burrell, David B. *Aquinas: God and Action.* Notre Dame, IN: University of Notre Dame Press, 1979.

Caputo, John. *The Insistence of God: A Theology of Perhaps.* Bloomington: Indiana University Press, 2013.

————, ed. *The Religious: Blackwell Readings in Continental Philosophy.* Oxford: Wiley-Blackwell, 2001.

————. *The Weakness of God: A Theology of the Event.* Bloomington: Indiana University Press, 2006.

Chang, Hasok. "Incommensurability: Revisiting the Chemical Revolution." In *Kuhn's "The Structure of Scientific Revolutions" Revisited*, edited by Vasso Kindi and Theodore Arabatzis, 153–76. New York: Routledge, 2012.

Clayton, John. *Religions, Reasons and Gods: Essays in Cross-Cultural Philosophy of Religion.* Cambridge: Cambridge University Press, 2006.

Clayton, Philip D. *God and Contemporary Science.* Grand Rapids: Eerdmans, 1997.

————., ed. *The Oxford Handbook of Religion and Science.* Oxford: Oxford University Press, 2008.

Cottingham, John. *Philosophy of Religion: Towards a More Humane Approach.* Cambridge: Cambridge University Press, 2014.

Craig, William Lane. *The Kalam Cosmological Argument.* London: Macmillan, 1979.

Curd, Martin, and J. A. Clover, eds. *Philosophy of Science: The Central Issues.* New York: W. W. Norton, 1998.

D'Andrea, Thomas D. *Tradition, Rationality, and Virtue: The Thought of Alasdair MacIntyre.* Aldershot: Ashgate, 2006.

Davies, Brian. *Aquinas.* New York: Continuum, 2002.

Davies, Brian, ed. *Aquinas's "Summa Theologiae": Critical Essays.* Toronto: Rowman & Littlefield, 2006.

———. *Philosophy of Religion: A Guide and Anthology.* New York: Oxford University Press, 2000.

———, ed. *Thomas Aquinas: Contemporary Philosophical Perspectives.* New York: Oxford University Press, 2002.

Davies, Paul. *The Mind of God: The Scientific Basis for a Rational World.* New York: Simon & Schuster, 1992.

Dean, Thomas, ed. *Religious Pluralism and Truth: Essays on Cross-Cultural Philosophy of Religion.* Albany: State of University of New York Press, 1995.

Descartes, René. *Discourse on Method.* Translated by Arthur Wollaston. Harmondsworth: Penguin, 1966.

———. *Meditations on First Philosophy.* Translated by Ronald Rubin. Claremont, CA: Areté Press, 1986.

Draper, Paul, and Ryan Nichols. "Diagnosing Bias in Philosophy of Religion." *The Monist* 96, no. 3 (2013): 420–46.

Dunn, John. *Democracy: The Unfinished Journey, 508 BC to AD 1993.* Oxford: Oxford University Press, 1994.

Embree, Ainslie T., and Carol Gluck, eds. *Asia in Western and World History.* New York: Armonk, 1997.

Evans, C. Stephen. *Natural Signs and Knowledge of God: A New Look at Theistic Arguments.* Oxford: Oxford University Press, 2010.

Everitt, Nicholas. *The Non-Existence of God.* London: Routledge, 2004.

Feyerabend, Paul K. "Explanation, Reduction and Empiricism." In *Minnesota Studies in the Philosophy of Science,* vol. 3, *Scientific Explanation, Space, and Time,* edited by H. Feigl and G. Maxwell, 28–97. Minneapolis: University of Minnesota Press, 1962.

Flew, Antony. *God and Philosophy.* London: Hutchinson, 1966.

———. "The Presumption of Atheism." In *God, Freedom, and Immortality,* 13–30. Buffalo, NY: Prometheus Books, 1984. First published in *Canadian Journal of Philosophy* 2 (1972): 29–46.

Flew, Antony, R. M. Hare, and Basil Mitchell. "Theology and Falsification." In *New Essays in Philosophical Theology*, edited by Antony Flew and Alasdair MacIntyre (London: SCM Press, 1955), 96–108.

Gale, Richard. *On the Nature and Existence of God.* Cambridge: Cambridge University Press, 1991.

Gutting, Gary. *Pragmatic Liberalism and the Critique of Modernity.* Notre Dame, IN: University of Notre Dame Press, 1999.

———. *What Philosophers Know: Case Studies in Recent Analytic Philosophy.* Cambridge: Cambridge University Press, 2009.

Hanby, Michael. *No God, No Science? Theology, Cosmology, Biology.* Malden, MA: Blackwell, 2013.

Hartshorne, Charles. *Anselm's Discovery: A Re-Examination of the Ontological Proof for God's Existence.* La Salle, IL: Open Court, 1965.

Hawking, Stephen. *A Brief History of Time: From Big Bang to Black Holes.* Expanded ed. London: Bantam Press, 1998. First published 1988.

Hawking, Stephen, and Leonard Mlodinow. *The Grand Design.* New York: Bantam Books, 2010.

Heidegger, Martin. "The Age of the World Picture." In *The Question concerning Technology, and Other Essays*, translated by William Lovitt, 115–54. New York: Harper and Row, 1977.

———. *Being and Time.* Translated by John Macquarrie and Edward Robinson. New York: Harper and Row, 1962.

———. *The Question concerning Technology, and Other Essays.* Translated by William Lovitt. New York: Harper and Row, 1977.

Hibbs, Thomas. *Dialectic and Narrative in Aquinas: An Interpretation of the "Summa Contra Gentiles."* Notre Dame, IN: University of Notre Dame Press, 1995.

Hick, John. *Arguments for the Existence of God.* New York: Seabury Press, 1971.

———. *Philosophy of Religion.* 4th ed. Englewood Cliffs, NJ: Prentice-Hall, 1990.

Hollis, Martin, and Steven Lukes, eds. *Rationality and Relativism.* Cambridge, MA: MIT Press, 1982.

Holmes, Arthur F. *Contours of a World View.* Grand Rapids: Eerdmans, 1983.

Hume, David. *Dialogues concerning Natural Religion.* Edited by Richard H. Popkin. Cambridge: Hackett, 1998.

———. *An Enquiry concerning Human Understanding.* Edited by Antony Flew. La Salle, IL: Open Court, 1988.

———. *The Natural History of Religion.* Edited by H. E. Root. London: A & C Black, 1956.

Husserl, Edmund. *The Crisis of European Sciences and the Transcendental Phenomenology: An Introduction to Phenomenological Philosophy.* Translated by David Carr. Evanston, IL: Northwestern University Press, 1970.

Kant, Immanuel. *Critique of Pure Reason.* Translated by N. K. Smith. New York: St. Martin's Press, 1965.

—. *Prolegomena to Any Future Metaphysics.* Translated by Gary Hatfield. Cambridge: Cambridge University Press, 1997.

Kenny, Anthony J. P. *Aquinas on Being.* Oxford: Oxford University Press, 2002.

—. *The Five Ways: St. Thomas Aquinas' Proofs of God's Existence.* London: Routledge & Kegan Paul, 1969.

Kerr, Fergus. *After Aquinas: Versions of Thomism.* Cornwall: Blackwell, 2002.

—. *Theology after Wittgenstein.* New York: Blackwell, 1986.

Kindi, Vasso, and Theodore Arabatzis, eds. *Kuhn's "The Structure of Scientific Revolutions" Revisited.* New York: Routledge, 2012.

Klima, Gyula. "On Kenny on Aquinas on Being: A Critical Review of A. Kenny, *Aquinas on Being.*" *International Philosophical Quarterly* 44 (2004): 567–80.

—. Review of *Aquinas on Mind*, by Anthony Kenny. *Faith and Philosophy* 15 (1998): 113–17.

Kraay, Klaas J. "Method and Madness in Contemporary Analytic Philosophy of Religion." *Toronto Journal of Theology* 29 (2013): 245–64.

Kretzmann, Norman. "Evidence against Anti-Evidentialism." In *Our Knowledge of God*, edited Kelly James Clark, 17–38. Dordrecht: Kluwer Academic, 1992.

—. "Evidence and Religious Belief." In *Philosophy of Religion: A Guide and Anthology*, edited by Brian Davies, 95–107. New York: Oxford University Press, 2000.

—. *The Metaphysics of Theism: Aquinas' Natural Theology in the "Summa contra Gentiles."* New York: Clarendon Press, 1997.

Kretzmann, Norman, and Eleanore Stump, eds. *The Cambridge Companion to Aquinas.* Cambridge: Cambridge University Press, 1993.

Kuhn, Thomas S. *The Essential Tension: Selected Studies in Scientific Tradition and Change.* Chicago: University of Chicago Press, 1977.

—. *The Structure of Scientific Revolutions.* 3rd ed. Chicago: University of Chicago Press, 1996. First published 1962.

Küng, Hans. *Does God Exist?* Garden City, NY: Doubleday, 1980.

—. *Theology for the Third Millennium: An Ecumenical View.* Toronto: Doubleday, 1988.

Küng, Hans, and Julia Ching. *Christianity and Chinese Religions.* New York: Doubleday, 1989.

Lakatos, Imre. *The Methodology of Scientific Research Programmes: Philosophical Papers.* Vol. 1. Edited by John Worrall and Gregory Currie. Cambridge: Cambridge University Press, 1978.

Lee, Richard A., Jr. *Science, the Singular, and the Question of Theology: The New Middle Ages.* New York: Palgrave, 2002.

Leplin, Jarett. *Scientific Realism.* Berkeley: University of California Press, 1984.

Locke, John. *An Essay concerning Human Understanding.* Edited by Peter Nidditch. Oxford: Oxford University Press, 1975.

Lonergan, Bernard. *Insight: A Study of Human Understanding.* Vol. 3 of *The Collected Works of Bernard Lonergan.* Toronto: University of Toronto Press, 1997. First published 1957 by Longman, Green.

———. *Method in Theology.* Toronto: University of Toronto Press, 1971.

———. *A Second Collection: Papers.* Edited by William F. J. Ryan and Bernard J. Tyrrell. Toronto: University of Toronto Press, 1996.

MacIntyre, Alasdair. *After Virtue: A Study in Moral Theory.* 2nd ed. Notre Dame, IN: University of Notre Dame Press, 1984.

———. "Epistemological Crises, Dramatic Narratives, and the Philosophy of Science." *The Monist,* no. 60 (1977): 453–72. Reprinted in *Paradigms and Revolutions: Applications and Appraisals of Thomas Kuhn's Philosophy of Science,* edited by Gary Gutting, 54–74. Notre Dame, IN: University of Notre Dame Press, 1980.

———. *First Principles, Final Ends and Contemporary Philosophical Issues.* Milwaukee: Marquette University Press, 1990.

———. *God, Philosophy, Universities.* Lanham, MD: Rowman & Littlefield, 2009.

———. "An Interview for Cogito." In *The MacIntyre Reader,* edited by Kelvin Knight, 267–75. Notre Dame, IN: University of Notre Dame Press, 1998. First published in *Cogito* 5, no. 2 (1991): 67–73.

———. "Is Understanding Religion Compatible with Believing?" In *Rationality,* edited by Brian R. Wilson, 62–77. Oxford: Blackwell, 1970.

———. *The MacIntyre Reader.* Edited by Kelvin Knight. Notre Dame, IN: University of Notre Dame Press, 1998.

———. "Nietzsche or Aristotle?" In *The American Philosopher: Conversations with Quine, Davidson, Putnam, Nozick, Danto, Rorty, Cavell, MacIntyre, and Kuhn,* edited by Giovanna Borradori, 137–52. Chicago: University of Chicago Press, 1994.

———. *Three Rival Versions of Moral Enquiry.* Notre Dame, IN: University of Notre Dame Press, 1991.

———. *Whose Justice? Which Rationality?* Notre Dame, IN: University of Notre Dame Press, 1988.

Mackie, J. L. *The Miracle of Theism*. Oxford: Clarendon Press, 1982.

Malachowski, Alan. *Richard Rorty*. Princeton: Princeton University Press, 2002.

Malcolm, Norman. "Anselm's Ontological Arguments." *Philosophical Review* 69 (1960): 41–62.

Marshall, Paul, Sander Griffioen, and Richard Mouw, eds. *Stained Glass: Worldviews and Social Science*. Lanham, MD: University Press of America, 1989.

Martin, C. F. J. *Thomas Aquinas: God and Explanations*. Edinburgh: Edinburgh University Press, 1997.

McGrath, Alister E. *Science and Religion: A New Introduction*. 2nd ed. Malden, MA: Wiley-Blackwell, 2010. First published 1999.

McInerny, Ralph. *Praeambula Fidei: Thomism and the God of the Philosophers*. Washington, DC: Catholic University of America Press, 2006.

Messer, Richard. *Does God's Existence Need Proof?* Oxford: Oxford University Press, 1993.

Milbank, John. *Theology and Social Theory: Beyond Secular Reason*. Oxford: Blackwell, 1990.

Moser, Paul K. *The Elusive God: Reorienting Religious Epistemology*. Cambridge: Cambridge University Press, 2008.

———. *The Evidence for God: Religious Knowledge Reexamined*. Cambridge: Cambridge University Press, 2010.

———. *The Severity of God: Religion and Philosophy Reconceived*. Cambridge: Cambridge University Press, 2013.

Murphy, Nancey. *Anglo-American Postmodernity: Philosophical Perspectives on Science, Religion, and Ethics*. Boulder, CO: Westview Press, 1997.

———. *Reconciling Theology and Science*. Kitchener, ON: Pandora Press, 1997.

———. *Theology in the Age of Scientific Reasoning*. Ithaca, NY: Cornell University Press, 1990.

Murphy, Nancey, and Warren S. Brown. *Did My Neurons Make Me Do It? Philosophical and Neurobiological Perspectives on Moral Responsibility and Free Will*. Oxford: Oxford University Press, 2007.

Murphy, Nancey, and George F. R. Ellis. *On the Moral Nature of the Universe: Theology, Cosmology, and Ethics*. Minneapolis: Fortress Press, 1996.

Murphy, Nancey, George F. R. Ellis, and Timothy O'Connor, eds. *Downward Causation and the Neurobiology of Free Will*. Berlin: Springer Verlag, 2009.

Nagasawa, Yujin. *The Existence of God: A Philosophical Introduction*. New York: Routledge, 2011.

Naugle, D. K. *Worldview: The History of a Concept*. Grand Rapids: Eerdmans, 2002.

Nielson, Kai. *Naturalism and Religion*. Amherst, NY: Prometheus Books, 2001.

―――. *Naturalism without Foundations*. Amherst, NY: Prometheus Books, 1996.

Nietzsche, Friedrich. *Gay Science, with a Prelude in Rhymes and an Appendix of Songs*. Translated by Walter Kaufmann. New York: Random House, 1974.

Olthuis, James. "On Worldviews." In *Stained Glass: Worldviews and Social Science*, edited by Paul Marshall, Sander Griffioen, and Richard Mouw, 26–40. Lanham, MD: University Press of America, 1989.

Oppy, Graham R. *Arguing about Gods*. New York: Cambridge University Press, 2006.

Orwell, George. *Nineteen Eighty-Four*. London: Secker and Warburg, 1949.

Peacocke, Arthur R. *Creation and the World of Science*. New York: Oxford University Press, 1979.

―――. *Theology for a Scientific Age: Being and Becoming—Natural, Divine and Human*. 2nd enlarged ed. Minneapolis: Fortress Press, 1993. First published 1990 by Blackwell.

Peterson, Michael L., and Raymond J. VanArragon, eds. *Contemporary Debates in Philosophy of Religion*. Malden, MA: Blackwell, 2004.

Peterson, Michael L., William Hasker, Bruce Reichenbach, and David Basinger, eds. *Philosophy of Religion: Selected Readings*. 4th ed. Oxford: Oxford University Press, 2010.

Philipse, Herman. *God in the Age of Science? A Critique of Religious Reason*. Oxford: Oxford University Press, 2012.

Phillips, D. Z. *The Concept of Prayer*. New York: Schocken Books, 1966.

―――. *Faith after Foundationalism*. New York: Routledge, 1988.

―――. *Faith and Philosophical Enquiry*. London: Routledge & Kegan Paul, 1970.

Pinsent, Andrew. Review of *God in the Age of Science? A Critique of Religious Reason*, by Herman Philipse. *Notre Dame Philosophical Reviews*, January 2013, n.p.

Plantinga, Alvin. *God and Other Minds*. Ithaca, NY: Cornell University Press, 1967.

―――. *God, Freedom, and Evil*. Grand Rapids: Eerdmans, 1974.

―――. *The Nature of Necessity*. Oxford: Oxford University Press, 1974.

―――. *Warrant and Proper Function*. Oxford: Oxford University Press, 1993.

―――. *Warranted Christian Belief*. Oxford: Oxford University Press, 2000.

―――. *Where the Conflict Really Lies: Science, Religion, and Naturalism*. New York: Oxford University Press, 2011.

Plantinga, Alvin, and Nicholas Wolterstorff, eds. *Faith and Rationality: Reason and Belief in God*. Notre Dame, IN: University of Notre Dame Press, 1984.

Plato. *The Republic of Plato*. Translated by Francis Macdonald Cornford. New York: Oxford University Press, 1945.

——. *Symposium*. Translated by Benjamin Jowett. New York: Liberal Arts Press, 1948.

——. *The Theaetetus of Plato*. Edited by Miles Burnyeat. Translated by M. J. Levett. Cambridge: Hackett, 1990.

Pojman, Louis P., and Michael C. Rae, eds. *Philosophy of Religion: An Anthology*. 5th ed. Belmont, CA: Wadsworth, 2008.

Polanyi, Michael. *Personal Knowledge: Towards a Post-Critical Philosophy*. Chicago: University of Chicago Press, 1958.

Polkinghorne, John. *Quantum Physics and Theology: An Unexpected Kinship*. New Haven: Yale University Press, 2007.

——. *Science and Creation: The Search for Understanding*. Philadelphia: Templeton Foundation Press, 2006.

Popkin, Richard H. *The History of Scepticism: From Savonarola to Bayle*. Oxford: Oxford University Press, 2003.

Putnam, Hilary. *Mind, Language, and Reality*. Vol. 2 of *Philosophical Papers*. Cambridge: Cambridge University Press, 1975.

Quine, W. V. O. "Two Dogmas of Empiricism." *Philosophical Review* 40 (1951): 20–43.

Quine, W. V. O., and J. S. Ullian. *The Web of Belief*. 2nd ed. New York: Random House, 1978.

Reichenbach, Bruce. *The Cosmological Argument*. Springfield, IL: Thomas, 1972.

Rogers, Eugene, Jr. *Thomas Aquinas and Karl Barth: Sacred Doctrine and the Natural Knowledge of God*. Notre Dame, IN: University of Notre Dame Press, 1995.

Rorty, Richard. *Objectivity, Relativism, and Truth*. New York: Cambridge University Press, 1991.

——. *Philosophy and the Mirror of Nature*. Princeton: Princeton University Press, 1979.

——. "Pragmatism and Philosophy." In *Contemporary Approaches to Philosophy*, edited by Paul K. Moser and Dwayne Mulder, 403–33. New York: Macmillan, 1982.

——. "Taylor on Truth." In *Philosophy in an Age of Pluralism: The Philosophy of Charles Taylor in Question*, edited by James Tully, 20–33. Cambridge: Cambridge University Press, 1994.

——. *Truth and Progress*. Cambridge: Cambridge University Press, 1998.

Rowe, William L. *The Cosmological Argument*. Princeton: Princeton University Press, 1975.

Russell, Bertrand. *A History of Western Philosophy*. New York: Simon and Schuster, 1972. First published as *A History of Western Philosophy, and Its Connection with Political and Social Circumstances from the Earliest Times to the Present Day*. New York: Simon and Schuster, 1945.

Russell, Robert John, Nancey Murphy, and C. Isham, eds. *Quantum Cosmology and the Laws of Nature: Scientific Perspectives on Divine Action*. Vatican City State: Vatican Observatory, 1993.

Schellenberg, J. L. "Philosophy of Religion: A State of the Subject Report." In *Toronto Journal of Theology* 25 (2009): 95–110.

———. *Prolegomena to a Philosophy of Religion*. Ithaca, NY: Cornell University Press, 2005.

———. *The Will to Imagine: A Justification of Skeptical Religion*. Ithaca, NY: Cornell University Press, 2009.

———. *The Wisdom to Doubt: A Justification of Religious Skepticism*. Ithaca, NY: Cornell University Press, 2007.

Scriven, Michael. *Primary Philosophy*. New York: McGraw-Hill, 1966.

Shults, F. LeRon, Nancey Murphy, and Robert John Russell, eds. *Philosophy, Science and Divine Action*. Boston: Brill, 2009.

Slagle, Jim. Review of *God in the Age of Science? A Critique of Religious Reason*, by Herman Philipse. *Philosophy* 88 (April 2013): 325–29.

Smart, Ninian. *Dimensions of the Sacred: An Anatomy of the World's Beliefs*. Berkeley: University of California Press, 1996.

———. "The Philosophy of Worldviews, or the Philosophy of Religion Transformed." In *Religious Pluralism and Truth: Essays on Cross-Cultural Philosophy of Religion*, edited by Thomas Dean, 17–31. Albany: State of University of New York Press, 1995.

———. *Religion and the Western Mind*. Albany: State of University of New York Press, 1987.

———. "Truth, Criteria, and Dialogue." In *Religious Pluralism and Truth: Essays on Cross-Cultural Philosophy of Religion*, edited by Thomas Dean, 67–71. Albany: State of University of New York Press, 1995.

———. *Worldviews: Crosscultural Explorations of Human Beliefs*. New York: Scribners, 1983.

Stannard, Russell. *The God Experiment*. London: Faber and Faber, 1999.

Stenmark, Mikael. *Scientism: Science, Ethics and Religion*. Aldershot: Ashgate, 2001.

Stump, J. B., and Alan G. Padgett, eds. *The Blackwell Companion to Science and Christianity*. Malden, MA: Wiley-Blackwell, 2012.

Swinburne, Richard. *The Coherence of Theism*. Oxford: Clarendon Press, 1977.

————. *The Existence of God*. 2nd ed. Oxford: Clarendon Press, 2004. First published 1979.

————. *Faith and Reason*. 2nd ed. Oxford: Clarendon, 2005.

————. *Is There a God?* Rev. ed. Oxford: Oxford University Press, 2010. First published 1996.

Taliaferro, Charles. *Evidence and Faith: Philosophy and Religion since the Seventeenth Century*. New York: Cambridge University Press, 2005.

Taliaferro, Charles, Paul Draper, and Philip L. Quinn, eds. *A Companion to Philosophy of Religion*. 2nd ed. Malden, MA: Wiley-Blackwell, 2010.

Taylor, Charles. "Charles Taylor Replies." In *Philosophy in an Age of Pluralism: The Philosophy of Charles Taylor in Question*, edited by James Tully, 213–57. Cambridge: Cambridge University Press, 1994.

————. "Overcoming Epistemology." In *Philosophical Arguments*, 1–19. Cambridge, MA: Harvard University Press, 1995.

————. "Rationality." In *Rationality and Relativism*, edited by Martin Hollis and Steven Lukes, 87–105. Cambridge, MA: MIT Press, 1982.

————. "Rorty in the Epistemological Tradition." In *Reading Rorty*, edited by Alan Malachowski, 257–89. Oxford: Blackwell, 1990.

————. *A Secular Age*. Cambridge, MA: Harvard University Press, 2007.

————. *Sources of the Self: The Making of the Modern Identity*. Cambridge: Cambridge University Press, 1989.

Taylor, Richard. *Metaphysics*. Englewood Cliffs, NJ: Prentice-Hall, 1963.

Torrell, Jean-Pierre, O.P. *Saint Thomas Aquinas*. Vol. 1, *The Person and His Work*. Translated by Robert Royal. Washington, DC: Catholic University of America Press, 1993.

————. *Saint Thomas Aquinas*. Vol. 2, *Spiritual Master*. Translated by Robert Royal. Washington, DC: Catholic University of America Press, 1996.

Toulmin, Stephen. *Cosmopolis: The Hidden Agenda of Modernity*. Chicago: University of Chicago Press, 1992.

Turner, James. *Without God, without Creed: The Origins of Unbelief in America*. Baltimore: Johns Hopkins University Press, 1985.

Van Biema, David. "God vs. Science." *Time*, November 5, 2006, 32–39.

Van Holten, Wilko. *Explanation within the Bounds of Religion*. Frankfurt: Peter Lang, 2003.

Wainwright, William. *Mysticism: A Study of Its Nature, Cognitive Value, and Moral Implications*. Madison: University of Wisconsin Press, 1981.

Walsh, Brian J., and J. Richard Middleton. *The Transforming Vision: Shaping a Christian World View*. Downers Grove, IL: InterVarsity Press, 1984.

Ward, Keith. *God, Chance & Necessity*. Oxford: One World, 1996.

————. *Religion and Creation.* New York: Oxford University Press, 1996.

————. *Religion and Human Nature.* New York: Oxford University Press, 1998.

White, Victor. "Prelude to the Five Ways." In *Aquinas's "Summa Theologiae": Critical Essays,* edited by Brian Davies, 25–44. Toronto: Rowman & Littlefield, 2006.

Wilson, Brian R., ed. *Rationality.* Oxford: Blackwell, 1970.

Winch, Peter. *The Idea of a Social Science.* New York: Humanities Press, 1958.

————. "Understanding a Primitive Society." In *Rationality,* edited by Brian R. Wilson, 96. Oxford: Blackwell, 1970. First published in *American Philosophical Quarterly* 1, no. 4 (October 1964): 307–24.

Wittgenstein, Ludwig. *Culture and Value.* Translated by Peter Winch. Chicago: University of Chicago Press, 1980. First published as *Vermischte Bemerkungen.* Frankfurt: Suhrkamp Verlag, 1977.

————. *Philosophical Investigations.* Oxford: Blackwell, 1967.

Wolters, Albert. *Creation Regained: Biblical Basics for a Reformational Worldview.* Grand Rapids: Eerdmans, 1985.

Wolterstorff, Nicholas. "Can Belief in God Be Rational?" In *Faith and Rationality: Reason and Belief in God,* edited by Alvin Plantinga and Nicholas Wolterstorff, 135–86. Notre Dame, IN: University of Notre Dame Press, 1984.

————. *Reason within the Bounds of Religion.* Grand Rapids: Eerdmans, 1976.

INDEX

Aertsen, Jan, 132, 137–38, 141–44, 165–67, 261n.62
Aeterni Patris, 117–18
agnosticism, 30–31
Allen, Diogenes, 202–3, 204
Alston, William, 20
Aquinas, Thomas, 114–19, 159, 179, 182–84, 200, 202–5, 210, 213, 214–15, 219; belonging to Aristotelian tradition, 140–46; belonging to Augustinian tradition, 140–46; bringing together Aristotelian and Christian positions, 142–46, 152–59, 165–77, 181–82, 196. *See also* Five Ways; *Summa Contra Gentiles*; *Summa Theologiae*; truth
arche, 149, 161–69, 215. *See also* first cause; intellectual inquiry
Aristotelianism, 123–24, 137–38, 148–49, 163–65, 185, 202–3, 264n.50; and Augustinianism, 112, 137–44, 149–54, 165–69, 174, 178, 181–84, 216, 219; as a comprehensive rational inquiry, 163–69, 173–76, 215; as naturalistic philosophy, 127–28, 149–52, 173–74, 177

Aristotle, 142–43, 149–50, 163–65, 173–74. *See also* Aristotelianism
atheism, 12, 127; as "default" worldview, 89–93, 178–80, 181, 212; implicit theological moves in its historical development, 200–202; modern historical emergence of, 178–80, 186–200; subtraction theory of, 179, 184, 205. *See also* atheism vs. theism; atheistic arguments; naturalism; presumption of atheism; scientism
atheism vs. theism, 1–10, 14–18, 43–46, 65–66, 157–58, 221–22; as comprehensive positions, 24, 42–46, 55, 66; as conflict between worldviews, 79, 82, 85–89, 94–95, 115–16, 178–79, 210, 212–13, 230, 248–49n.6; difficulties in the debate, 43–46
atheistic arguments: from evil, 25, 120, 127–28, 170, 195, 228, 234n.5, 236n.9, 236n.13; for the incoherence of the concept of God, 118, 199–200, 236n.9, 248n.6. *See also* presumption of atheism
Augustinianism. *See* Aristotelianism
Averroes, 138, 142–43, 182

PAUL SEUNGOH CHUNG is a sessional lecturer at St. Michael's College in the University of Toronto.

CPSIA information can be obtained
at www.ICGtesting.com
Printed in the USA
LVOW13*1516030517

533129LV00011B/264/P